Toward Inclusive Schools for All Children

Toward Inclusive Schools for All Children

Developing a Synergistic Social Learning Curriculum

Herbert Goldstein

pro·ed
An International Publisher

8700 Shoal Creek Boulevard
Austin, Texas 78757-6897
800/897-3202   Fax 800/397-7633
www.proedinc.com

© 2006 by PRO-ED, Inc.
8700 Shoal Creek Boulevard
Austin, Texas 78757-6897
800/897-3202   Fax 800/397-7633
www.proedinc.com

LC 1201
.G63
2006

0 6 0 8 2 4 1 5 9

Library of Congress Cataloging-in-Publication Data

Goldstein, Herbert, 1916 –
    Toward inclusive schools for all children : developing a synergistic
social learning curriculum / Herbert Goldstein.
        p.   cm.
    Includes bibliographical references and index.
    ISBN 1-4164-0068-0 (soft cover : alk. paper)
    1. Inclusive education—United States.   2. Special education—
Curricula—United States.   3. Social learning—Study and teaching—
United States.   I. Title.
LC1201.G63 2006
371.9'046—dc22

2005018387

Art Director: Jason Crosier
Designer: Nancy McKinney-Point
This book is designed in Minion, Nexus, Math Pi.

Printed in the United States of America

1 2 3 4 5 6 7 8 9 10   10 09 08 07 06

I dedicate this book to all the teachers of children
and youth with disabilities.
To this day, special education teachers are the only teachers
in our schools who have not been provided with a
comprehensive curriculum upon which they can
base their instruction.
Individually, and sometimes in small groups,
they have provided the substance of education for their students.
They continue to fill the curricular gap
with instructional materials they have scavenged
and adapted from diverse sources
to fill their students' instructional needs,
augmenting these with educational content
and teaching aids of their own design.
They would be the first to agree that the time
and energy consumed by this task
would be better spent working directly
with their students.

Contents

Preface

The Inclusive School Movement (ISM) is approaching its third decade in our schools. It ranks second to P.L. 94-142, the Education of All Handicapped Children Act, as the largest and most pervasive effort to reform special education. ISM's entry to the educational scene coincided with my retirement after almost 40 years in special education. As a bystander, I was able to observe the battle for dominance in the education of students with disabilities take shape. My first inclination was to join the conflict on the side of conventional special education by preparing a scathing article predicting the devastating results of the wholesale placement of students with disabilities in general education classes. It quickly became apparent, however, that indignation was my only ammunition. I was faced with an undeniable fact—there are no data demonstrating that special education is more effective for students with disabilities than general education. It immediately became my goal to learn why.

Thus began a round-trip back through history to the late 17th century and John Locke's "An Essay Concerning Human Understanding," where I found what proved to be the conceptual basis for the education of all children. Because the essay is available in its entirety on the Internet, I will state Locke's reasoning simply. He argued against the prevailing belief that knowledge and the authority to disseminate it were vested in the church, crown, and guild. He took the position that (a) knowledge was the outcome of learning, (b) learning was acquired through the senses in the course of one's experiences, and (c) because everyone had senses, the ability to learn was a universal human characteristic.

This was the basis for the sensationalist movement, and the first step toward special education occurred when Dr. Jean-Marc Gaspard Itard, chief physician at the National Institution for Deaf-Mutes in Paris in the early 19th century, tested its relevance to human growth and development in his effort to educate Victor, a feral boy who was presumed to have retarded intellectual development. In Chapter 1, I base a brief history of special education on Itard's work and that of his student, Dr. Edouard Seguin, who proposed a cure for mental retardation.

Seguin's work introduced a half century in which physicians became the authorities in the education of children with disabilities. They diagnosed and prescribed the treatment for individuals with mental retardation and assumed the leadership of state schools for individuals with mental retardation. Their influence ended early in the 20th century with the failure of the state schools in their goal to educate individuals with mental retardation and to return them to society, the rise of the mental test movement, and the reluctant acceptance by the public schools of the obligation to educate children with disabilities.

Logic would suggest that the ensuing vacuum in leadership in the education of children with mental retardation would be filled by the public school administrators. After all, the children were in their schools, and they had society's mandate to educate all of its young. Unfortunately, school administrators and their boards found it more expedient to segregate children with mental retardation into special classes and to leave their instruction to their teachers rather than to provide them with a comprehensive educational program based on a curriculum consistent with their learning needs and with the goals of education. Thus, this opportunity to develop a curriculum for students with disabilities that would parallel the general education curriculum and serve as the basis for their integration into the school was lost. Since then, students with disabilities have had no equivalent of Brown v. Board of Education, the 1954 Supreme Court decision that dismantled racial segregation in public schools in this country. Accordingly, students with disabilities have remained joined with their nondisabled peers by little more than a common geography. The Inclusive School Movement of the 1980s demonstrated that simply bringing students together in the same room makes no difference in their educational outcomes and in their ability to attain social inclusion in society.

The leadership vacuum in special education was quickly filled by psychologists. Unlike the physicians they replaced, their diagnoses were based on objective measures of students' intellectual, behavioral, and academic aptitudes and performance. The psychologists' reports to teachers included deficits detected in students' performance, their conclusions about the conditions that caused the deficits, and suggestions for remediation. Without a curriculum as a frame of reference used to assess students' progress in their performance, the reports to teachers did not include the relationship between students' deficits and the content of their instruction.

At this point in my travels through the literature, it became clear that without the foundation of a comprehensive curriculum relevant to the education of students with disabilities, the simplest pre–post test of students' performance is impossible, as is a longitudinal assessment of the efficacy of their educational program, the quality of their instruction, and the relationship between their schooling and their ability to achieve social inclusion in school and society. Nor is it possible to ascertain the concordance between the rate of students' learning and the sequencing of the curriculum's content or the effect of the curriculum's structure on students' learning.

The implementation of the No Child Left Behind (NCLB) legislation indicates that there may be a conflict between the structure of the general education curriculum, the loose assembly of its elements from disparate sources, and the learning characteristics of students with disabilities. The general education curriculum places a huge premium on students' ability to synthesize, to see the relationship between curricular areas, each developed temporally and conceptually distant from each other and taught independently of each other, and to select from each area those concepts and facts that, when assembled correctly, comprise solutions to problems.

Experience and the recent results of neurological studies indicate that central nervous system disorders, typically the basis for children's disabilities, militate against their facility to acquire new knowledge and to combine elements of this knowledge into a coherent whole. The results of the implementation of the No Child Left Behind Act indicate that this theory also could apply to the many marginally disabled students and other underachievers who join children with disabilities in their schools' dropout data, the ranks of the unemployed, dependence on their families and their communities, and the inability to achieve social inclusion in society.

The accountability provisions of NCLB have exposed the fact that our schools have never provided students with disabilities with a curriculum. Looking back to the origins of special education, it is clear that Dr. Seguin, in pursuit of a cure for mental retardation, prescribed activities that he believed would stimulate the senses. Public school administrators were not inclined to do much more than that when they accepted children with disabilities into their schools, and educators everywhere have adhered to the "one curriculum fits all" concept with the expansion of ISM and as their response to the requirements of NCLB. Their solution is either the academic content of the general education curriculum to all but 1% of the students or nothing.

The purpose of this book is to provide students with disabilities with an alternative to the general education curriculum that is responsive to their learning needs and characteristics and consistent with the goals of education, the prerequisites society has set for social inclusion. There are presently many precedents in the curricula that are tailored to the needs of students with special skills, talents, and interests as well as in the variations found in charter schools and home schooling.

In particular, this book presents a rationale for a curriculum for students with disabilities and their underachieving peers and a strategy for developing a curriculum based on social sciences constructs. Its frame of reference is social learning, ensuring its relevance to students' attainment of social inclusion. The proposed curriculum's content and learning activities are synergistic in order to enhance students' abilities to synthesize solutions to life's problems. And it is designed as a computer program with its own Web site so that it can be implemented by individual teachers and adapted to the demands of their students and their communities.

As a computer program, the proposed curriculum can be easily updated on a day-to-day basis in order to accommodate social and technological change. At the same time, it provides teachers and administrators everywhere with a facile and rapid means of coordination and communication. Most important, because it is consistent with the goals of education for all children, it allows for options in the deployment of children to the instructional settings within our schools where the curriculum can be implemented most effectively. Given these parameters, the availability of the proposed curriculum disposes of the educationally irrelevant distinction between special and general education.

As formidable as the development of a comprehensive curriculum may appear, it is the only means of providing students with disabilities and their underachieving peers the education promised to all children who enter our schools. I hope that the plan offered in this book will provoke educators to think about the diversity in students' learning characteristics and needs and the role curriculum can play in integrating them in our schools. Some will undoubtedly design curriculum development processes that are less time and labor intensive. If this book facilitates their emergence, it will have served its purpose.

Acknowledgments

I am grateful to Sam Ashcroft for his vision and his encouragement to expand an article into what much later became this book. Thanks to Mel Semmel's confidence in my scholarship, it found a publisher. No one was more patient and constructive than my highly respected colleague, Nicholas Anastasiow. He read and critiqued each of the many drafts of the manuscript and contributed invaluable suggestions. To my wife and colleague, Marjorie, go my thanks for her unflagging support, her suggestions to strengthen the message in my book, and her remarkable ability to unravel and make sense out of the uncountable conceptual Gordian knots in my writing.

Introduction

Early in the 20th century, state schools for individuals considered to be mentally retarded had become so overcrowded that admissions were reduced drastically. While children admitted to these institutions were diagnosed as mentally retarded, we now know that they were far from homogeneous. Children with a variety of disabilities, including epilepsy, cerebral palsy, auditory deficits, and a host of neurological disorders, were subsumed under the rubric of mental retardation and constituted a notable proportion of the state school's population.

Denied access to state schools, families of children with disabilities turned to their local schools. This created problems for administrators and school boards who were aware that these children could not cope with the general education curriculum. Educators had two alternatives to resolve this dilemma. One was to include these children in following society's mandate to the schools to socialize all of its young and to provide them with an educational program that was consistent with the goals of education for all students. The other alternative, far more expedient, was to separate them from general education programs into special classes where educational accommodations could be effected. This would allow general education to continue uninterrupted. Expediency won out. Administrators provided children with disabilities with classroom space in their schools, recruited volunteers to act as teachers, and encouraged them to do the best they could to educate these children. Some notion of the degree of commitment to the education of these students is seen in the fact that a decade passed before the first effort to provide professional preparation for teachers of children with disabilities emerged.

There is no doubt that fulfilling society's mandate by developing a comprehensive educational program for these children, as an alterative to the general education program, would have been difficult, time-consuming, and expensive, but it would have made special education unnecessary and society would have been spared the price it has paid over the past century. In the long run, schools would not have been overwhelmed by legislation and regulation, and, more important, it is likely that many people with disabilities and their families would be enjoying the quality of life they merited. In comparison, the cost of finding an educational solution to the challenge presented by children with disabilities would have been infinitesimal.

While children with disabilities have been the most conspicuous victims of expediency, they are far from the most numerous. The implementation of the No Child Left Behind (NCLB) legislation indicates that they are far outnumbered by underachieving students with disabilities whose measured sensory, cognitive, and behavioral deficits exceed the legal limits for acceptance into special education. These children remain in general education along with students whose underachievement appears to be related to socioeconomic and cultural factors. In less politically correct times, they were referred to as slow learners. In numbers more than twice those of students with disabilities, they remain in general education classes and contribute disproportionately to the schools' dropout rate and, ultimately, to the ranks of the unemployed (Alexander, Entwistle, & Kabbani, 2001; Griffin, 2002).

Change and reform designed to reduce the proportion of underachieving students in general and special education have taken many forms. Early education programs have increased in number and quality and are presently commonplace throughout the country for all children. From the first days of educational programs for students with disabilities to the present, there has been the conviction that a precise diagnosis of students' learning and behavioral deficits would reveal the relevant educational or, more realistically, remedial program for each student. The search for tests that would make diagnosis of students' disabilities more precise has dominated special education efforts. For other underachievers, educators have turned to a variety of remedies ranging from ways of increasing students' motivation to distinctive instructional materials.

Some changes and reforms have been successful. In special education, however, the results have been far from satisfactory. The President's Commission on Excellence in Special Education (2002) reported that the dropout rate of students with disabilities alone is double that of students in general education and that their unemployment rate persists at 70%. Accordingly, schools have augmented their programs with add-ons such as transition programs to help school-leavers with disabilities attain social inclusion in adult society. Vocational training and occupational placement assistance is provided for other underachievers. Like earlier attempts at change and reform, these have helped some students but not in numbers that have affected unemployment data.

Many in special education looked to the enactment of P.L. 94-142 and its successor, the Individuals with Disabilities Education Improvement Act of 2004 (IDEA), with optimism. Despite opening the schools to all students, increasing financial support for state and local education agencies, and requiring compliance with an extensive array of procedural changes, the data reflecting success in attaining social inclusion by school-leavers with disabilities has not improved. The dramatic rise of the Inclusive School Movement (ISM) a decade later raised hopes in many educators and parents of children with disabilities that these students' educational outcomes would improve if they were assigned to general education classes. They proposed that association with students without disabilities would create a climate of understanding and acceptance that would facilitate social inclusion in adult society. Twenty years later, ISM has demonstrated that physical inclusion, by itself, rarely leads to social inclusion. Its most notable outcome is the schism created in special education when a notable proportion of special educators and their school boards rejected the notion of discontinuing traditional special education.

Adding ISM to a century of attempts to effect change and reform had no noticeable effect on the education of students with disabilities. Instead, these efforts contributed to the evidence that education has not lived up to its claim that the schools do not fit educational programs to children but instead tailor programs to meet students' needs. This contradiction is confirmed by the 1997 reauthorization of IDEA, which included the requirement that students with disabilities be viewed as general education students and that they participate in the general education curriculum. More recently, it was reinforced in the NCLB legislation that requires that all students with disabilities to participate in statewide reading and arithmetic achievement tests.

The widespread conflict that NCLB created in schools prompted the U.S. Department of Education to relax and revise some of its criteria for compliance. Among the first changes was allowing schools to exclude 1% of their student population from their aggregate achievement test data. This is, coincidentally, close to the proportion of students with severe and moderate disabilities. Historically, excluding students with severe disabilities from educational assessment has been the precursor to ultimately excluding all students with disabilities who are significant underachievers in academic content areas.

There are no signs that educators are entertaining the possibility that their "one curriculum fits all" policy may be the source of our inability to change educational outcomes for underachieving students and those with disabilities. In fact, the unquestioning compliance with the 1997 reauthorization of IDEA, the NCLB criteria for adequate schooling, standards-based reform (Kendall & Marzano, 1997; Stodden, Galloway, & Stodden, 2003), and the trend toward an increasing number of local and state agencies adopting ISM policies clearly indicate that our schools do not acknowledge that the general education curriculum may be inappropriate for students with disabilities and their underachieving counterparts. Instead, they are preparing to begin another century of high costs and low results for all students who cannot profit from the general education curriculum.

This book proposes that there is an alternative—that schools are not limited to one approach for meeting society's commitment to its young. The alternative proceeds from the premise that when change and reform prove ineffective, schools should discontinue programs that do not fulfill their commitment to society and invent programs that will. In the case of students with disabilities and other underachievers, this means recognizing that limiting their instruction to the general education curriculum perpetuates their failure in school and in society. Furthermore, it denies them the wherewithal to achieve a quality of life commensurate with that of people without disabilities—those for whom the general education curriculum is intended (U.S. Census Bureau, 2002).

Curriculum Development

The foundation of any educational program is its curriculum, a body of knowledge and behaviors to be imparted to its students. All other elements in the educational program, including the preparation or training of those who will implement the curriculum or contribute in some way to its implementation, are shaped by the nature of the curriculum content. Accordingly, this book is devoted to the development of a curriculum that will meet the needs of children with disabilities and can be generalized for all other children for whom the general education curriculum has been irrelevant. Because programs for students with disabilities are the most prominent, the book focuses on the well-documented needs of students with disabilities as the framework for the development of a synergistic curriculum that capitalizes on communication technology. It documents a century of educational experiences and rationale, uses social learning theory as its theme, and recommends social science concepts rather than the current medical model for its frame of reference. It includes strategies for organizing educational teams to ensure synergy in its content, for developing and validating the curriculum, and for capitalizing on communication technology in the curriculum's implementation.

The Criterion for an Effective Education

Academic achievement has been the criterion against which the outcomes of special education have been measured throughout its history. It was the criterion in the efficacy studies of the mid-20th century and is presently the standard for success in the No Child Left Behind legislation. While tests of academic achievement reflect students' progress through the schools, they do not measure the extent to which education prepares them to attain the autonomies that underlie social inclusion and their participation in and contribution to adult society. The ability to secure and sustain gainful employment that subsidizes social inclusion is the more appropriate criterion to determine the extent to which education fulfills society's expectations.

Follow-up studies of school-leavers with mild disabilities span special education's history in our schools. In combination, they report that the unemployment rate among adults with mild disabilities is as much as 10 times greater than that of the population as a whole, that the large majority of those who are employed full time are paid the minimum wage or less, and that within a year or two, most become dependent on their families and community agencies. These results indicate that special education has failed to meet society's expectations.

The Source of Failure

The inevitability of special education's failure to meet its commitment has its origins in the early 20th century. There was an interval of a few years during which a decision was made that determined the nature of the experiences that children with disabilities would have in our public schools and, ultimately, the quality of their lives. This occurred at the time that the public schools were almost overwhelmed by the arrival of large numbers of children of European immigrants and of children with mild disabilities whose admission to state schools for individuals with mental retardation had been discontinued due to overcrowding.

The schools accepted the immigrant children in customary fashion even though many were illiterate. Those who had been diagnosed as having mental retardation were less welcome because there was little precedent for their attending the public schools. The decision confronting the schools involved establishing the status of these students within the school. Should they be considered members of the conventional student body, or should they be set apart from other students because they were so different in learning characteristics and, in many cases, in their behaviors?

How State Schools Influenced Schooling Decisions

The fact that students with mild mental retardation had been or could have been committed to state schools played a role in shaping the decision that affected their status in the school. Most children and youth with auditory and visual disabilities, as well as those with mental retardation, attended separate residential schools within their states. State schools for children with auditory and visual disabilities were provided by state education agencies and were administered by educators. However, state schools for individuals with mental retardation came under the aegis of the state medical services and were administered by physicians.

Furthermore, while the mission of state schools for students with auditory and visual disabilities was identical to that of local schools, the mission of state schools for individuals with mental retardation was to admit those whose maladaptive behaviors made them unwelcome members of their communities, teach them acceptable behaviors, and return them to their communities to live as productive citizens.

From the mid-19th century, when Dr. Seguin theorized that mental retardation could be cured by engaging these children in activities that required acceptable behaviors, to the maturation of the mental measurement movement in the early 20th century, the diagnosis of mental retardation was made subjectively by physicians. As intelligence tests and behavioral measures improved in objectivity, reliability, and validity, diagnoses appeared to become more accurate. Even so, the deinstitutionalization movement of the 1960s uncovered a notable number of adult residents whose intelligence had been underestimated. As children, they had exhibited emotional problems, communication disabilities, and/or sensory disorders that were mistaken for mental retardation. There were also many with cerebral palsy whose inability to respond to ordinary tests of intelligence was equated with mental retardation, in addition to children with autism and other forms of central nervous system malfunctions.

These children's poor performance on intelligence tests and behavior checklists led to their assignment to state schools. Almost a century later, similar discoveries were made in public schools with the emergence of specific learning disabilities as a special education category and the subsequent retesting of students in special classes for children with mild mental retardation.

State schools never realized their goal because the medical model that guided their operations did not require the development of a curriculum and instructional methods to serve as a framework for the experiences that would "cure" their residents' mental retardation and return them to their communities. Without a comprehensive educational program designed to socialize residents, discharges from state schools were reduced to a trickle. What was originally expected to be a transient population settled in as lifelong residents. By the early 20th century, the state schools were so seriously overcrowded and moribund that admissions were limited to one-for-one replacements.

The Public Schools as Educational Settings

The perceptions of children with mental retardation held by school administrators and their school boards were reinforced by the medical and psychological literature that underscored their behavior disorders, their antisocial tendencies, and the difficulty in remedying them (Fernald, 1912; Kerlin, 1887; Doll, 1921). The proposition that mental retardation was hereditary (Dugdale, 1877; Estabrook, 1915; Goddard, 1910, 1913, 1914; Osborne, 1894) caused a radical change in attitudes toward people with mental retardation; earlier concerns for their welfare were often displaced by fear and rejection. The "exploited innocents" whose needs provoked the state school movement as a benign alternative to their placement in almshouses and jails (Dix, 1904) were portrayed by Barr (1904), Goddard (1920), and others as depraved and criminal parasites whose breeding propensities threatened to overwhelm society.

Most public school administrators were swayed by these reports and by the conclusion of influential psychologists that it would be detrimental to nondisabled students if they and students with mild retardation attended the same schools (Goddard, 1913). Many school administrators argued vigorously, but to no avail, against accepting these students in their schools (Hendricks & MacMillan, 1989).

Faced with the mandate to accept students with mild retardation in their schools, administrators and their school boards were confronted with two choices. They could subscribe to the philosophy that governs education in a democratic society and accept these children as students who were included in society's expectation that its schools socialize all of its young. Or they could adopt the medical model governing state schools' programs and provide activities designed to remediate their maladaptive behavior.

Had they opted for the former, they would have been obligated to provide these students with an alternative to the general education program—an educational program based on a comprehensive curriculum that was consistent with the goals of education for all students. This curriculum could have been designed to fulfill their learning needs and to accommodate their learning characteristics. Most important, at the time, the development of this curriculum would not have been influenced by any presuppositions or projections of their limitations as adults. Opting for the latter would allow the admission of students with mild retardation to their community's schools. However, they would be isolated from other students in small, manageable groups in their own classrooms. Thus, the tranquility of the school would be preserved at the minor cost and inconvenience of providing classrooms or equivalent space and hiring teachers.

In the short run, providing these students with an appropriate educational program would have been costly. The conventional operations of the schools would have been disrupted because there were no reliable precedents for identifying strategies for accommodating students with mental retardation or other disabilities in ongoing instructional programs. Trial and error would have governed most decisions. Integrating children with disabilities into the educational scene would have required the development of curriculum prototypes as alternatives to the only curriculum in the schools, the general education curriculum. Professional staff would have required extensive preparation, and reliable ways for identifying students and grouping them for instruction would have been needed. As challenging as these tasks may seem, they were nevertheless doable.

In the long run, providing these students with an appropriate education would have resulted in savings to schools and communities. Special education would have been unnecessary. Children with disabilities and their families would have been spared stigmatization. And it is likely that, given an appropriate education, a notable proportion would have been able to complete their education and achieve many of the autonomies typical of employed, participatory citizens who have attained social inclusion.

The General Education–Special Education Dichotomy

Administrators opted for the second alternative, and public school education evolved into a general education–special education dichotomy. Consistent with the medical model upon which it was based, special education subscribed to the theory proposed by Seguin, a century and a half earlier, that an accurate diagnosis of each student's disability would lead to a system of classification that would enable each student to be placed in an appropriate educational setting (Seguin, 1841). Special education has yet to realize this goal because the disabilities in question—mental retardation, emotional problems, and learning disabilities—derive from central nervous system conditions and have never been relevant to educational placement and instruction. To put it another way, within the context of education, disability is not a defining variable. Labels specifying central nervous system disorders that result in sensory, cognitive, or behavioral deficits and disorders, individually or in combination, say nothing about what students need to learn or how they should be taught.

Had schools accepted children with disabilities as bona fide members of the student body, educators would have had to design an educational program for them based on a comprehensive curriculum that was consistent with the goals of education for all students. This would have led to the instructional objectives necessary for their attainment of these goals.

Without a commitment to the goals of education and the educational criteria for classifying students, special education has spent the last century fixed firmly in a taxonomic state in an ongoing endeavor to find the ideal classification system: one that would unequivocally place children's learning and/or behavioral deficits within one or the other parameters of mental retardation, sensory disabilities, emotional disorders, or specific learning disabilities. Consequently, special education became, and continues to be, an array of remedial and ameliorative treatments and procedures rather than an educational program that imparts a body of knowledge organized in curricular form.

History Repeated

The quality of life and the experiences of students with mild disabilities attending schools in their communities were far superior to those sent earlier to state schools. However, the outcomes of their schooling were not superior. The medical model locked special education into a closed cycle of screening, testing, and classifying students according to their central nervous system disorders. Children who met the arbitrarily established criteria were assigned to special education classes accompanied by reports of their deficits. Because their performance in a comprehensive curriculum was not part of the screening, testing, and classifying process, their teachers had only the details of students' deficits to guide their instruction.

Teachers adopted the instructional programs that originated in the state schools, in which the emphasis was on manual activities to sharpen motor skills associated with the kinds of jobs they might obtain. When machines replaced handwork in factories, these activities were replaced by arts and crafts projects. However, when it became obvious to teachers that students needed more than an array of motor skills to obtain employment, they looked to their only known source, the general education curriculum, as the framework for their classroom instruction. Reading proficiency became the major goal. This has been the status quo for over half a century.

Follow-Up Studies

Studies of the status of school-leavers provide evidence that public school special education programs for students with mild disabilities have not been any more effective than those provided in the state schools. The first follow-up studies reported the failure of the majority of former residents of state schools to secure gainful employment and a good quality of life (Fernald, 1919). Later, the focus of these studies was on public school-leavers with mild disabilities (Goldstein, 1964). The ability of adults with mild disabilities to get and hold remunerative employment was a critical factor in all studies. A series of follow-up studies that spanned the better part of a century reported that, like their state school counterparts, the vast majority failed to get and keep employment. Recently, Blackorby and Wagner (1996) found, in a similar study, that (a) students with disabilities are significantly overrepresented among school dropouts, (b) as adults, they are the largest unemployed group in American society, (c) their arrest rate is greater than that of their peers without disabilities, and (d) they are less likely to live independently in their communities.

In mid-2004, a National Organization on Disabilities news release reporting results of the Harris Survey of Americans with Disabilities revealed that, in addition to data congruent with earlier follow-up studies, three times as many people with disabilities live in poverty, only 35% are employed full or part time, and only a third report a satisfactory quality of life.

Efficacy Studies

The constantly upward spiraling expenses for maintaining the state schools and, later, special education in public schools were not supported by evidence of effective educational programs. This prompted a lengthy sequence of efficacy studies, which were initiated in the 1930s when it was estimated that at least 50% of students with mild disabilities who were eligible for placement in special education classes were attending regular education classes because of a shortage of qualified special education teachers and classroom facilities (Bennett, 1932; Pertsch, 1936). The studies were designed to test the assumption that programs in special education classes were more responsive to the learning needs and characteristics of students with mild mental retardation than programs in general education classes.

These studies compared the performance of students with mild disabilities in special education classes with their counterparts in general education classes. None found that special classes were better educational settings for these students than general education classes. At best, the results were equivocal.

Together, the follow-up studies of school-leavers with mild disabilities and the efficacy studies are evidence to critics of special education of the results of a century of ineffective educational programs. The follow-up studies were instrumental in the extinction of the state schools. Both were instrumental in the emergence of the Inclusive School Movement (ISM) which could be interpreted as a vote of no confidence in public school programs for students with mild disabilities. Had there been solid evidence of effective educational programming for these students and their more disabled counterparts, the arguments of ISM advocates that children with disabilities have a right to be educated in the company of their nondisabled peers might not have attracted the support that has polarized special education.

Cost and Effect

In the 75 years preceding the enactment of the Education of All Handicapped Children Act of 1975 (P.L. 94-142), the cost of special education was borne by state education agencies and local school districts. In the years that P.L. 94-142 and IDEA have been in force, the U.S. Congress has contributed over $50 billion to help states and their local school districts meet the expenses of special education. Local schools together with state and regional educational administrations have contributed considerably more. During the 1999–2000 school year alone, they expended more than $77 billion, for an average of over $12,000 per student with disabilities, almost twice the amount spent for each general education student (Chambers, Parrish, & Harr, 2002).

While expenditures for education increased significantly, the unemployment rate for individuals with disabilities continues to be more than 10 times that of the population as a whole. In the equation that determines social inclusion and quality of life, education and gainful employment are the two most important factors. An appropriate education is the foundation for gainful employment. In turn, gainful employment subsidizes one's social and personal autonomies, thereby affecting quality of life.

The persisting high unemployment rate of adults with disabilities indicates that a century of schooling provided for students with disabilities has made no discernible difference in their employability or in the quality of their lives. In this sense, special education has failed to fulfill society's mandate to the schools to socialize its young.

Invention as an Alternative to Change and Reform

Over time, special education's inability to fulfill society's mandate has provoked a wide array of changes and reforms but none have reached the proportions and impact of IDEA and ISM. In the tradition of change and reform in special education, IDEA deals exclusively with procedures—the how-tos of special education. The law details who will be involved in its implementation and where and when procedures will take place. IDEA makes no reference to what children and youth with disabilities need to learn to go into the adult world armed with the knowledge and skills they need to achieve a measure of autonomy consistent with social inclusion. Thus, IDEA is emblematic of the fact that there is no substance to special education that rationalizes the changes and reforms in the law and provides a framework for evaluating the outcomes of their implementation.

Similarly, ISM deals only with procedures—where students with disabilities should get their schooling, the procedures for locating them in accordance with ISM policies, and who should be involved. And like IDEA, ISM does not concern itself with what students with disabilities need to learn other than insisting that they participate in the general education curriculum. Their performance on reading and arithmetic achievement tests required by the No Child Left Behind legislation is a commentary on the wisdom of this policy. Consequently, there is no way to ascertain the merits of the procedures it recommends. The outcomes of IDEA and ISM indicate that both fall short of being effective vehicles for change and reform.

When change and reform are unproductive, there is a third option available—invention. It may be assumed that when it becomes necessary to invent a program, it is because the program in force was irrelevant from the onset or because it became so irrelevant over time that changing or reshaping it piecemeal would not make enough difference to warrant the effort.

The prospect of returning to square one within the present complex and costly structure of special education to invent an alternative to the general education program may seem daunting. However, ethics and morality leave educators no alternative. To ignore the evidence that what passes as educational programs for students with disabilities are ineffective and to nevertheless continue present practices would be a betrayal of society's trust, and it would deny students with disabilities social inclusion and the opportunity to achieve a quality of life of their own making.

Laying a Foundation for Invention

If the invention of educational programs is to be effective, it is imperative that the condition which makes the process necessary is identified and avoided. While the inadequacy of special education programs is rarely addressed in the literature or at professional meetings, there is, nevertheless, a sense among most educators that the source of the problem is in the fact that special education has its roots in a medical model. This is alluded to in a report from the National Early Childhood Technical Assistance System (NECTAS): "for a growing number of students with disabilities, special education today is not preparing them for increasingly rigorous graduation requirements and career skills that are based on problem solving, collaboration, and technology. Why is this? Special education has typically been viewed as an intervention of remediation" (NECTAS, 1999, p. I-21). Similarly, Gersten (1998) writes that while nondisabled students hone their skills through practice in problem-solving activities, students with disabilities receive remediation interventions. In their assessment of the effectiveness of special education, Kavale and Forness (1999) underscore the fact that the focus of special education is on remediation.

Recognizing the disparity in the models that govern the operations of general and special education and in their outcomes is the first step in uncovering the underlying problem. The next step is to understand how a medical model became the basis for the education of students with disabilities. The ultimate step is to correct the condition by replacing the medical model with an educational model that will serve as a framework for inventing educational programs for these students.

Looking Ahead

The ensuing chapters first address the need for the invention of a curriculum that will be an alternative the general education curriculum—one that (a) will accommodate the learning needs and characteristics of students with disabilities and those of their underachieving counterparts and (b) will be consistent with the goals of education for all students. These chapters are followed by the design and explication of an educational model based on social sciences constructs to replace the medical model that has persisted since the early 1880s. The basis for a comprehensive, synergistic curriculum as a foundation for the education of students with mild disabilities is discussed. The last chapters present a detailed development, implementation, and dissemination strategy for the development of a computer-based curriculum for children and youth with mild disabilities.

All of these chapters often draw from the literature related to students with mild mental retardation for two reasons. First, educational provisions for children and adults with mental retardation have a much longer and much more elaborate history than do programs for children with mild behavior disorders and learning disabilities. Throughout this history, there are indications that diagnostic procedures related to the intellectual abilities of children result in a notable proportion of false positives—children who have learning disabilities, behavior disorders, and/or a variety of central nervous system malfunctions. Second, until recently, there has been a dearth of cross-categorical exploration and, therefore, only the first signs of an emerging literature. Readers are urged, therefore, to look at references to individuals with mental retardation as being relevant to a remarkably heterogeneous school-age population because of the problems in social and personal adaptation that they have in common with other categories of students with disabilities and with a significant proportion of underachievers in general education (Gresham & MacMillan, 1997; Walker & Bullis, 1991; Gresham, Sugai, & Horner, 2001).

It is likely that some readers will be confronted with some of the foregoing issues for the first time. The special education literature dealing with curriculum development is minuscule. A Google search establishes this fact clearly. It is likely that coping with the concept of a synergistic, computer-based curriculum will provoke anxiety caused by the many logistical and legal unknowns. Similarly, finding educationally relevant classifications for the students most suitable for participating in an alternative to the general education curriculum will conflict with the requirements in P.L. 94-142 and IDEA that these students be identified by the traditional labels associated with their central nervous system disorders.

To solve this problem and others yet to emerge, convention and tradition will have to be overcome as educators explore and experiment with educationally productive ways of imparting the proposed curriculum effectively and economically. To put it in practical terms, the bad news is that efforts to provide students with mild disabilities and their underachieving peers with an appropriate curriculum will present educators with more problems than they can anticipate. The good news is that all such problems have solutions and that they must and can be solved.

Dealing with the Unconventional

Some readers may object to the idea of combining of students with mild mental retardation, behavior disorders, learning disabilities, and academic underachievement in the same educational program. If this were proposed under the present conditions in schools, their objections would be justified. After all, untold energy, time, and funds have been dedicated to finding ways to distinguish these students from each other, even though a sizable literature underscores the fact that they have in common serious and persisting problems in their personal, interpersonal, and social relationships (Forness & Knitzer, 1992; Gresham, 1992; LaGreca & Stone, 1990; Skiba & Grizzle, 1991). Nevertheless, while we wait for other professions to resolve the central nervous system disorders that are likely the basis for the learning characteristics and behavior of children and youth with mild disabilities, educators can deal with their personal and interpersonal development by engaging them in a curriculum based on the social learning principles proposed in this book. The educational program proposed is not another kind of special education program. It should be perceived, along with general education, vocational education, college prep, and advance placement programs, as one designed to meet the needs of students who do not fit the conventional mold.

There is no doubt that once the proposed curriculum takes shape and programs for these students are invented, we will be able to devise educationally relevant identities for them. Until then, they will be referred to as students with mild disabilities for lack of a more appropriate term.

Before you turn the page, a caveat. If you read this book with an eye toward simply remedying the status quo or if you judge the merits of the outcomes of this book by the likelihood that they could be implemented in today's special education programs, you have missed the point of the book. The operative concept is neither to repair nor to reshape—it is to invent.

The Context
for Invention

Chapter

Educational programs in public schools take place within a social, political, and economic context that characterizes the society that the schools serve. The events and conditions in society that make up this context have an impact on decisions which affect the strategies and tactics employed in the invention of programs for students with mild disabilities. In particular, they influence the selection of the knowledge, behaviors, skills, and proficiencies that, in combination, become the curriculum that is the foundation for the invention process.

Technological and Social Change

Of the many factors that make up this context, technological and social change are the most important because of their role in determining the extent to which students with mild disabilities will achieve independence in adult society. Automation and robotization, for example, have eliminated many jobs that were once within their capabilities. Among many occupations that remain accessible, the ability to use relatively simple devices such as scanners and calibrators has become a prerequisite.

Regarding social change, the deinstitutionalization movement of the 1960s has had an impact on individuals with mild disabilities and their families, shifting responsibility for the care and shelter of individuals with mild disabilities from institutions to their home communities. In a notable

17

proportion of families, the aging of the parents and their diminishing ability to provide care and shelter has led to a crisis. Advocacy groups, state agencies, and communities are responding by providing community residences for small groups of adults who need supervision. For those who have attained the necessary level of independence through employment or family subsidies, apartments as well as guidance and some supervision are being provided. In both situations, this is a new way of life for those whose experiences have been limited to the privacy, customs, and mores of their homes. Their adaptability to these changes in residence and the quality of their lives will be determined by the quality of their educational programs.

The direct implication of technological and social change on the education of students with mild disabilities has always been evident in society as their educational programs evolved. Within this context, the proliferation of their programs over the course of the 20th century was remarkably rapid and dramatic. In just over 100 years, education of students with mild disabilities grew from a scattered patchwork of classrooms and services to one of the most complex, expensive, and controversial aspects of public school education.

The century was marked by events and conditions in society and in public school education that influenced the growth and configuration of educational programs for students with mild disabilities. Some events and conditions had and continue to have both direct and indirect implications for curriculum development—some positive and some not.

When inventing educational programs for students with mild disabilities, being able to capitalize on the positive while avoiding the negative can make a remarkable difference in both the procedures for developing curriculum and in the decisions that affect curriculum content. The enabling factor is the awareness of the history of educational programs for students with disabilities. Toward this end, a brief history follows.

A Select History of Educational Programs in the United States for Students with Mild Disabilities

Although the existence of individuals who are disabled by intellectual deficit and affective disorders is as old as humankind itself, the history of societies organizing and supporting comprehensive educational programs designed to reduce the dependency of its constituency by ameliorating the effects of disability is only about 150 years old. Prior to the pioneering work of Jean-Marc Gaspard Itard (1894) and Edouard Seguin (1841), philanthropic individuals and religious groups were the main source of help and support for individuals with disabilities (Scheerenberger, 1983).

The Origin of the Medical Model in Special Education

Early in the 19th century, Seguin proposed that dysfunctional senses constituted a peripheral nervous system that resulted in retarded mental development, of which children's maladaptive behavior was the major symptom (Seguin, 1841, 1846).

The mainstays of Seguin's theory and treatment and his legacy to special education were a medical model for the diagnosis and treatment of mental retardation in educational settings and the notion that the maladaptive behavior of individuals with mental retardation requires such distinctively different treatment from others with identical symptoms but different etiologies (e.g., emotional disorders) that they need separate educational settings. These beliefs have persisted to the present.

Early in the 19th century, Seguin proposed a method for curing mental retardation that became the model for special education programs for all children with disabilities. He proposed that the key to successful treatment was a careful diagnosis of the sensory deficits associated with each child's condition that would lead, in turn, to the prescription of appropriate treatment activities (Seguin, 1907). The purpose of these treatment activities was to "bombard" the senses and jar them into a normal state.

Accordingly, Seguin prescribed a physiological method for engaging children in the acquisition of the social skills that had escaped them in the ordinary course of their maturation. He claimed that this procedure would serve two purposes simultaneously: it would stimulate the peripheral nervous system and return it to its normal functions and teach children social skills that would replace the maladaptive behaviors symptomatic of mental retardation.

The popularity of Seguin's physiological method for the treatment of mental retardation spread to the United States, where he became influential in the emerging state school movement. (For a comprehensive history of Seguin's role in the education of children with intellectual, affective, and sensory disabilities, see Talbot [1964].)

The State School Movement

In this country, Dr. Samuel Howe (1849), impressed by Seguin's work, was instrumental in launching the state school movement. Howe, director of the state-run Perkins School for the Blind in Massachusetts, was successful in educating children with visual impairments. He contended that state schools should also be established for children with mental retardation.

Howe was successful in persuading the Massachusetts legislature to fund a three-year experimental social skills training program for these children. He opened a wing of the Perkins School to 10 children with mental retardation. After two years, a committee appointed to assess Howe's effort found the results promising. Accordingly, the state legislature appropriated funds for a residential school for children with mental retardation (Richards, 1935). The goal of state schools for individuals with mental retardation was to remove them from the home and community conditions that fostered their condition, provide them with social skills training, and return them to their communities. The state school movement spread quickly.

The state school movement was on a shaky foundation from the outset. No state school came close to replicating the experimental model established by Howe. Most were more like hospitals than schools. Physicians were the principal administrators. Most were built in remote, sparsely populated areas that made it difficult to attract capable professional staff. As the population of state school residents grew, the ratio of professional staff to residents was reduced significantly. Accordingly, managing residents and maintaining the buildings and grounds took precedence over education.

The state schools' social environment had no resemblance to residents' homes and communities. Male and female residents, grouped by sex and age, lived in large buildings. Almost all functions were performed as large group activities: residents slept in dormitories, used large toilet and bathing facilities without privacy, and ate what was prepared for them in large dining halls. As a result, the customs and mores in state schools and the knowledge and behaviors needed to survive there had no relevance to life in their homes and communities.

Consistent with the medical model, state school programs did not develop curricula. Instead, in order to maintain order in the state school, staff concentrated on immediate goals designed to extinguish maladaptive behaviors and replace them with the knowledge, skills, and behaviors that were consistent with the social, psychological, and physical adaptive abilities demanded by their life conditions.

As a result, state schools were unable to help students attain the long-term educational goals that would enable them to make the transition from school to society effectively: to become productive and participating members of their communities. As a result, the anticipated cycling of individuals with mild mental retardation through the state schools never materialized, and most became lifelong residents. The evolution and demise of state schools for individuals with mental retardation that followed is now a matter of record and well documented (Tylor & Bell, 1984).

Public School Programs for Students with Mild Disabilities

When state schools for children and adults with mental retardation curtailed admissions late in the 19th century, communities had no recourse but to turn to their public schools for the education of children with mild disabilities. Public school administrators were far from enthusiastic about this turn of events. They were ill prepared for children with questionable reputations who arrived at a time when their schools were being overwhelmed by a sizeable influx of non-English speaking, illiterate, immigrant children. Grudgingly, public school administrators made room for these children in their schools, but they did not make substantive educational provisions of the same quality as those made for nondisabled students (Connors, 1989; Hendricks & MacMillan, 1989). As a result, students who were unable to cope with the curriculum in their general education classes due to deficits in intellectual and emotional aptitudes were removed and grouped in special classes.

During the first half of the 20th century, the number of children with mild disabilities eligible for enrollment in special classes exceeded the number of available places. There is no direct way to account for the increase in the number of school-age children with mild mental retardation, apart from the fact that as special education became more commonplace in local schools, teachers and administrators became more knowledgeable about the characteristics of their students and more accurate in identifying them.

Early in the 20th century, intelligence tests became more reliable and psychometricians became more skilled. Accordingly, more accurate distinctions were made between students who scored at or near the upper limit of intelligence quotients used to define mild retardation and those with other mild disabilities. Nevertheless, some students with emotional problems and learning disorders were misdiagnosed and assigned to special classes for students with mild retardation.

Because there had never been agreement on the prevalence of students with mental retardation or with other mild disabilities in public and private schools, educators and psychologists used a bell-shaped distribution of intelligence as the basis for estimating the proportion of children with mild mental retardation in the school age population. The results ranged from 3% (Mort, 1928) to 5% (Hilleboe, 1930), with the former becoming the conventional estimate.

In time, this estimate was treated as fact, and it became a benchmark when making decisions about students with mild retardation. It should be noted that only these children, referred to in some state educational codes as Educable Mentally Retarded (EMR) and in others as Educable Mentally Handicapped (EMH), were accepted into the schools. Children with moderate or severe mental retardation were turned away (Scheerenberger, 1983; Zedler, 1953).

The Context for Invention

Public School Programs for Students with Moderate to Severe Disabilities

School administrators and many educators of teachers in colleges and universities argued against the admission of children with moderate and severe disabilities to public schools. They contended that schooling for children with moderate and severe disabilities was inappropriate because they could not master academic subject matter. Furthermore, they maintained that children with moderate and severe disabilities were hazardous to their own well-being and, in some instances, to that of their schoolmates because many lacked the language ability to communicate their needs, few were toilet trained, and many had physical disabilities that limited their mobility.

Parents of children with severe and moderate disabilities and advocates of children's rights maintained that these children were, like all children, entitled to equal protection under the law and, therefore, to a public school education. In addition, they pointed out that in spite of the fact that the goal of education is to socialize all of our young, the schools were rejecting these children for being deficient in the very social skills that should be included in their curriculum (Goldberg, 1959).

Presently, children with moderate and severe disabilities are actively engaged in educational enterprises in the public schools as a result of their parents forming support groups in their communities in the early 1930s. Having been turned away by their community's schools, parents raised funds to underwrite educational programs for their children. They found classrooms wherever they could and often took turns teaching until they were able to hire someone to assume this role (Boggs, 1954; Hay, 1952). In time, these parents' groups coalesced into a powerful national organization, the National Association for Retarded Citizens (NARC), which played an important role in promoting P.L. 94-142, legislation that opened the schools to all children with disabilities. Similar parents' organizations have formed since to provide advocacy for children with mental health disorders and those with learning disabilities.

Problems in Special Education

By the mid-20th century, it was estimated that more than 50% of students with mild mental retardation were biding their time in regular classes, waiting for their school district to find a qualified teacher or an available classroom or both so that additional special education classes could be started.

Competition for certified teachers of children with mild mental retardation among school districts was keen. Local education agencies in rural areas and in states with low salary schedules had the most difficulty acquiring qualified teachers and support personnel such as school psychologists and school social workers.

The shortage of teachers and classrooms for students with mild disabilities all but disappeared with the passage of P.L. 94-142. Since that time, legislation for expanding educational provisions and related services has become commonplace at all levels of government. An elaborate infrastructure of educational and related services that accommodates the full range of children with mild disabilities has become a part of almost every school district.

Educational Outcomes

Despite vast outlays of funds and other resources to underwrite the growth of programs for students with mild disabilities, the public schools have been no more successful than the state schools in fulfilling society's expectation that these students would leave school with the ability to take on constructive and participatory roles in society. A remarkably large proportion of school-leavers with mild disabilities, like their state school counterparts in prior years, has been unable to secure and sustain employment that would ensure them a reasonable degree of autonomy (Hasazi et al., 1985; Mithaug, Horiuchi, & Fanning, 1984; Sitlington, Frank, & Carson, 1993; Wagner et al., 1991; Wagner & Shaver, 1989). Other follow-up studies indicated that students with disabilities had difficulty adjusting to life in the community. Their educational programs did not include tactics and strategies for self-advocacy (Mithaug, Martin, Agran, & Rusch, 1988). Accordingly, in their final year of school, they looked to IEP committees to make decisions and connections for them with service agencies in their communities (Chadsey-Rusch, Rusch, & O'Reilly, 1991).

While the proportion of unemployed school-leavers with mild disabilities varies somewhat from one follow-up study to another, it is consistently and markedly greater than that of the population as a whole (Blackorby & Wagner, 1996; Goldstein, 1964; Hasazi et al., 1985; Sitlington, Frank, & Carson, 1993; Wagner et al., 1991; Wagner & Shaver, 1989).

Until recently, the public schools have never been held accountable for the ineffectiveness of their programs for these students. As stated earlier, commissions appointed from time to time to assess the effectiveness of public school education consistently ignored programs for children with disabilities. Also, when performance standards such as competency testing have been imposed on the public schools, the vast majority of students with mild disabilities have been exempted. In those few instances when these students were required to participate in statewide testing, they were given specially designed tests, and the results were usually reported in an alternative or separate format (Ysseldyke, Thurlow, & Shriner, 1992).

Heterogeneity in Special Education Classrooms

By the mid-20th century, the heterogeneity in classes for students with mild mental retardation was becoming increasingly obvious. Without a comprehensive curriculum and the accountability that accompanies its implementation, there was little to prevent the expediency of using the special classes for children with mild mental retardation as repositories for problem children for whom the administration was unwilling or unable to provide an appropriate educational setting. It was not uncommon, therefore, to find one or more emotionally disturbed or behaviorally disordered children in these classes as well as some who were later diagnosed as having learning disabilities.

The remarkable heterogeneity in learning and behavioral attributes that characterized these classrooms frustrated teachers' attempts to provide relevant educational experiences for such a mixture of students. Because of the broad range of student aptitudes, many classrooms for students with mild retardation were reminiscent of the huge differences in age and ability of the one-room schoolhouses of early rural America.

The rationalization for assigning students with behavior disorders to educational settings for students with mild retardation was simply that regular classes were too stimulating and goal oriented. In other words, the general education classes couldn't provide students with behavior disorders or with serious deficits in reading or arithmetic abilities with the kind of structure or attention they needed. It was argued that special classes for students with mild retardation had fewer students and were managed by teachers who were experienced in dealing with behavior problems. In such settings, the argument went, students with behavior problems were more likely to get the attention they needed.

If teachers of students with mild retardation had had a comprehensive curriculum to meet the educational needs of their students, they would have been protected from the expediency that led to the placement of students with behavior disorders and learning disabilities in their classrooms. That is, they could have referred to the curriculum and documented the fact that the content of instruction appropriate for students with mild mental retardation would not meet the unreasonably wide range of educational objectives that more heterogeneous groups demanded. The futility of trying to implement a curriculum under such conditions would have been evident, and the practice of using the special classes for students with mild retardation as a catch-all would have been halted.

Conflicts in Terminology

Presently, the term *mentally retarded* has reached a new low in reputation. In many communities, the schools and other agencies go to some lengths to avoid its use. Thus far, none of the schemes to avoid the label has succeeded fully because the federal and state legislation concerning the reimbursement of expenses connected with educational programs for these students requires that the term be used for reporting and accounting purposes. Nevertheless, while many school systems report their census of students with mild mental retardation to state and federal agencies, they proscribe the use of the term *mentally retarded* in their instructional settings.

The use of euphemisms such as *intellectually challenged, handi-capable,* and *differently able* has been illusory. There is no evidence that such language has contributed significantly to improvement in the aptitudes or self-concepts of children with mild retardation or in the attitudes of their non-disabled schoolmates (Gottleib, 1975; Gottleib & Corman, 1985; Goodman, Gottleib, & Harrison, 1972; Siperstein, Leffert, & Wenz-Gross, 1997). Similarly, efforts to obscure their presence by inventing a catch-all group called noncategorical, which allowed schools to combine children with mild retardation and children with behavior disorders and with mild learning disabilities in the same classroom, did little more than add problems of classroom management to teachers' already complicated instructional burden.

The history of special education for students with mild disabilities in public schools is far from that of a vital, goal-oriented member of the educational establishment. Because they conform with a medical rather than educational model, programs for these students are remarkably different from those provided for students without disabilities. That is, programs for children with intellectual and behavioral deficits and learning disabilities are remedial rather than educational. They are not based on a comprehensive curriculum. Instead, they focus on the remediation of manifest maladaptive behaviors as well as deficits in academic achievement (Gersten, 1998; Kavale & Forness, 1999; NECTAS, 1999). In contrast, programs for nondisabled students are educational, based on comprehensive curricula that span the students' entire school experience.

Another way of distinguishing between special and general education is the fact that in special education, remediation is an end in and of itself. In general education, remediation is a means to an end: activities are designed to improve students' academic and behavioral skills and to expedite their attainment of the goals of education.

Providing educational programs for students with mild disabilities that are comparable qualitatively to those provided for students without disabilities will require the replacement of their present school experiences with an educational program that is entirely new. This program should be based on a comprehensive, developmentally organized curriculum that addresses their educational needs and learning characteristics. The content of such a curriculum and strategies for its development is discussed in detail in subsequent chapters.

Missed Opportunities for an Appropriate Education

The first opportunity to devise an appropriate education for children with mental retardation came at the turn of the 20th century when the limiting of admissions to state schools for people with mental retardation confronted local schools with large numbers of children with mild retardation. The second opportunity came some 70 years later when the Pennsylvania Association for Retarded Children (PARC) (1971) accepted a consent decree as a settlement of its suit against the Commonwealth of Pennsylvania. At both of these critical moments, administrators and school boards had the same options: to assess the effectiveness of the educational programs they were acquiring before accepting them and to explore other formulations.

PARC v. the Commonwealth of Pennsylvania

At the turn of the 20th century, the failure of the state schools was far from a secret. Recognizing that children with mental retardation and, parenthetically, children with other disabilities, would soon be entering the public schools in large numbers, public school administrators had the opportunity to familiarize themselves with the conditions that led to the failure of the state schools and to avoid these conditions in planning their own school programs for these children. Over half a century later, PARC charged that the state and its department of education were denying children with moderate and severe mental retardation their right under the law to an education at public expense. The PARC case was pivotal because its outcome set the scene for P.L. 94-142 and for P.L. 101-476 Individuals with Disabilities Education Improvement Act of 2004 (IDEA). When the authors of P.L. 94-142 prepared the legislation for which the PARC case was a precedent, the failure of the large majority of adults with disabilities to gain the kinds of remunerative employment that would support an acceptable quality of life was prominent in the literature of special education and vocational rehabilitation.

Had the authors of P.L. 94-142 been attentive to these data, they might have expanded the parameters of conventional public school education to accommodate all children with disabilities. That is, they might have started with the presumption that educational programs for these children, like those for all children, need to be consistent with the goals of education.

Accordingly, educators could have designed programs in which the educational experiences of students with disabilities would be based on a curriculum that was appropriate to their maturational needs and learning characteristics rather than on the medical model that was the downfall of the state schools' programs and subsequent programs in the public schools.

In all likelihood, had educators opted for this alternative, the troublesome distinctions between general and special education would not have materialized. However, at the turn of the 20th century and again 75 years later, they elected to maintain the status quo, thereby perpetuating the aberration of using a medical model to provide the framework for educational enterprises.

The rationale for maintaining the status quo became evident in the course of the hearings required by the consent decree agreed to by both PARC and the Pennsylvania department of education. In reporting on their progress in meeting the mandates of the decree, a notable proportion of school administrators and representatives of their boards of education were candid about their conviction that few of the children with mental retardation in their schools would become as productive in adulthood as their nondisabled peers.

Many administrators objected to the costs of educational programs for these children, claiming that the funds would be better spent on the education of gifted students who, they argued, would some day have to provide for the students with disabilities. As distasteful and unprofessional as this presumption may be, it is nevertheless given credibility by the follow-up studies of school-leavers with mild disabilities discussed earlier.

The Impact of the Deinstitutionalization Movement

The population of state institutions for individuals with mild mental retardation and for those who were mentally ill remained unchanged until the mid-20th century. Efforts to limit admissions to replacements for deaths and escapes were somewhat successful. Nevertheless, the overpopulation of such institutions became acute. Services and programs were overwhelmed and the residents stagnated. Advocacy groups initiated campaigns to protect the rights of residents, demanding that the state agencies that managed institutions direct their efforts to providing a system of community residences and services. The strategy was to accommodate institutionalized people in their home communities with their families, if possible, or in state-supported neighborhood residences. Thus, residents would be living near agencies that were already well staffed and capable of providing a wide variety of services. The campaign was successful first for people in institutions for the mentally ill and shortly after for those with mild mental retardation.

With the rapid depopulation of state institutions in the 1960s and 1970s and the abrupt arrival in communities of a large number of individuals of all ages with mental retardation and with mental illness, families were affected in ways that would soon have implications for education. Some parents found it very difficult to accommodate their offspring in their homes. Some teenagers and adults had acquired serious behavior problems and were difficult to control. In some households, both parents were employed, while in others only one parent was present. A notable proportion of parents were in their declining years. This made the care and supervision of their sons and daughters extremely difficult.

The serious physical disabilities and the death of some parents exacerbated the problems for older adults with mental retardation and with mental illness. Some were fortunate enough to have had parents with the resources and the foresight to establish trust funds or the equivalent to provide for their care. Unfortunately, the families of a substantial number of individuals with mild disabilities lacked and continue to lack the wherewithal to invest in such protection for their children. To this state of affairs, we can add the fact that there was then, and continues to be, relatively little advocacy and painfully few community accommodations available for older adults with mild disabilities.

Apart from a few effective post-school training and support programs for adults with mild disabilities (Halpern, Close, & Nelson, 1986), the literature on community residence programs and supported employment suggests that, with few exceptions, these accommodations are not only slow in coming about but are reserved mainly for people with moderate or severe disabilities, for those convalescing from mental illness, and for recovering substance abusers.

Presently, there is little in the political scene that warrants optimism regarding the rapid spread of community residences for adults with mild disabilities. While some states have appropriated funds to purchase and activate community residences for adults with disabilities, such funds are difficult to obtain because of the not-in-my-backyard sentiments in many neighborhoods. To complicate matters, in places where residences have been established, they are often impossible to staff because of the low salaries that prevail. In those that have been staffed, the turnover of workers is so rapid that sustaining continuity in programs is difficult.

Misconceptions of the Deinstitutionalization Movement

Those who promoted the long-overdue closing of state institutions for people with mild mental retardation and with mental illness did not plan ways to facilitate their transition from institutional to community life. Like their counterparts in the deinstitutionalization movement, people in the mental health services presumed that community social service and health agencies would find the resources to add the newcomers to their already crowded caseloads. That is, they believed that the abrupt release of people with disabilities into the community would create stresses of such proportion that the community would find it necessary to respond with personnel and services to care for these troubled and troublesome newcomers. This strategy makes no concessions to the needs of others in the community, to the strain on available resources, or to the capacity of the community to absorb the added costs.

Effects of Technological Change on the Employment of Adults with Mild Disabilities

Technology, particularly as it relates to the means of production, has always had bearing on the quality of life of individuals with mild disabilities. Beginning with the Industrial Revolution, the increasing sophistication of technological devices at work, in the home, and throughout the community has determined the extent to which people with mild disabilities achieve autonomy. For example, until the 1930s, farmwork was an ideal occupation for men with mild mental retardation. Workers typically received room and board as part of their compensation, and they benefited from the guidance and supervision of the farmer and his family. Household helper was a popular placement for women with mild mental retardation for the same reason.

Then came the mechanization of farming equipment. The requirements for operating and maintaining this equipment not only challenged the competencies of farmworkers in general, but it ultimately rendered most of them redundant. Tractors required less daily care than horses and performed more work. At about the same time, the electrification of homes and the resulting availability of appliances such as toasters, vacuum cleaners, washing machines, and dryers revolutionized housekeeping and drastically reduced the need for household helpers.

From World War II to the present, the proliferation of automation and robotization, the computerization of sales and inventory management, and the exportation of fabrication and assembly jobs to countries where labor costs were minimal helped to change the focus of the U.S. economy from manufacture to service. Accordingly, many jobs that were once well within the capabilities of adults with mild disabilities are now either performed by computers and machines or in the hands of workers elsewhere in the world.

However, the effects of these changes in technology do not end with the reduction of work opportunities for people with mild disabilities. These changes in technology and the export of jobs to foreign lands have also ended the employment of a large part of the conventional workforce. Like adults with disabilities, many nondisabled workers have turned to the service sector for employment. As a result, competition has increased for many jobs well within the capabilities of people with mild disabilities. It is becoming increasingly difficult to find career ladders with bottom rungs that are within reach of most adults with mild disabilities and other undereducated adults. If adults with mild disabilities are to succeed, they will need to enter the job market equipped with a higher level of skills and proficiencies than are presently provided by their educational programs.

Individuals with Mild Disabilities in the Criminal Justice System

In the late 1940s, visitors to Sonoma State School, an institution in California for children, youth, and adults with mental retardation, were surprised to find three widely separated buildings, each surrounded by high chain-link fences, among the facilities. The ominous appearance of the buildings, the barred windows, and a guard at the entry gate was in stark contrast to the otherwise verdant, rolling, Valley of the Moon campus. Two of the buildings housed about 40 male residents each, juveniles in one and adults in the other. The third building was reserved for adolescent and adult females.

The residents in these buildings had in common the fact that they had been committed to Sonoma State School following arrest and conviction for crimes that would have earned them quarters in San Quentin or Folsom Prison had they not been diagnosed as individuals with mild retardation. Some could have been sent to death row. Similar accommodations could be found in institutions for people with disabilities in other states.

Most visitors to Sonoma State School in the 1940s were surprised to see these grim, maximum security buildings because the link between mental retardation and crime has been tenuous. It is rarely discussed in educational circles except in the aftermath of spectacular crimes. Nevertheless, as Fitch (1989) reports, many societies have a long history of efforts to reconcile the legal defense of accused individuals with their questionable ability to distinguish right from wrong.

Ray (1831), Seguin (1846), Ireland (1877), Barr (1904), and Goddard (1914, 1920) subscribed to the concept of moral imbecility as an aspect of mental retardation. All were concerned with instances in which individuals with mental retardation engaged in criminal activities and how this condition should be taken into account by the courts. On a more positive note, the trend in recent years has been in the direction of advocacy for offenders with disabilities (Edwards & Reynolds, 1997; Norley, 1997).

Increase of Adults with Mild Disabilities in Prison Populations

Because the criminal justice system and the public schools rarely intersect, few educators are aware of the overrepresentation of adult offenders with mental retardation and learning disabilities in correctional facilities (Brown, 1989). Cohen (1985) and Steelman (1987) have reported that the number of inmates with mild retardation has doubled since the early 1970s. They see a connection between the increase in prison inhabitants and the deinstitutionalization movement.

One growing concern is the fact that although the flow of residents from state institutions has abated, there has not been a reduction in the number of prisoners with mild mental retardation. Hall (1989) suggests that the rising crime rate, pessimism about rehabilitation programs, and an advocacy of punishment reduce alternatives to incarceration for offenders with mild retardation.

Hall (1989) has found that because of the narrow purpose of correctional institutions, the constant potential for violence within these institutions, and the resulting stringency of rules, prisoners with mild disabilities are more than ordinarily capable of disrupting prison activities. This can make them difficult to manage. Moreover, in the ordinary course of life in the correctional institution, they are inclined to cause damage to property and injure other inmates, staff, or themselves.

Contrasting Goals of Schools and Correctional Institutions

Because of the differences in the goals of schools and of correctional institutions, behaviors that are tolerable in one can be intolerable in the other. That is, the goal of education is to send students into the community as functioning adults. Toward this end, educational institutions direct their resources to providing students with the knowledge and skills that provide the foundations for socially acceptable behavior. In contrast, the primary responsibility of correctional institutions is the secure containment of individuals remanded to their custody (Snarr & Wolford, 1985). Thus, the concern of the administrators is the security of their institution and the protection of both staff and inmates, in that order. Any behavior, innocent or not, that threatens the tranquility of correctional institutions provokes immediate, and often forceful, responses from staff.

Furthermore, adult inmates with mild disabilities in correctional institutions live, simultaneously, in two social systems. One is the visible, codified system that is part of the criminal justice system, within which each inmate lives as a condition of having achieved the status of prisoner. The second is the less visible, uncodified system that is designed and administered informally by the inmates. This system governs many of the behaviors of inmates by establishing acceptable and unacceptable ways for doing things as well as its own system of rewards and punishments. The authority to manage this system is often achieved and maintained through raw power. The authority may rest in an individual and his or her entourage, or it may be shared by a coalition of special interest groups.

Stress in Prison Life

Living within the law in two sometimes conflicting social systems must be very stressful for inmates with mild disabilities, particularly when security considerations do not allow for second chances or flexibility in the enforcement of rules. Corrections officers implement legally sanctioned methods of control that do not require concern for whom or what provoked the inmates' behavior. Accordingly, corrections officers are more concerned with the fact that inmates broke rules than with the reasons why they were broken (Hall, 1989).

Because of their difficulty adapting to the inmate society, poor judgment, and aggressiveness, inmates with mild disabilities are often abused or victimized by other inmates. Others make off with their personal property or lead them into homosexual acts or relationships, or they are used by wily inmates as cat's-paws in violating the institution's rules (Santamour, 1989). Consequently, prisoners with mild disabilities require greater attention and, therefore, an increase in staffing (Rowan, 1976; Santamour & West, 1977; Steelman, 1987).

Juvenile Offenders with Mild Disabilities

Drawing a connection between public school educational programs and the overrepresentation of adults with mild disabilities in prisons is extremely difficult. However, for juvenile offenders, school records are more readily available and with them the basis for their classification as students with disabilities. Schwartz and Koch (1992) point out that, nationwide, more than 300,000 juveniles are imprisoned on any given day. Wolford (1987) reported that the prison population in the United States had doubled over the preceding 15 years. From 1980 to 1995, arrests of juveniles age 10 to 17 for committing violent crimes increased by 70%, with indications that the numbers will continue to rise (Ransom & Chimarusti, 1997).

The Overrepresentation of Adolescents with Mild Disabilities in Correctional Institutions

Juveniles with mild disabilities are remarkably overrepresented in the populations of correctional institutions. In a national survey of youth correctional agencies, Bullock and McArthur (1994) found that 23% of incarcerated juveniles had disabilities. In a meta-analysis of the available prevalence studies, Casey and Keilitz (1990) reported that some 12.6% were classified as mentally retarded, 35.6% had learning disabilities, and more than 22% had mental health problems.

Theories that account for the overrepresentation of youths with mild disabilities underscore the relationship between students' educational experiences and their delinquent behavior. Some experts contend that a disproportionate number of students with learning disabilities and behavioral disorders experience academic failure, drop out of school, and become delinquents. Others feel that certain cognitive and behavioral deficits predispose some students with mild disabilities to delinquency (Fink, 1990). Keilitz and Dunivant (1986) claim that students with learning disabilities commit more acts of stealing from home and school, shoplifting, and property damage and that they are more likely to be apprehended by police than those without disabilities because they lack the skills to plan strategies, avoid detection, and understand questions and warnings during encounters with police. Bryan, Pearl, and Herzog (1989) conclude that students with learning disabilities are more likely to commit violent acts and abuse alcohol and drugs.

Education as Prevention

The data from adult and juvenile correctional institutions and theories about the conditions that lead to delinquency add a frequently overlooked dimension to the context for the reinvention of educational programs for students with mild disabilities. The data add weight to the argument that an appropriate education might reduce the proportion of youthful offenders with mild disabilities.

While it is reasonable to presume that students with mild disabilities who are beneficiaries of an appropriate education are less likely to become inmates of the criminal justice system, this presumption has no basis in fact until correctional agencies recognize that IDEA applies as much to prison programs as it does to the public school educational programs (Ransom & Chimarusti, 1997).

The Twenty-First Annual Report to Congress on the Implementation of the Individuals With Disabilities Education Act, submitted by the U.S. Department of Education in 1999, stated that the number of students with disabilities in correctional institutions increased at over twice the rate of those in the overall special education population between 1992 and 1997—an increase of 28% in correctional institutions compared with 13% in schools. The increase was most notable among youth with emotional problems and learning disabilities.

It is very likely that if educational programs for students with mild disabilities continue to be unstructured, undefined, and unresponsive to their needs, the data that characterize the outcomes and conditions of their education will only show continuing deterioration in their social status and the quality of their lives. Kauffman (2001) points out that in students with behavior problems, academic and social failures are almost inseparable. About 50% of these students are school dropouts (Wagner et al., 1991) and, as a result, are overrepresented in the ranks of the unemployed (Carson, Sitlington, & Frank, 1995).

Conclusion

34

The development of a curriculum for students with mild disabilities must take into account the fact that, like their nondisabled counterparts, they must establish themselves in a society that has become increasingly complex because of rapid and dynamic social and technological change. Thus, the content of their instruction needs to be based on a conceptual and factual formulation of social learning rather than on the present "school-to-work" exercises in social skills training that presently typify the last few years of their schooling.

Reports of the post-school experiences of individuals with mild disabilities indicate that most do not succeed in attaining the quality of life and autonomy that are underwritten by remunerative work. The data also show that if they do not have the support and guidance of their families, their options are reduced to (a) placement in a community residence with a work assignment in a supervised or supported, competitive work setting; (b) life in the underclass, often among homeless people, with total dependence on Supplemental Security Income (SSI) and the largesse of public and private social welfare agencies; or (c) confrontations with the law and confinement in the criminal justice system.

The condition of people with mild disabilities in society justifies our speculation about the extent to which a significantly greater number of school-leavers might have enjoyed a more positive outlook on life had we provided them with an appropriate education from the day they entered school. Twelve years or more of intensive and focused participation in an appropriate education might have had consequences that made a difference.

The results of follow-up studies and training programs justify the presumption that a program which puts literacy and other content into a social learning context might equip more students with mild disabilities with the skills and proficiencies needed to compete for, obtain, and sustain employment and to manage their personal and social affairs competently. Those able to achieve these autonomies would experience a more satisfying quality of life.

The Context for Invention

The Structure of an Appropriate Education

Implications for Planning and Decision Making

The mandate in P.L. 94-142 and Individuals with Disabilities Education Improvement Act of 2004 (IDEA) that all children with disabilities be provided with an appropriate education has been all but ignored by administrators of public school programs and by educators in institutions of higher education (IHEs). Some argue that this charge is unjustified, that evidence of schools providing children with mild disabilities with an appropriate education is readily available in the form of Individualized Education Programs (IEPs). They claim, in fact, that the specific curriculum that is the keystone of an appropriate education is ascertained simply by assembling each child's IEP in temporal order from the time he or she enters school to the time he or she leaves.

If we presume that each IEP is a curricular element, we ascribe to each a degree of validity and reliability that is inconsistent with the remarkable variability in the amount and quality of the data used to report each student's performance as well as the equally remarkable variability in the competencies and motivations of the individuals comprising the committees that design IEPs. That is, without a curriculum as a stable framework for assessment, the diverse sources of data—the tests, observations, experiences, and biases which influence the selection of the teaching and learning objectives for each IEP—along with the personnel changes from one IEP committee to the next do not make for the kind of consistency and continuity in content that characterizes a curriculum.

Fulfilling two of the three P.L. 94-142 and IDEA requirements cannot be construed as full compliance. The fact that accountability was not allowed to become an issue in the implementation of the law (Hocutt, Martin, & McKinney, 1991) does not absolve educators from their moral and ethical obligations to fulfill the law's intent. Thus, there is no avoiding the fact that the vast majority of, if not all, school districts are out of compliance with P.L. 94-142 and IDEA because they cannot provide evidence of their compliance with the substantive mandate of the law—to provide all children with disabilities with an appropriate education. Nor can we avoid the conclusion that the disregard of this mandate has led to something remarkably less than an appropriate education.

The Nature of an Appropriate Education

An appropriate education is an extraordinarily complex entity that is affected by every person, place, and thing in the classroom and as distant from the classroom as the professional preparation programs and research enterprises in IHEs. Some appreciation of the complex and dynamic nature of an appropriate education can be gained if we isolate a single teaching–learning moment, examine each of its elements individually, and then observe how they relate to each other. This is analogous to studying a single physical act such as throwing a ball in order to better understand how muscles, bone, sensorimotor elements, the central nervous system, and other factors combine to generate force and accuracy in the performance of this seemingly simple skill.

38

Each teaching–learning transaction can be viewed as an equation consisting of the same six elements. The equation, stated operationally, is "somebody is teaching something to someone somehow, sometime, somewhere." In this equation, *somebody* represents a teacher or teacher surrogate with the professional pedagogic skills that enable successful learning. *Something* is the content of instruction or the curriculum component that is relevant to the student's educational objectives. While this element can vary from a simple fact to a complex collection of facts, concepts, skills, and behaviors, its relevance to the student must be constant. *Someone* is the learner whose learning characteristics are known to and understood by the teacher. A competent teacher expects some variability in this element among students and incorporates and adjusts for similarities and differences in the teaching–learning activity. *Somehow* represents the instructional methods and aids, including technologies, that are germane to both the nature of the content to be imparted and the characteristics of the student(s) participating in the transaction. The mark of the competent teacher is the ability to make the best match of the content, the student's characteristics, and the teaching method. *Sometime* represents that point in a learner's development of knowledge and behaviors when the content to be learned represents the next logical acquisition in the student's knowledge bank. This is typically called readiness. If all of the elements of the equation are continuously in sync, readiness for learning is a steady state. The last element of the equation, *somewhere,* represents the teaching–learning environment—its physical, social, and psychological characteristics.

No significance should be attached to the fact that the place of instruction is discussed here as the last element in the equation. However, it is all too often the last requirement to be considered when educational programs for students with disabilities are designed. As a result, special classes and resource rooms for students with mild disabilities sometimes have a restricted range of learning activities and experiences because the location, size, or configuration of the classroom that is available cannot accommodate all of the conditions and activities that effective instruction requires.

The Role of Curriculum in an Appropriate Education

Curriculum is the keystone of the teaching–learning equation. While there are often alternatives and accommodations in all other elements of the teaching–learning equation, there is no substitute for a comprehensive curriculum nor are there ways for converting the disparate activities that presently characterize instructional practices in educational programs for students with mild disabilities into a curriculum.

Because there are no comprehensive curricula in special education, we can turn to existing curricula in general education to understand the attributes of a curriculum and how central it is to the implementation of an appropriate education. In reviewing the general education practices, our purpose is not to adopt them so much as to gain a sense of how general education organizes itself to provide its students with an appropriate education. A comparative view of programs for students with mild disabilities and those for general education students may reveal some important differences that could be instructive. For example, one need only compare the curriculum of the general education program in any community, large or small, with its program for students with mild disabilities to find differences that have serious implications for the success or failure of the educational programs.

Curriculum in General Education

The curriculum in general education is the body of knowledge that the schools impart to their students in order to fulfill their commitment to society to educate its young. While all curricula are similar in important ways, elements within each curriculum may vary among school systems. That is, while all curricula include the teaching of reading, they often vary remarkably in the nature of the instructional programs they adopt for this purpose.

Curricula typically consist of a continuum of developmentally organized content in each subject area that extends from the time a child enters school to graduation. Some content areas may have been developed or updated under the aegis of such prestigious organizations as the National Science Foundation or the National Foundation for the Humanities. Others benefit from the contributions of learned societies such as the International Reading Association and the Association for Supervision and Curriculum Development. Still others are the products of departments of curriculum and instruction at IHEs and, in some content areas, are the collaborative efforts of a number of diverse instructional content specialists.

While we do not have a uniform or national curriculum for our public schools, the similarities in curricula and instructional methods in local school districts throughout the country have resulted in educational programs that are more alike than different. Because these curricula are developmentally organized, students in general education are assured continuity in their educational experiences as they move from elementary school to middle school and on to high school.

Furthermore, should their family move across town or across the country, the probability is very good that they will be able to resume their education at essentially the same grade level in their new educational setting. Odds are that they will have to make fewer adaptations to their instructional content areas than they will to their new neighborhood, their classmates, and their teacher.

Limitations in Instructional Programs
for Students with Disabilities

There is no organized body of knowledge that special education is committed to imparting to students with mild disabilities. Nothing approximating the continuity and developmental organization of content that characterizes the general education curriculum is to be found in programs for these students. As a result, there is no curricular infrastructure in their educational programs. Instead, the curriculum in most classrooms is assembled by the teacher or a small group of teachers. It is not unusual to find that the curriculum consists of a patchwork of mail-order packages and kits of instructional materials intended for social skills training, remedial reading, and arithmetic. These are augmented by bits and pieces of academic materials assembled from general education textbooks and workbooks.

The configuration of this montage of subject matter areas varies from class to class in accordance with teachers' experiences, aptitudes, and biases. As a result, there is little continuity in the educational experiences of students with mild disabilities as they advance from primary to inter-mediate and then to secondary classes in their schools. Continuity in their educational experiences is even less likely if their family moves to another community.

We know relatively little about the specific effects of discontinuities in content on the learning of students with mild disabilities, how gaps or redundancies in their educational experiences affect their performance as students and later as adults. Continuity in instructional experiences can be a powerful reinforcer of learning. In contrast, inconsistencies and disparities in the educational experiences of students with mild disabilities can diminish the quality of their education and may intensify their learning and behavioral problems. The impact of discontinuities in the education of these students may contribute to their dissatisfaction with their schooling and, as a consequence, to their high dropout rate and their disproportionately high unemployment rate.

Defining an Appropriate Education

For present purposes, an appropriate education for students with mild disabilities is defined as one in which the curriculum, the content of instruction, the methods of instruction, the competencies of personnel, the nature of facilities, the technologies that support and enhance teaching and learning, and the strategies for the systematic evaluation of the outcomes of teaching and learning all correspond with the learning characteristics and developmental needs of students with mild disabilities and are consistent with the goals of education and with the objectives of education by which these goals are attained.

A *curriculum* is appropriate when (a) it contains the concepts, facts, and skills that, once learned, lead to the realization of the goals of education, namely, students' successful adaptation to their immediate environment and, at maturity, to the adult community, and (b) concepts, facts, and skills in the curriculum are organized developmentally and stated in terms that are consistent with the learning characteristics of students.

Methods of instruction are appropriate if they maximize the learning and retention of the curriculum's content by capitalizing on established principles of teaching and learning. Toward this end, they are consistent with the nature of the content as well as with the learning characteristics of children with mild disabilities. That is, methods of instruction are appropriate if (a) they introduce knowledge and skills in ways that ensure both immediate and long-term retention and combine situationally to form concepts and (b) they deal with the teaching and learning of concepts and abstractions in ways that enhance reasoning and problem-solving strategies and facilitate their generalization to practical situations. The common denominator for the appropriate teaching of concepts, facts, and skills is the student's learning characteristics.

The *competencies of personnel* are appropriate when (a) teaching, supervisory, administrative, and supportive staff comprehend and subscribe to their local education agency's (LEA's) conceptualization of the goals of education, (b) they are committed to the attainment of these goals, (c) they have the professional training, experience, and predisposition required to contribute to the realization of the goals of education, and (d) they are thoroughly familiar with the content and organization of the curriculum adopted by the school. Within this context, all personnel should be conversant with their colleagues' contributions to students' education and to the evaluation of the program's effectiveness.

Facilities, classrooms, and other instructional settings are appropriate when their design, location, size, and availability, accommodate teaching–learning and other curriculum-related activities prescribed by the curriculum. The size and configuration of facilities should not limit students' learning activities, hamper their deployment, or restrict their interactions with classmates, schoolmates, teaching personnel, and technologies. The physical properties of facilities should provide favorable light, acoustics, and working conditions, be readily accessible to everyone, and be conducive to the deployment and use of technologies and other instructional equipment.

Evaluation in educational programs for students with disabilities is appropriate when it is based on the curriculum and when it measures and communicates in useful ways the accomplishments of students in all aspects of their curriculum. To be appropriate, evaluation should be a formalized and frequent aspect of the total education program. The results should be reported in practical terms as they relate to the content of the curriculum and its implementation in the classroom and should lead to the most effective strategies for assigning students to instructional settings so that differences in their learning needs and characteristics are minimized.

Because of the symbiosis between schooling and life in the community, a system of evaluation that is consistent with an appropriate education includes the evaluation of the performance of school-leavers in important aspects of their activities in the community. This provides a measure of the educational program's effectiveness as well as data reflecting social and technological change and their implications for curriculum reform. Furthermore, such data provide direction for in-service education of professional staff. Thus, an appropriate evaluation system contributes to the vitality and effectiveness of educational programs.

With the attainment of the goals of education the basis for judging the relevance of educational practices, the configuration of an appropriate education is shaped by the nature of all of the decisions and actions, and by the characteristics of the people, things, and places that are required for education to fulfill its function efficaciously and economically.

An Appropriate Education and the Individualized Educational Program (IEP)

The gaps and ambiguities in the conceptualization of the IEP and its functions within the context of P.L. 94-142 help to explain why the literature on the effectiveness of IEPs provides little credibility to claims that IEPs, as they are presently developed, have notable pedagogic value (Billingsley, 1984; Carrell, Kayser, Mason, & Haring, 1987; Gallagher & Desimone, 1995; Welton, 1981; Ysseldyke, Algozzine, & Mitchell, 1982).

Development of an IEP

The process for developing IEPs for students with mild disabilities reflects precisely this state of affairs. For example, selection to serve on the committee entrusted with this important task is, more often than not, based on occupational titles rather than the more exacting criteria that participants are (a) knowledgeable about the general and specific aspects of educational programs for students with mild disabilities and (b) aware of and in accord with the immediate and long-term goals for each student. One can infer from the foregoing an expectation that the same or a comparable version of the IEP would be written irrespective of the nature of the committee's membership. This has yet to be substantiated.

The development of IEPs for students with disabilities is, for the most part, a highly subjective undertaking in which need to comply with the requirements in IDEA often take precedence over the IEP's relevance and quality. Nevertheless, the concept and intent of the IEP is, prospectively, one of the best aspects of IDEA. The IEP has the potential to be an indispensable element in an appropriate education. The vast majority of problems that emerge during the development and implementation of IEPs could be circumvented if educators of students with mild disabilities thought of the IEP as part of the total educational process, as an element of an appropriate education rather than as an artifact of legislation.

Contents of an IEP

The ideal IEP is a plan within a plan. That is, the huge and complex nature of the goals of education requires that those who are responsible for the fulfillment of these goals organize a plan under which the goals can be reached by the time the student graduates. While educational plans or programs throughout the country have a great deal in common, they vary in certain ways from one school district to another because they are affected by the LEA's philosophy and values.

In a school district where the community believes that students should become entrepreneurial, it is anticipated that most will go on to college and become professionals or business executives. Such districts generally have a plan and curriculum in their schools coinciding with this goal. The plan and curriculum are reflected in the conceptual basis of academic subject matter and in the kinds of facts, skills, and proficiencies that their curriculum imparts to their students.

The same is true of the district's other associated goals: those designed to give rise to as many fine musicians and artists, superior athletes, and great writers as can be found in the student body. This kind of school district is likely to foster magnet schools, intramural orchestras, and highly competitive debate and athletic teams.

In another school district, where the community values employability and craftsmanship, the proportion of students going on to colleges and universities is likely to be notably smaller. Accordingly, the community's curriculum focus will be on occupational education, and most students will attend the community's vocational or technical school. Those who aspire to the status of artisan will likely engage in the advanced vocational specializations offered by their community college or by private trade schools.

The IEP as a Component of the Curriculum

Regardless of the local district's philosophy of education or its values, the curriculum is the keystone of its educational plan because it consists of the knowledge, skills, and behaviors that lead to the attainment of the goals of education. In this sense, the curriculum is the substantive metaphor of the philosophic statement of values to which the school district subscribes.

Within this scheme of things, if an IEP were required for nondisabled students in general education classes, it would encompass the segment of the curriculum that prescribes the student's readiness to learn as an outcome of their instruction and experiences to this point in their education. Accordingly, the content of the IEP should be drawn from the developmentally ordered sequence of educational objectives in the subject matter areas that make up the curriculum. The operational details of the IEP (i.e., the specific amount of content to be learned, the method of instruction, and the technological support) are determined by each student's learning characteristics.

Thus, in general education classes, the curriculum serves as the frame of reference for the overall planning in each class as well as for the instructional plan for each student. If the time comes when our schools require general education teachers to formulate IEPs for nondisabled children, this could be done immediately because all of the ingredients for an appropriate education for these children are firmly in place. The curriculum and each child's achievement within its total context are a matter of record and immediately available.

The Importance of the Role of the IEP

The requirement in IDEA for a formalized IEP for each student with disabilities is unequivocal. However, the reliability of those that are developed is not. This is because the only objective, stable, and, therefore, constant factor in the IEP process—the curriculum—is absent from the equation. Without the scope and sequence of the curriculum as the framework for stating short- and long-term objectives in educational settings for students with mild disabilities, the accuracy and relevance of instructional objectives is too often a matter of opinion, persuasion, and chance (Cone, 1987). Even when the results of achievement tests and other assessments are available, these often have greater influence on decisions than their reliability and validity warrant.

There is no middle ground for IEPs. They either enhance or diminish educational practices for students. If an IEP is not in harmony with and directly responsive to the student's needs, its execution engages the student in activities that may be interesting and stimulating but that contribute little, if anything, to the student's growth and development. For example, in one analysis of IEPs, Weisenfeld (1987) found that 80% of the stated goals and objectives lacked any contextual or functional relationship to the competencies expected of students in their life activities. Alper's (1978) examination of over 250 IEPs disclosed that only 25% of the objectives specified an observable and measurable behavior with specific criteria for their mastery.

Inadequate IEPs can waste valuable and irretrievable teaching–learning time. If an IEP is appropriate and prescribes the next stage in learning as indicated by the student's place on the continuum of curriculum content and if its implementation employs the most effective conditions for teaching and learning, the student is likely to acquire another solid component in his or her knowledge and behavioral repertoire. Each component thus acquired contributes to an accumulation of the knowledge and skills that ultimately lead the student to attaining the best approximation of the goals of education that he or she can.

An Appropriate Education in the Least Restrictive Environment (LRE)

Section 117 in the consent decree for PARC v. Commonwealth of Pennsylvania stated that placement of children with disabilities in a general education public school class is preferable to placement in a special school and placement in a public school special class is preferable to placement in any other type of program of education or training (PARC, 1971). Subsequently, section 612(5) of P.L. 94-142 required that, *to the maximum extent appropriate,* children with disabilities be educated with children who are not disabled and that they be placed in special classes or special schools only when the nature or severity of the their disability is such that educational goals cannot be fulfilled in a general education class.

In effect, section 612(5) underscores the point that society makes no exceptions when it directs schools to socialize all of its young. It accepts the notion that the schools need to distinguish between children's specific learning needs and learning characteristics because these, unlike the demographics of race, religion, gender, and socioeconomic status, have a direct impact on how the educational system goes about fulfilling society's mandates.

The conditional "to the maximum extent appropriate" in P.L. 94-142, section 612(5), reminds educators that there can be no compromise of the priorities associated with education's goals; that, in actuality, a student's instructional placement is a means to the end of the student receiving an appropriate education. This means that regardless of the intensity of wishful thinking or how appealing and attractive the interactions of children with and without disabilities may be, these are not grounds for reducing or altering the scope, quality, or intensity of instruction. In other words, no matter what the character or location of the instructional setting is, the outcomes of the educational placement of children with disabilities and that of their nondisabled classmates have to be consistent with the schools' mandate to attain the goals of education.

This concept of the least restrictive environment (LRE) presumes that all options for students' educational experiences need to be kept open if students are to receive an education appropriate to their learning and maturational needs. At one extreme, some students' educational placement may be such that many of their interactions with their nondisabled counterparts must be limited to extracurricular activities in the school building and in their neighborhood. At the other extreme, some students with disabilities may pursue equivalent educational objectives as full-time students in general education classes.

The Reality of LRE

Within the context of the conventional public school, the constraints on students without disabilities are no more or less restrictive than they are for their counterparts with disabilities. That is, the vast majority of third graders spend almost all of their instructional time together, much more than they do with first and fifth graders, and, like students with mild disabilities in special education classrooms, they interact with older and younger schoolmates at recess and during other school activities such as assemblies, sporting events, and school plays. At the same time, there are students without disabilities who are so advanced in one or more subject matter areas that special arrangements such as Advanced Placement classes are made to accommodate their aptitudes. For students with achievement deficits, tutorial experiences are provided.

The Learning Environment in an Appropriate Education

Before we assign students with mild disabilities to general education classes on a full- or part-time basis, we need to be able to ensure that the proposed instructional environment is such that it does not restrict the delivery of an education that is appropriate to their needs. We need to ascertain precisely what is to be learned, the characteristics of the learner, and other pertinent elements of an appropriate education. Early on, we need to verify that either the general education curriculum offers each student with mild disabilities learning experiences consistent with the objectives of education as stated in his or her IEP or, alternatively, that it is possible to implement the student's special education curriculum in the course of general education class activities.

This is no simple undertaking. Conventional learning environments such as general education and special education classrooms and specialized learning environments such as music and art centers, the gymnasium, and resource rooms are remarkably complex. As learning environments, each has physical, psychological, and social attributes that are dynamic and interactive. The physical characteristics of a learning environment include its size, configuration, furniture, equipment, light, and temperature. Psychological attributes include a collective understanding by students and the teacher of the status of the classroom in the total school, a wide range of teacher and student attitudes and motivations, relationships between the teacher and students, each student's feelings about the subject matter of learning, and each student's self-concept based on his or her status in the class. Social attributes stem from the fact that people in the learning environment act on their ascribed and achieved statuses and roles and, associated with these, their special interests, biases, and values, which may or may not be influenced by ethnic and socioeconomic phenomena.

47

The Effects of the Learning Environment

Individually and in combination, attributes of the learning environment can have remarkable effects on educational enterprises. Experience indicates that quantitative change in one or more of these environmental attributes may induce qualitative change. Adding one more student to an already established class, for example, can result in a reshuffling of students' interrelationships, changes in how the class is organized for instruction in whole or in part, and reconsideration by the teacher of plans and expectations for the class as a whole. Any one or combination of these changes can alter learning conditions in the classroom and, as a consequence, the results of teaching and learning.

Similarly, in the physical aspects of the environment, something as simple as a change in the classroom's temperature can alter the focus of some, if not all, children's attention. Discomfort can be distracting. Students' motivation can be affected. Their work and their interactions with class-mates may become qualitatively different. Sensitivity to annoyances often becomes intensified and tempers flare. Overall, students' accomplishments may suffer. The old aphorism "the straw that broke the camel's back" and the minimalist notion that "less is more" are apt depictions of quantitative change creating qualitative change. Thus, the classroom is not simply a place where teachers and learners come together to do things. In its own way, it is actually as much an educational instrumentality, a means toward an end, as a textbook, a competent teacher, or an effective teaching strategy. Despite the classroom's importance in teaching–learning transactions, however, it is often the last educational variable to be taken into account and the first on which we compromise.

Problems in General Education Class Placements

In schools where the terms *least restrictive environment* and the *general education class* are synonymous, relatively few educational factors or expectations for performance are employed as criteria for placement. Instead, there seems to be an abiding faith that once the student with disabilities is settled in a general education class, an educational plan will emerge and good things will happen. The attitude of advocates of the notion that the general education classroom is the least restrictive environment seems to be, Place the student, and all else will follow.

In such schools, expediency frequently reigns in assigning unusually large numbers of students with mild disabilities to general education classes. In these settings, more so than in those where rigorous criteria govern the general education class placement of students with mild disabilities, the onus is on the students to demonstrate their unquestioned incompatibility with the program and /or with the accomplishments of other students in the general education class before another accommodation for them is considered.

Unfortunately, by the time this incompatibility is recognized and addressed, serious, if not irreversible, damage may have been done to the self-concepts, attitudes, and motivation of some children with mild disabilities. Furthermore, it is not unlikely that their general education classmates are left with unflattering and possibly long-lasting impressions of the mal-adaptive behavior and the academic incompetence of these students—a result contrary to the rationale for placing students with mild disabilities in general education classes.

If the placement of students with disabilities in general education classes is made within the context of an appropriate education, the decision must take into account the extent to which each of the elements vital to an appropriate education can be implemented in the general education class. These include the relevance of curriculum to the immediate and long-term needs of students, the attitude of the general education teacher and classmates, the competency of teachers and support staff, the social and academic sophistication of students with mild disabilities, and other equally important variables. The standard, of course, is the extent to which these elements contribute to or detract from the fulfillment of educational objectives for each of these students as well as for the general education class as a whole.

Thus, assigning students with mild disabilities to a general education class simply because the classroom is considered to be the least restrictive to their association with their nondisabled peers may not turn out to be an educationally meaningful act. Unless their educational needs and learning characteristics are taken into account, these students are likely to find themselves in a situation that is contrary to their best educational interests and to the quality of their lives in their adult years.

Time wasted in irrelevant activities cannot be recaptured. Consequently, the process for developing the LRE must be as educationally rigorous as that for hiring a teacher, designating a learning objective, or selecting a teaching aid. The fact that schooling has built-in, inflexible time constraints instructs us that every available teaching–learning transaction for students with mild disabilities must contribute to their education if they are to meet their educational objectives.

49

Transition

Follow-up studies of school-leavers with mild mental retardation, behavioral disorders, and learning disabilities indicate that these students have always needed help in effecting a successful transition from school to adult society (Blackorby & Wagner, 1996; Hasazi et al., 1985; Mithaug, Horiuchi, & Fanning, 1984; Wagner & Shaver, 1989). These studies, along with the experiences of many employers, indicate that most of these school-leavers find the work environment far more demanding and much less forgiving than their school experiences. Also, many have difficulty capitalizing on their free time and in managing their personal affairs effectively (Blackorby & Wagner, 1996). Adults with mild disabilities who are accommodated in community residences may benefit from the guidance and supervision of residence staff and job coaches.

However, because adults with more moderate and severe disabilities are often given priority in community residences, most adults with mild disabilities have to get along as best they can at home or elsewhere. For this reason, state and federal vocational rehabilitation agencies have, since the 1960s, provided assistance to school-leavers with mild disabilities in the form of counseling, placement, and post-secondary vocational training programs. The entrance of the Office of Special Education Programs in the U.S. Department of Education into this area has made available more funds and more forms of assistance than ever before for all school-leavers with mild disabilities.

The fact that the results of recent follow-up studies of school-leavers with mild disabilities indicate persistent high rates of unemployment and dependency suggests that providing services and training to adults whose schooling has been ineffective has had remarkably little impact on their competencies. The foundation for the acquisition of marketable work and social skills that form the basis of the transition of all students from school to adult society is laid in the course of their schooling. It is on this foundation that skills and proficiencies can be expanded and refined.

The Impact of Technology on Employability

The trend toward complex mechanization, automation, and robotization and their contribution to the reduction in work opportunities for adults with mild disabilities is a matter of history. In a recent op-ed news article, the principal of a vocational secondary school discussed how technological change influenced the rising standards for admission to his school. He pointed out that in 1990, teachers in the school's tool and die shop taught students how to set up a metal turning lathe and how to adjust and readjust the machine to produce work within prescribed tolerances. Today, he reports, students no longer deal directly with the lathe. Instead, they are taught how to program a computer that not only directs the lathe's operations, including the monitoring of quality control, but also senses wear on the cutting tools and either adjusts them or alerts the operator that a replacement is necessary. The implication of this technological advance for the careers of students whose aptitudes do not measure up to the new job description is clear.

To this illustration of the impact of technological change, we can add the increase in the number of manufacturers exporting vast numbers of assembly, sorting, and fabricating jobs to countries with large, low-salaried labor pools. A notable proportion of these jobs are well within the abilities of adults with mental retardation as well as many with behavioral disorders and learning disabilities.

If technological change and the export of jobs are not damaging enough, there is the fact that both have added to the job-hunting scene workers of considerable competence whose jobs have been either replaced by automated or robotic devices or exported elsewhere. These unemployed workers intensify the competition for jobs that are within the competencies of adults with mild disabilities.

The Challenges in the Transition from School to Adult Society

There is no escaping the fact that the transition from the teen years to adulthood, from the school to full membership in the community, is no mean feat even under the best of conditions. The distinctions between the specifications for success in schooling and for success in the community, particularly in work settings, exemplify the conditions that make this transition arduous. In school, for example, much of the preparation for the transition of students with mild disabilities to the adult world doesn't begin until students are in secondary school, where a significant amount of their learning is either in the abstract or vicarious. Both represent the kind of learning that research has confirmed as unusually difficult for students with mild disabilities to assimilate and act on.

Typically, students read and talk about things and events that are happening beyond the school walls in the adult world. They also attempt to synthesize real life by engaging in class or group projects, viewing videotapes, and participating in the occasional field trip during which they may have real but relatively brief and often superficial experiences. The expectations of teachers and others is that much of what is learned through these experiences will be stored in children's memories for future reference, usually in response to questions on a test of some sort, but also as the basis for generalization within conventional problem-solving situations.

Beyond the classroom, the mix of problems that characterize the transition from school to work consists of genuine experiences. These provide a dynamic context for the generalization of many principles and rules for social adaptation that were learned in school if, of course, they were taught at all. The critical factor here is the extent to which students, having learned and stored these important principles and rules over the 12 or more years of their schooling, can (a) recognize that they are being confronted with a problem and, having identified it, (b) retrieve and apply the appropriate principles or rules needed to solve the problem, and, having examined the results of their actions, (c) make whatever adjustments that are needed to close the transaction.

Transition Programs in the Schools

Even though we are familiar with the learning characteristics of children with mild disabilities and their need for intensive experiences from the time they enter school onward, transition plans are typically confined to secondary and post-secondary programs (Kohler & Chapman, 1999). At the same time, studies show that many states are failing to meet the transition requirements included in the 1997 reauthorization of IDEA (Johnson & Sharpe, 2000; National Council on Disability, 2000).

The mind-set of many local schools and state education agencies results in beginning the transition planning at age 14. Apart from minimizing the importance of students building a solid base for transition in their primary and elementary school experiences, this view of transition programs presumes that students with mild disabilities can learn, in the few years they are in secondary schools, a critical mass of facts, concepts, rules, and principles vital to social adaptation in work and community settings as well as skills in the transfer and generalization of learning.

Some may take exception to this view of transition programs and argue that much of the learning ascribed to secondary school programs actually begins in earlier school experiences and that it is more visible in the secondary school because learning is organized into more lifelike experiences there. Ordinarily, this explanation would be acceptable. However, conventional knowledge tells us that teachers in primary and elementary programs for students with mild disabilities are, with few exceptions, absorbed with teaching academic skills, particularly reading. This preoccupation with academics persists irrespective of the placement of students with mild disabilities in a special or general education class or in a resource room. This preoccupation is reinforced by the standards for success mandated in NCLB.

In light of the usual elementary school experiences of students with disabilities, expecting them to learn and retain the vast array of facts, concepts, and principles that are critical to their transition to adulthood in the course of their secondary school experiences is difficult, if not impossible, to justify. This incongruity has not gone unnoticed (Clark, 1979, 1980; Clark, Carlson, Fisher, Cook, & D'Alonzo, 1991; Cronin & Patton, 1993; Patton & Dunn, 1998).

Transition: A Continuing Process

For children with mild disabilities, as for all children, readiness for the transition from school to the larger community begins with their admission to school. It then continues daily as they apply and practice their newly acquired social adaptive skills and proficiencies in their personal and social interactions in their homes, neighborhoods, and communities before and after school hours.

If we use the conventional definition of sophistication—the process or result of change from the natural or simple to the knowledgeable or cultured—as an index for the rate and breadth of children's transition from school to community, we get an appreciation of the importance of an appropriate education within the context of their social growth and development. Those who lack sophistication in the conventions of ordinary neighborhood and community activities such as shopping, dining out, and using public transportation will be slow in making the transition from home to neighborhood or community, if they make it at all.

With the onset of schooling, the transition from school to community is coupled with the unfolding of children's social environments (their home, school, neighborhood, and community) as they accumulate knowledge and behaviors that are normative in the social, psychological, and physical aspects of their environment. To put it another way, as children with mild disabilities accumulate knowledge and increase and upgrade their social adaptive skills and proficiencies, their interactions with more numerous and more varied people, places, and things become feasible.

These experiences then add to and expand the base on which subsequent learning and experiences accrue. In this way, if an appropriate education is in place, school and community become complementary. That is, as students put abstract and vicarious school learning to practical use in the community, the results reinforce both the learning and the utilization of learning. It is on these school-to-community experiences that the ultimate transition from school to adult life is built.

Transition as Recurring Developmental Stages

Transition is a periodic process that probably starts with conception. Graphically, it resembles a helix more than a straight line because, with maturation, the learner returns to learned concepts and facts but at a more complex and abstract level. For example, in a process as straightforward as personal cleanliness, infants are bathed. As youngsters, they are told when to bathe and they participate in the process. After a few years, they are told when to bathe or shower and left to comply on their own. There comes a time when they are expected to use their own judgment to decide the time and conditions for this personal activity.

Readiness for transition implies that the individual has acquired the knowledge and skills necessary for making the transition to the next developmental stage. Within this framework, transition from school to the adult community is a sequence of stages through which most children and adults pass, and the readiness to do so with poise and purposefulness hinges in great part on the extent to which they have been the beneficiaries of an appropriate education.

At the same time, there is an undercurrent of pessimism among some who are engaged in the many aspects of transition programs for people with disabilities. Questions have arisen about the merits of programs whose costs are a serious burden to their communities. Some suggest that, notwithstanding job coaches and other support measures, the technologies of work settings have outdistanced the competencies of most workers with mild disabilities. Others argue that more effective educational programs would reduce the need for job coaches and other costly supports.

In their review of the transition literature, Kohler and Chapman (1999) conclude that empirical support for practices and interventions is difficult to ascertain—that there is, at best, guarded support for some practices and that some remain indeterminate. They note that their conclusions are little different from those reported in an earlier review of the transition literature (Kohler, 1993).

The fact is, we will not be able to resolve the debate about transition until a sizeable number of students with mild disabilities have graduated from an educational program that is appropriate to their needs and have lived in the community long enough to provide data that bring time, costs, incomes, and other factors into reliable relationships. Only then will we be able to determine whether transition problems have their source in a society too complex for their talents and whether they are by-products of an inadequate educational program.

Transition to Community Residences

There will always be some individuals with mild disabilities whose aptitudes are such that they are good candidates for competitive employment. At the same time, there will always be others whose skills and proficiencies are marginal at best. The latter are the people who need supported employment of some kind. Public school programs and community agencies need to be responsive to the social adaptive needs of both groups because both will remain in their communities.

An Appropriate Education for Life in Community Residences
It is unlikely that individuals with mild disabilities who are not good prospects for competitive employment and independent living will be institutionalized. Instead, their presence in the community and their opportunities for a productive way of life will likely be assured because of the proliferation

of community residences and related community programs for those whose families are unable to provide shelter and supervision. This means that the curriculum needs to include concepts of social adaptation that are responsive to many employment alternatives, including supervised work. The conventional supported employment setting for less-able workers is unsuitable as the sole resource because there are sure to be some candidates for supervised work whose competencies will increase to a level that makes a transition to competitive employment and increased autonomy possible.

Irrespective of the kinds of autonomy and work placement that school-leavers with mild disabilities achieve, the vast majority become, in one way or another, members of their neighborhood and community. At one extreme, the fact that every follow-up study of school-leavers has been unable to locate a notable number of former students suggests that some leave school and achieve an active and productive life in their community subsidized by their success at remunerative work.

It is likely, therefore, that some shed school-based labels and reputations and become assimilated into society. At the other extreme, there are those who persist as dependent adults, some of whom probably never capitalize materially on their capabilities. They spend their adult years in community residences where they are helped to live active and productive lives to the extent that they can.

The vast majority of people with mild disabilities stand somewhere between these extremes. Just where they fall on the dependency continuum depends on a number of factors. Prominent among these are their school experiences, which determine the kinds of personal, social, and occupational skills they bring to the transition from school to adult life. Because most of these attributes take root and flourish, to some degree, in the course of school experiences, the extent to which they do so is determined, in great part, by the appropriateness of their educational program.

Conclusion

In this chapter, the concept of an appropriate education has been discussed as the frame of reference for the invention of educational programs for children with mild disabilities. Some improvements have been mandated by P.L. 94-142 and IDEA. Others stem from the experiences of school-leavers with mild disabilities as reported in the many follow-up studies completed over the better part of the 20th century. By using long-established elements of general education programs as models against which programs for children with mild disabilities can be compared, it becomes clear that the curriculum, the substantive infrastructure of all educational programs, was and continues to be the missing element in programs for students with mild disabilities.

Without the structure or framework provided by curriculum, the determination of each element of an appropriate education discussed earlier is default to whatever the people in leadership roles feel they ought to be, and their decisions are based on biases, opinions, and wishful thinking. This fact is observable in ongoing efforts to comply with P.L. 94-142 and IDEA, particularly in the development of IEPs and the implementation of LREs. The framework provided by a curriculum allows for consistency in the designation of the elements of an appropriate education and in their implementation.

Elements of a Curriculum for Students with Mild Disabilities

More often than not, curriculum reform in educational programs entails altering the prevailing content of instruction to conform with a reconceptualization and restatement of the school's goals. Because there is no comprehensive curriculum in educational programs for students with mild disabilities, a curriculum needs to be developed that is consistent with the goals of education and the educational objectives by which the goals are achieved and is, at the same time, harmonious with students' learning characteristics.

These are demanding criteria under the best of conditions. Curriculum development and adaptation in general education, for example, has a long and productive history with proven strategies and tactics available to curriculum developers in the various subject matter areas. Even so, curriculum development in general education remains a time-consuming, intensive, and costly enterprise. To educators of students with mild disabilities, these criteria must appear daunting. Those who are sensitive to the need for a curriculum are aware of the fact that, apart from a handful of well-organized curriculum projects (Hungerford, 1948; Hungerford, DeProspo, & Rosenzweig, 1952; Mayer, 1975), there are no precedents on which they can build.

Educators of students with mild disabilities have no alternative but to start the curriculum development process from square one. This entails establishing an operational definition of curriculum. This is an important first step because it enables us to define the term curriculum so that it aligns with the goals and objectives of an educational program for students with mild disabilities.

Defining Curriculum

Curriculum is defined here as a systematic organization of the knowledge, behaviors, concepts, facts, skills, and proficiencies that, in combination, represent the content of instruction through which the goals and objectives of the educational program are achieved. The criterion of systematic organization distinguishes a curriculum from other collections or configurations of instructional content. Furthermore, by systematizing the curriculum content along both developmental and characterological lines, developers not only align content with the principles of human growth and development, but also with those aptitudes of students that help to determine the relevance of the content and the methods and rate in which it is imparted to learners. Ultimately, the systematic nature of the curriculum provides a matrix for the decisions and actions that are basic to its implementation as well as for the evaluation of its outcomes.

Defining curriculum within the context of the goals and objectives of education for students with mild disabilities is advantageous to the process of curriculum development in two ways. First, it legitimizes curriculum developers making the most of the subjective experiences and observations of teachers, psychologists, rehabilitation workers, and other professionals whose careers are linked directly to the successes and failures of individuals with mild disabilities. We can use the information they provide along with the objective data that supports their observations and experiences as criteria in selecting and organizing the concepts, facts, skills, and proficiencies that make up the content of instruction.

Second, by linking the nature of the instructional content with the goals and objectives of education, the definition establishes a template with firmly fixed temporal boundaries within which the instructional content must fit. The concepts, facts, skills, and proficiencies that, in combination, form a curriculum must be selected from the infinite array of information that represents our culture, and in the process, curriculum developers need to take into account the fact that the time allocated for the schooling of students with mild disabilities is the same as that for their nondisabled peers. These time constraints are compounded by the fact that children with mild disabilities learn at a significantly slower rate than that of their nondisabled peers.

Thus, while educational programs are available to these students for the conventional 12 school years (in some schools slightly longer), their rates of learning are such that their actual learning time is reduced significantly to more like six to nine years. These conditions mean that there is no room for error in either the makeup of the curriculum or in its implementation.

It follows, then, that curriculum developers need to establish priorities and rigorous selection procedures for determining which of the many knowledge and behavior elements that appear relevant to the growth and development of children with mild disabilities should be given a place in the curriculum. This is not to suggest that the curriculum needs to be narrow or linear. To the contrary, a multidimensional curriculum not only offers more teaching alternatives, but also uses time more efficiently. Some designs that accommodate alternatives already exist. For example, the curriculum can signal to the teacher that children who demonstrate mastery of concept X should proceed to concept Y, while those who do not should move laterally to concept X prime for additional instruction and practice.

The Nature of Curriculum for Students with Mild Disabilities

The observations and data emerging from the assessment of the outcomes of educational programs for students with mild disabilities are the most fruitful source for the specific knowledge and behaviors that merit inclusion in the curriculum. This is not to say that the school performance of students with mild disabilities is of little value. Comparatively, however, the real measure of the effectiveness of educational programs is found in the extent to which their graduates adapt, as adults, to their physical, psychological, and social environments and achieve functional levels of independence.

In weighing the relevance of concepts, facts, skills, and proficiencies for inclusion in the curriculum, it is important to recognize that in the conventional view, the social adaptation of people with mild disabilities is too often equated with getting and keeping a job and with all that this implies for their quality of life.

While data describing the occupational accomplishments of people with mild disabilities are essential, they provide only one form of evidence that an individual has adapted to a certain aspect of his/her combined physical, social, and psychological environments. Limiting the concept of social adaptation in this way oversimplifies a very complex process.

While securing employment is a noteworthy accomplishment, it is only the prelude to what can be a lifetime of coping with work-related and work-associated conditions that can, individually or in combination, threaten an individual's status as an employee. A single event such as a delayed bus, a misunderstood assignment, a hostile fellow employee, or the misinterpretation of a facial expression can precipitate an avalanche of conflict. Such incidents, if ineptly managed, can escalate into unpleasant confrontations that may lead to the termination of employment. The knowledge and behaviors that are imparted to children with mild disabilities and the strategies and tactics used to implement them allow these children to confront and overcome such challenges and other aspects of living and earn them the acknowledgment of being socially adaptable.

Moving Beyond a Curriculum of Discrete Subject Matter

The popular notion that a curriculum for students with mild disabilities should parallel the general education curriculum implicitly endorses the practice of arranging the school day as a mosaic of instructional content: the arbitrary compartmentalization of subject matter areas into discrete instructional blocks. Because this results in unavoidable conceptual and temporal dissociation between subject matter areas, such an endorsement says, in effect, that there is little or no relationship between how the content of instruction is organized and how children with mild disabilities learn. This contradicts research about their learning characteristics.

In particular, organizing a general education curriculum so that reading, arithmetic, science, and other content areas are taught independently of each other exacerbates the difficulty that most learners with mild disabilities have in the transfer and generalization of learning. This effect on their problem-solving ability is inevitable because facts, concepts, and reasoning skills that are important to problem solving in general are often taught as separate elements in each subject matter area. For example, a certain inductive strategy that is relevant to solving arithmetic problems as well as to "reading for meaning" is often taught in such a way that students view the strategy as useful only for the subject matter area in which it is being presented.

To make matters even more difficult for students with mild disabilities, the curriculum for students in general education classes is based on presumptions about the learning characteristics of nondisabled children. Accordingly, some thinking skills, facts, and concepts are often taught in the abstract because it has been found that most nondisabled children can make the generalization from the abstract to the concrete on their own. Many students with mild disabilities who are far less facile in their ability to generalize abstract experiences to life situations are bound to end up seriously limited in their problem-solving abilities.

In addition, the practice of isolating the content of the conventional general education curriculum into discrete subject matter areas is more than a little unrealistic. Rarely do the solutions to problems in life rely exclusively on skills in a single subject matter. To understand and solve many everyday problems, we must often combine skills and proficiencies in reading and reckoning with skills in other substantive areas, such as practical knowledge of science, geography, or civics. In such situations, most of us see the relationships between the diverse subject matter skills, facts, and concepts even though we learned them separately. With practice, we learned to weave discretely learned subject matter into the problem-solving process. Over time, we became so adept at solving conventional problems that we are almost entirely unaware of the stress that accompanies the process. It isn't until the unusual happens, such as oversleeping because of an unexpectedly dysfunctional alarm clock or a computer crash, that the pores open and the pulse accelerates.

Some students with mild disabilities who are educated by means of a curriculum modeled after the general education curriculum may become somewhat proficient at conventional problem solving despite the hurdles imposed by such a curriculum, providing that rote instruction equips them with enough relevant problem-solving formulas. However, to maximize their ability to solve conventional problems and enhance their social adaptation, students with mild disabilities must become competent problem solvers. We need to provide them with a curriculum in which the content of instruction and its organization are compatible with their learning needs and characteristics because these have implications for their transition from school to their neighborhoods and communities.

Social Adaptation as a Curricular Theme

Political theorists, social scientists, and philosophers, recognizing that schooling influences the values that people acquire and how they conceive of their roles in society, prescribe curricular themes that are consistent with their notions of how and why societies organize and how members contribute to the strength and durability of their society. Few, if any, of these have any discernible relevance to the education of students with mild disabilities.

This does not mean that curriculum for students with mild disabilities should be thematically neutral. To the contrary, knowing what we do about the experiences and accomplishments of school-leavers with mild disabilities, a theme that guides both the selection of instructional content and the curriculum development process, is indispensable. In particular, students with mild disabilities need a curricular theme that is compatible with the knowledge and experiences that are basic to their transition from school to society, to becoming participating and contributing members of their community, and to achieving an acceptable quality of life. Thus, the theme of a curriculum for students with mild disabilities needs to be as utilitarian as it is theoretical.

Curricula for the vast majority of students are in accord with their aspirations for professional careers, occupations, and entrepreneurial pursuits. These encompass a wide range of statuses and the accompanying quality of life. In contrast, while gainful employment is also a major objective for school-leavers with disabilities, it is part of an equation that has as its overall goal the attainment of an effective level of adaptability in a socially and technologically complex society. The other variables in the equation include skills and proficiencies in self-care, management of personal matters, interpersonal relationships, and the worthwhile use of leisure time.

Thus, a curriculum for students with disabilities must hew closely to the line of social survival—a social sciences concept that is a metaphor for the Darwinian biologic concept of survival of the fittest. Survival, in this sense, means achieving a level of personal and financial autonomy that permits self-advocacy and self-determination and that reduces dependence on the community for the essentials of life. Without a sound foundation of social adaptive concepts, facts, and behaviors, there is little likelihood that much of the good life will follow. Given the constraints imposed on schools by the combination of the rigid time frame for their education and their reduced rate of learning, the curriculum for children with mild disabilities must be thematically focused if they are to attain their educational goals.

The concept of survival of the fittest provides the frame of reference for such a theme. Some may find the notion of survival too extreme or too limiting to warrant consideration as a factor in the growth and development of children. However, when we consider the steadily rising tide of technological and social change and the rate at which it is engulfing heretofore competent individuals, survival predicated on keeping one's head above water is not an overly dramatic way to envision a theme. Because the role of education is to socialize all of society's young, it follows that the curricula in our schools should be designed to impart to children the knowledge and behaviors that are basic to social adaptation.

Social Adaptation Defined

We can define social adaptation, operationally, as the dynamic state that evolves from an individual's efforts to attain the best approximation of a comfortable and tolerable balance between his or her personal and social needs and the conditions in his or her social, psychological, and physical environments. The best approximation of balance is achieved as a consequence of one's ability to respond effectively to environmental demands in socially acceptable ways.

The action–reaction exchanges that characterize social adaptation can vary considerably in the amount of stress they generate in individuals and in groups, ranging from almost indiscernible to extremely intense. As a result, the problems that emerge in the ordinary course of the day can vary in their ability to capture our attention. That is, subtle or low-key problems may escape detection. This has implications for the design and content of a curriculum for students with mild disabilities. Because of individual differences, important distinctions exist in people's abilities to sense and to comprehend what is occurring in their environments. In the vernacular, problems can stem from the fact that people do not realize that they have a problem.

Including Problem-Solving Skills in the Curriculum

Like others, students with mild disabilities need to be aware of the hurdles in their lives. They need to develop thinking skills that will help them cope with life problems. Within the context of curriculum development, this means achieving a realistic balance between content areas such as reading, science, and arithmetic and the development of cognitive or thinking skills. Instruction in both is necessary if children with mild disabilities are to cultivate the ability to think critically and act independently.

The curriculum content—the concepts and facts—provides the vehicle for acquiring critical thinking skills. The problem-solving strategies shaped by thinking skills are the tools for acting independently. Therefore, beyond conventional subject matter areas, the curriculum for students with mild disabilities must contain the knowledge and experiences that will help them to understand that the process of social adaptation usually begins with the awareness of a problem or, more important, the likelihood of its emergence.

Reality dictates that a curriculum for students with mild disabilities needs to be carefully detailed if errors of omission are to be avoided. When teaching children with mild disabilities to think within a problem-solving frame of reference, we must organize activities so that they lead to the perception of a problem; thus, the activities take the shape of a strategy—a systematic way for solving problems. The presumption here is that over time, students will learn the elements of the strategy and internalize it as a component of their problem-solving repertoire.

As an example, one form of task analysis reveals that awareness of a problem leads to a search of one's knowledge bank for information that can contribute to (a) a more thorough understanding of the elements of the problem and the consequences of its being ignored or otherwise going unsolved, (b) a sense of options or alternative directions for contending with the problem, (c) a selection or commitment to a strategy for solving the problem, (d) the implementation of the strategy, (e) an assessment of the effectiveness of the strategy, and, if called for, (f) adjustments and refinements to either optimize the results or simply confirm the appropriateness of all preceding steps. If one concludes that the problem has not been solved satisfactorily, it is often necessary to return to step (a) and develop an alternate problem-solving strategy.

Of course, not all problems call for this deliberate route to their solution. Many are so much a part of our experiences that we solve them almost reflexively. Others fall somewhere between these extremes. In either case, given the learning problems of children with mild disabilities, such as limitations in retention and in the ability to generalize, there is no justification for the assumption that intuition or incidental learning will fill in the gaps caused by curriculum developers' errors of omission.

A highly desirable outcome of problem solving, and one that sometimes escapes the most astute among us, is the discovery of the rule or principle that governs the solution of certain types or classes of problems so that the rule or principle can then be transferred or generalized to other situations for a more expeditious solving of analogous problems.

A curriculum developed for students with mild disabilities needs to include well-designed opportunities for learning inductively the rules or principles that underlie the solutions of common problems. Without this ability, students are left with the far more laborious and time-consuming alternatives of trial and error and emulating the behaviors of someone who appears to know what he or she is doing on the chance that it will work for them as well.

Developers of a curriculum for students with mild disabilities must be aware that the definition of social adaptation discussed earlier is easily oversimplified to the point that it does not do justice to the actual complexity of the process. For example, problem solving is not always as linear, in substance or solution, as it is often portrayed. That is, more often than not, there are alternative interpretations of both the problem and its consequences or implications that can lead to different approaches to solving the problem, including, in some instances, the decision to ignore or abandon it.

Taking the economy of time and effort into account, some problems are best solved by using rote or memorized procedures. Thus, engaging in inductive reasoning to determine the cost of one orange if the going rate is four for a dollar is intellectual overkill. Learning how to recognize both the nature of a problem and the most effective route to its solution are salient objectives of an appropriate curriculum.

Some may be inclined to question the wisdom of devoting valuable instructional time to cultivating the thinking skills of students with mild disabilities, of teaching them how to reason inductively and deductively. They often argue that in the time that it would take most children with mild disabilities to learn a strategy for inductive reasoning, they could memorize any number of "if . . . then" procedures. This may or may not be correct. We have no reliable way of knowing how productive the teaching of thinking skills to students with mild disabilities might be until we provide them with an appropriate education that necessarily includes intensive efforts at enhancing their reasoning and problem-solving skills.

Synergy in Curriculum Content

The "one curriculum fits all" concept underlying the recommendation that the curriculum for students with mild disabilities should parallel the general education curriculum has little basis in fact. The learning characteristics of students with mild disabilities indicate that these students require a synergistic curriculum organized in a way that unifies traditional subject matter areas to represent the best approximation of reality allowed by the uniqueness and constraints of the school environment.

The recommendation that the curricular content of educational programs for children with mild disabilities should be organized so that the concepts, facts, and thinking skills are synergistic does not mean that students with mild disabilities should no longer engage in instruction in reading, arithmetic, and other familiar subject matter areas. As proposed earlier, the extrinsic value of literacy skills is determined by their effectiveness as problem-solving tools. As such, they can be a powerful means toward reaching the goal of social adaptation. It is important, then, that all children learn to read and reckon as well as they can. No less important is their acquisition of useful knowledge about their physical, social, and psychological environments. The challenge to curriculum developers is to deploy the content of instruction in such a way that learning, the retention of learning, and the exploitation of learning are employed effectively in the ordinary course of life events.

The development of a curriculum for students with mild disabilities is a pioneering enterprise. We need not be defensive about disregarding the precedents established in the development of curricula, teaching materials, and teaching aids for use in general education classrooms. For example, we can set aside the conventional, discrete subject matter format that is typical of most general education programs and explore designs for a seamless, synergistic curriculum in which the subject matter is interactive and mutually reinforcing. In a synergistic curriculum, skills in reading and arithmetic, for example, are deployed within the context of the problem to be solved. This type of curriculum will provide students with mild disabilities with continuing lifelike problem-solving experiences in the ordinary course of their schooling, beginning at the earliest possible moment.

Although once limited to school-based audiovisual teaching aids, we now have access to an expanding array of communication resources and hardware that challenge our creativity. With the technologies now available,

Elements of a Curriculum for Students With Mild Disabilities we can capitalize on the capabilities of computers to help manage rote learning and on the flexibility of interactive TV to contribute to the learning of concepts, rules, and generalizations. These teaching aids, along with access to the Internet, cable, and satellites, can provide the vicarious experiences that students with mild disabilities need to help them make the transition from the abstractions of the classroom to the realities of the larger, more encompassing world.

The Challenge of Selecting Curriculum Content: The Abundance of Culture

Irrespective of philosophical and conceptual differences, those who plan to engage in the development of a synergistic curriculum for students with mild disabilities will be faced with the same four tasks: (a) specifying the content of instruction; (b) organizing the content into a format that facilitates instruction and the assessment and evaluation of outcomes; (c) developing the teaching materials, aids, and technologies that are used to impart the curriculum to students; and (d) validating the curriculum through field tests, evaluations, and revisions in preparation for its publication and dissemination. The specific content of instruction is discussed in the remainder of this chapter. The other tasks are discussed in detail in a subsequent chapter.

Specifying Curriculum Content
As discussed earlier, the difficulty in choosing the content of instruction is not solely a matter of finding it within the huge context of our culture. There is also the matter of the time constraints that impose a certain period during which the content is to be taught (that is, the number of years children are accommodated in our schools), which is affected, in turn, by the learning characteristics of students with mild disabilities.

Curriculum developers need to remember that our culture and subcultures confront us with an infinite array of information from which we must extract the knowledge that is relevant to the socialization of students with mild disabilities. Furthermore, as Postman and Weingartner (1969) point out, the task of identifying the concepts and facts that the school intends to impart to its students is complicated by the fact that many concepts and facts no longer have survival value due to social and technological change. They suggest that education must sometimes include in its programs the "unlearning" of obsolete or marginally useful knowledge and behaviors.

The encyclopedic accumulation of facts and concepts that constitutes our culture complicates the selection of content. In fact, coming to a decision about where to break into this vast assortment of information is so imposing that those who have engaged in the process have, more often than not, compromised by drawing solely on their own experiences and beliefs as a basis for determining what students with mild disabilities need to learn. Others, looking for a broader range of data, have sent questionnaires to educators and rehabilitation workers as well as to employers of workers with mild disabilities asking them to list the deficits in social and personal behavior that interfere with their clients' or employees' adaptability to work. Some also inquire about the abilities of their employees to participate in community life outside the work setting.

Education Versus Remediation

The influence of the medical model on this procedure for identifying the content of instruction for students with mild disabilities is obvious. As a nominally clinical technique, the procedure makes no distinctions between the competencies and biases of observers, presumes that the observed deficits in behaviors are typical of the performance of people with mild disabilities regardless of differences in their work conditions, and concludes that instruction designed to remediate these deficits is generalizable to students everywhere.

All things considered, the "find the flaw and fix it" dogma of the medical model is in direct opposition to the purposes of a curriculum. Attempting to tailor a curriculum to the maladaptive behaviors of adults with mild disabilities assumes that they will fail to make a successful transition from school to society. Built into this approach is the hope that a critical mass of adult maladaptive behaviors has been detected and addressed by learning activities that will extinguish them, much as Seguin hoped to do a century earlier.

A curriculum, on the other hand, is a totally positive educational instrument. Because the content of the curriculum reflects the customs and mores of society, it offers to all students the knowledge, behaviors, skills, and proficiencies that, having been learned, promise success in many enterprises in their careers as students and later when they enter adult life. Within this context, if students fail to attain the goals of education, it may be because the curriculum developers applied the wrong strategy to identify the content, because the organization of the curriculum is flawed, or both. On the other hand, if the strategy and organization of the curriculum are correct and some students nevertheless show signs of failure to learn certain of its content, educators have the specifics of the curriculum as their point of departure for revising the curriculum by assessing students' problems and designing solutions.

Compared with what is presently available as a curriculum for children with mild disabilities, the proposed curriculum is far more positive and constructive because it is based on the presumption that students with mild disabilities can acquire the knowledge and behaviors important to social adaptation if the content of their curriculum is organized developmentally and if their learning characteristics are taken into account. In practical terms, a curriculum that is appropriate to the learning needs and characteristics of students with mild disabilities anticipates and prepares them for the many interactions they will have with the physical, social, and psychological aspects in their environment. It also prepares them for the many and varied interactions that they will have with each other and with the adults in their schools, homes, and neighborhoods.

The vast majority of these interactions are scenarios lifted out of our customs and mores. Some reflect only the locale within which they take place, others are regional, and some are typically American. Most spell out the nature of the interaction down to the smallest detail, colloquialism, and inflection. Some have become such referents for behavior that a minor deviation from the scenario can jar other participants. People who deviate remarkably from expected behaviors or who are clearly unfamiliar with conventional ways for interacting with others are more often than not seen as strange if not maladaptive.

Those who are unaware of the established patterns for interpersonal transactions have but one of two choices. They must either improvise behavior or find a socially acceptable way for withdrawing from the interaction. Odds are that neither will be appropriate to the situation, and the behavior will be seen by others as maladaptive. It is worth repeating that the follow-up studies of school-leavers with mild disabilities indicate with remarkable consistency that their problems at work and other important social settings very frequently stem from breaking conventional rules such as arriving at work on time, staying on task, maintaining good hygiene, being civil to authority figures, and being able to engage in "small talk" with coworkers.

Preventing Socially Maladaptive Behavior

The conventional curriculum in general education classrooms, which is the basis for much of the education of children with mild disabilities, does not devote much time or effort to instruction in the substance and process of interpersonal interactions. Deviations in such interactions are dealt with, for the most part, in classroom management procedures because curriculum developers in general education presume, justifiably, that most children learn these behaviors, in terms of both substance and style, in their homes and in other settings outside the school by observing others and by direct instruction from parents and other authority figures. In fact, school personnel expect children to enter school with a well-established repertory of social adaptive, interpersonal skills.

However, many students with mild disabilities have either missed the kinds of experiences and instruction that have socialized most of their nondisabled peers in their formative years or they have been unable to acquire enough of the knowledge and behaviors that are required for successful interactions with their physical, social, and psychological environments. To put it in practical terms, it is likely that (a) their experiences in their homes, neighborhoods, and schools have been lacking the kinds of guidance and education that would equip them with the basic skills for conventional interactions with others and (b) their learning problems have interfered with their acquisition of expected knowledge and behaviors.

The results of preschool studies suggest that both explanations are true for a sizable proportion of students with mild disabilities. It follows, then, that if school-leavers with mild disabilities are to make a satisfactory transition from school to adult society, the school must play a leading role in their socialization. Accordingly, their curriculum must be designed to accommodate their need to learn how to acceptably fulfill their roles in interpersonal transactions.

Unlike a clinical strategy for resolving the social adaptive deficits of individuals with mild disabilities, a culturally based curriculum provides a body of knowledge and behaviors that serves as the foundation for a program that can be imparted from the moment students enter school to the time they leave school to enter the adult world.

Such a program is based on two related presumptions. First, it presumes that the schools need not wait for individuals with mild disabilities to demonstrate their social adaptive deficits before they can be addressed. Instead, children with mild disabilities are believed to have the ability to acquire the knowledge and behaviors relevant to their social adaptation in the ordinary course of their classroom instruction, providing that their educational program offers a curriculum that accommodates their developmental needs and the nature of their learning characteristics.

Second, it presumes that if children with mild disabilities acquire a functional repertory of social adaptive skills, the frequency with which they will need to improvise in the course of their interactions with others will be reduced significantly. In other words, children and youth with mild disabilities who learn socially acceptable responses to the conditions in their social, physical, and psychological environments are less likely to make improper responses.

The precision of the procedure used for selecting the content of curriculum has a substantial influence in determining the relevance and reliability of the instructional content. Conventional practices in curriculum development for other subsystems of education do not provide the rigor that the development of curriculum for students with mild disabilities requires. Other subsystems do not function under the same time constraints as programs for students with mild disabilities. Furthermore, the prevailing practice of developing subject matter areas independently of each other

Elements of a Curriculum for Students With Mild Disabilities works against the assembly of a seamless, synergistic curriculum for these students.

To construct a synergistic curriculum, we need a format that provides the curricular boundaries within which we can position content. We also need a process for the selection of content that minimizes errors of omission and commission. Curriculum developers are always vulnerable to these errors because subjectivity plays such a large role in the decisions about what content is included. Being forewarned helps one remain constantly aware of the vulnerability of the selection process. Both types of errors have undesirable consequences. Errors of omission lead to gaps in the curriculum that teachers and IEP committees may not be able to fill or bridge because they are difficult to detect. Errors of commission lead to the inclusion of content that, despite its apparent appeal, is nevertheless superfluous or irrelevant to students' needs and therefore is a diversion that wastes valuable energy and time.

Conditions other than errors in the selection of the content of instruction can also complicate the development effort and ultimately diminish the effectiveness of the curriculum. In addition to depending on educators to select the information from our culture that our young need to learn in order to contribute to the strength and durability of our society, society looks to other social institutions, most notably family and church, to contribute to this mission. Compared with the contribution of the family, education's share is expected to be more comprehensive and less provincial. At the same time, as change in the family and other social institutions reduces or otherwise alters their contribution to the upbringing of our young, communities frequently turn to the schools to fulfill the responsibilities abandoned or mishandled by others.

Without a curriculum in place to document the school's mission and the programs leading to its fulfillment, it becomes almost impossible to counter arguments that these functions are and should remain the responsibility of the local school. Administrators of programs for students with mild disabilities need to protect the integrity of the curriculum development effort by standing firm against the efforts of other social institutions, agencies, and services to indiscriminately dump additional responsibilities on their programs. They can, however, help the community to arrive at a more productive solution to such problems.

Conclusion

A curriculum that is appropriate to the educational needs of students with mild disabilities will be notably different from curricula now being used in other subsystems of education. The goal of curriculum reform in general education is to improve students' academic achievement. The goal of Education 2000, for example, was to improve the instruction of students in general education so that American students will be superior to their counterparts in many parts of the world in the major academic areas.

This goal is not as compatible with the educational and developmental needs of children with mild disabilities as a curriculum that underscores social adaptation. This is not to suggest that children with mild disabilities do not need to acquire academic skills. To the contrary, reading and arithmetic are powerful problem-solving tools. In combination, their mastery is one of the primary resources for social adaptation.

A curriculum based on social adaptation is therefore more relevant to the educational needs of students with mild disabilities. Such a curriculum gives a distinct focus to the contribution of schools to the growth and development of students with mild disabilities. Unlike curricula for nondisabled students, a curriculum for students with mild disabilities need not make presumptions about the contributions of other social institutions to the socialization of our young. Instead, it can be single-minded about educational objectives and their effect on students' ability to acquire the concepts, facts, and skills that are fundamental to the autonomies that define an acceptable quality of life for adults in our society.

A Social Sciences Basis for Curriculum Development

■   ■   ■   ■   ■   ■   ■   ■   ■   ■   ■

Culture has been defined in many ways. Some definitions are so overly simplified as to do an injustice to culture's complexity. Others are so complex as to defy understanding by ordinary mortals. The *Oxford Dictionary of Sociology* (Marshall, 1994), for example, states that culture, to social scientists, is everything in human society that is socially rather than biologically transmitted. Much earlier, Tylor (1913), who was more explicit in his definition, wrote that culture was a complex whole that includes knowledge, belief, art, morals, law, customs, and any other capabilities acquired by man as a member of society. Presently, most students of culture subscribe to similarly detailed definitions.

An Educationally Oriented Definition of Culture

For our purpose, we can define culture as the knowledge and learned behaviors that a group provides to its members so that their interactions with their social, physical, and psychological environments are consistent with the group's and its individual members' needs for tranquility and durability. Durkheim (1972) conceived of "social facts" in these terms when he wrote:

> *When I carry out my obligations as brother, husband, or citizen, when I comply with contracts, I perform duties which are defined externally to myself and my acts, in law and in custom. Even if they conform to my own sentiments and I feel their reality*

subjectively, this reality is still objective, for I did not create them, I merely received them through my education. (p. 63)

Likewise, Malinowski (1944) maintained that we live by norms, customs, traditions, and rules that are the results of interactions between organic processes and humankind's manipulation and resetting of his environment. Segerstedt (1966) pointed out that the importance of social norms and their key positions in social life have been widely recognized by social scientists. Typically, societies look to their schools and social institutions for the dissemination of this information and for its transmission to succeeding generations. Curricula are major tools in this process.

The Constancy of Social and Technological Change

The notion that people are able to manipulate and change their environments highlights the dynamic nature of culture. That is, although much of our culture seems to be fixed in place by tradition and habituation at any given moment, it is nevertheless in the process of changing in response to the fluctuations in our physical, social, and psychological environments.

Within this context, imparting an oversimplified version of the general education curriculum to students with mild disabilities cannot be justified. Nor can one justify the presumption that engaging these students in extensive rote learning of rules for getting along in society will, in the long run, be of any value to them. Both of these approaches tend to be static. That is, the simplification of the general education curriculum is too often achieved by eliminating concepts that are considered beyond the learning capabilities of students with mild disabilities. With the reduction of concepts, rote learning, or the memorization of facts, becomes the indicated method of instruction.

Constant social and technological change means that new knowledge is being added to our culture, ineffective ways for doing things are being culled, and familiar procedures are being revised. The change in the status of women over the last few decades is a good example. No longer considered the weaker sex, many women are offended by courtly treatment that was once considered appropriate. In technology, the slide rule is no longer a ubiquitous tool of engineers, and typewriters have all but disappeared from offices and homes. In industry and commerce, outsourcing and downsizing have introduced novel ways for changing configurations of the workforce. Because constant social and technological advances result in ongoing change in culture, any curriculum that is designed must be capable of addressing these changes quickly.

Behavior as a Cultural Response

Looking to culture rather than to the medical model as a frame of reference for the development of curriculum for students with mild disabilities represents a complete turnabout. Presently, educators of children with disabilities view their behavior almost exclusively within a psychological framework—as the aggregate of their responses to internal and external stimuli. This concept of behavior leads to the cataloging of behaviors as items in a checklist of socially acceptable and sometimes fixed ways or formulas for individuals and groups to meet their basic physical, social, and psychological needs.

Concepts of behavior have implications for the stability and predictability of a curriculum. In looking to the normative behaviors that characterize culture, curriculum developers are selecting instructional objectives that have a well-established consensual basis. A notable majority of people in a society accepts these behaviors as normative for the society as a whole. In contrast, basing instruction on the remediation of manifested maladaptive behavior introduces conjecture as to what behavior or behaviors are being observed as well as to what need is being met. Conjecture is unavoidable because of the differences in the biases and competencies of observers as well as in the conditions that evoke the child's behavior. Thus, making a decision to include the learning of a specific behavior that has been recognized by society as an acceptable way of meeting one's needs is very different from observing an inappropriate or defeating behavior, speculating as to what motivated the individual to behave in this way, and using these speculations as the basis for organizing instruction in order to extinguish the behavior and replace it with one that is presumed to be more positive.

In short, using clinical and educational psychological theory as a framework for understanding observed maladaptive behavior can result in as many conclusions as there are diagnosticians and children. In the classroom, establishing instructional priorities often depends on the teacher's tolerance. A behavior that is obnoxious to one teacher may be whimsical to another. This is not to say that psychologically based behaviors are irrelevant—in fact, they are critical to classroom control and to the management of children's learning. However, they are much less relevant as the sole frame of reference for the curriculum development process and the instruction that follows.

The concept of behavior as a cultural response is based on the presumption that culture itself is an artifact of humankind's struggle for biological survival that has evolved along with the ascendancy of the species (Malinowski, 1944). We need to be reminded that our problems initially arose directly from our organic needs and that many still do. Equally important is the fact that we have always lived, and continue to live, in an environment that is, at the same time, both hostile and friendly: hostile because it threatens us with many dangerous and sometimes lethal forces but friendly because it provides nourishment and the raw materials for the invention and construction of the tools and mechanisms that we use to confront and overcome the lethal forces and other threats to our survival.

In the process of dealing with both the hostile and friendly aspects of our environment, we, like all societies, have invented and continue to invent procedures, devices, and artifacts and the rules on how they are to be used as well as sanctions for their misuse. At the same time, we dispose of or in some way discontinue unproductive ways of coping with our environments because they can mislead or divert us from discovering or inventing effective ways. In some cases, then, we unlearn certain behaviors.

Societies have found it necessary to regulate many procedures as well as the use of devices in order to preserve and protect its citizens and to ensure that valued ways of doing things can be transmitted to succeeding generations. To these ends, some procedures have been codified and become the law of the land. Others have gone uncodified but have nevertheless become distinctly recognizable as society's customs and mores. Behaviors that lead to the misuse or abuse of procedures and devices in our individual and collective confrontations with our environment attract formal sanctions in the case of codified procedures and informal sanctions in the case of uncodified procedures.

Curriculum developers who draw on cultural responses for instructional content will rarely find that only one behavior is associated with a problem-solving protocol or a single procedure for the use of devices. For example, the behavior involved in ordering a meal in a restaurant is influenced by a number of factors, including the kind of restaurant (e.g., fast food or conventional), type of cuisine, and pricing. Some restaurants have dress codes, and some enforce a policy on smoking. Then there are regional and local differences in the ways that eating places provide services. Similarly, the expected behaviors for using public transportation vary according to local and regional customs and regulations. In some communities, for example, the exact fare is required and disabled or elderly passengers are given priority for seats at the front of the bus.

Defining Appropriate Social Behavior

In a complex society such as ours, the original rationales for many of our laws, customs, and mores, have been lost over time. Apparently, the only characteristic needed to qualify as subject matter to be learned and acted on in our curriculum is that these laws, customs, and mores serve society well. It is within this inordinately complex context that we define an appropriate cultural response as a learned behavior that is a socially normative reaction to a physical, psychological, and/or social environmental stress. An approved response is one that has a history of being perceived as effective in the ordinary course of events. A novel response may startle observers because of its originality. Nevertheless, it too can be acceptable if it does not appear to violate law or custom.

From this enormous accumulation of things to know, things to do, and ways of doing them, curriculum developers are expected to specify and justify what students need to learn as well as the conditions of learning. In educational terms, the elements of culture that educators, as society's surrogates, regard as essential to the socialization of society's young become the substance of learning to be taught in the public schools.

Accordingly, the culture of each society is the source of the knowledge and behaviors that are requisite to social adaptation, and it is the obligation of the educational system to interpret culture toward this end. The conventional outcome of this process is a curriculum. In complex, technological societies in which there is marked variability in students' aptitudes, abilities, and aspirations, curricula are likely to reflect as many variations on the same theme of social adaptation as there are variations in the characteristics and aspirations of students.

Cultural Response as a Curriculum Format

For the purposes of curriculum development, viewing behavior as a cultural response is more than a convenient way of explaining the relationship between culture, behavior, and the fulfillment of our physical, social, and psychological needs. The ways that cultural responses are organized or categorized can also serve as a format for organizing knowledge about the ways that people meet their basic needs. Such a format can be generalized to societies of all sizes irrespective of their structure or their geography, based on the presumptions (a) that basic human needs are universal and (b) that each group's culture provides its membership with prescribed ways of meeting these needs.

There is a well-established link between behavior cataloged as a cultural response and the psychodynamic concept of behavior that is popular in educational programs for children with mild disabilities. The link is in the performance schedules that are typical of child development literature as well as in the informal but often rigorous behavioral criteria of the lay community. These are often implicit in aphorisms such as "you have to be able to walk before you can run" and "the child is father to the man" as well as in admonitions such as "act your age."

In their present form, cultural responses and psychodynamic conceptualizations of behavior confront curriculum developers with the challenge of organizing them in a way that is consistent with the goals of education. A format for organizing cultural responses that has the capacity to accommodate social and technological change would be responsive to such a challenge. Marshall (1994) points out that apart from the basic human biological needs that have direct bearing on survival, there is little agreement among social scientists as to what constitutes human needs and desires.

Nevertheless, a clinical approach to understanding and changing students' behaviors has dominated the instructional scene in educational programs for students with mild disabilities. Maslow (1970), for example, provides a comprehensive treatment of this issue. He proposes that human needs are hierarchical, with the basic biological needs as the foundation. Once these needs are met, safety and security fulfill the need for order, which then makes way for fulfilling the need for belonging and love. Fourth in the hierarchy is the need for self-esteem. Only when all of the foregoing have been fulfilled does the need for self-actualization take over.

Experience has shown that arranging needs in a hierarchical form creates problems in the curriculum development process and its implementation. In an earlier curriculum development project, efforts to use Maslow's concepts of needs as instructional goals created many ambiguities in definition and in implementation. In fact, it was difficult to relate the nature of the instructional content at the development stage with the results of instruction in the classroom (Goldstein, 1974, 1975; Goldstein & Alter, 1980) because the curriculum activities were sometimes based on needs that were contradictory to the teachers' knowledge about the student. That is, teachers sometimes found that their knowledge about the basis for a student's inappropriate behavior did not match the presumptions of the curriculum writers.

It is clear that the development of instructional materials for a curriculum does not require behaviors to be organized within the psychological categories of needs they purportedly fulfill because, at best, observers can only infer the need that is being fulfilled. In the classroom, using a curriculum that categorizes behavior by needs can be distracting and often frustrating. Suppose that a young child is unwilling to share his or her toys. Does the teacher need to know what need the child is attempting to fulfill in order to ameliorate the child's behavior?

Paradoxically, our society's remarkable complexity is the mitigating factor in the resolution of conflicts about how to develop instructional content. Generally, we expect that complexity leads to so many choices that confusion and conflict are inevitable. In this case, the almost infinite number of ways to do things includes a multiplicity of acceptable ways to get them done. This means that attempting to isolate the *best* cultural response would be futile. It also means that the most constructive approach to developing instructional content is to offer teachers and their students with mild disabilities the best array of options for fulfilling needs.

Obviously, the more worthwhile cultural response options that people with mild disabilities have available in their response repertories, the greater their flexibility and maneuverability in interpersonal and environmental transactions will be. Not being committed to the single best response allows the curriculum developer to broaden the scope of the curriculum by including responses that are appropriate across society, including those dictated by local and regional customs. As Steward (1963) points out:

> All men eat, but this is an organic and not a cultural fact. It is universally explainable in terms of biological and chemical processes. What and how different groups of men eat is a cultural fact explainable only by cultural history and environmental factors. (p. 8)

Malinowski's (1944) construct offers two attributes that would benefit a curriculum for students with mild disabilities. First, it focuses on basic physiological or survival needs while omitting difficult-to-define psychological needs such as belonging, love, and self-esteem. As a result, curriculum developers are spared the conflicts that arise when trying to make unnecessary distinctions between cultural responses to physiological needs that can be generalized to people in all cultures and those that have their origins in the customs and mores of some cultures but not others.

Second, the construct provides categories of responses that are relevant to needs, but it can be left to others (to curriculum developers in this instance) to specify the responses intended to occupy each category. This flexibility allows cultural responses to be organized within categories in a developmental sequence that is congruent with children's maturation and their progress in school—a characteristic that distinguishes curricula from therapies and remedial instruction.

This flexibility allows curriculum developers to take into account the fact that culture provides different ways for children, teenagers, and adults to respond to the same needs. The expectations are different for a child, a teenager, and an adult. For example, children have a need for nourishment, but they are not expected to be hunters and gatherers in either the primitive or modern sense. If they are engaged in such activities at all, it is usually in peripheral or minor roles in which they are expected to acquire the knowledge and skills that will one day allow them to assume more mature and helpful roles. The child who rides in the shopping cart while mother tours the supermarket aisles finding and collecting the needed provisions is expected to "grow" into the role of shopper at the appropriate stage in his or her development.

A Social Sciences Basis for Curriculum Development

Physiological Needs and Their Cultural Responses

Malinowski (1944) connects human physiological needs and the broad categories of corresponding cultural responses as follows:

Physiological Need	Cultural Response
metabolism	commissariat
reproduction	kinship
bodily comfort	shelter
safety	protection
movement	activities
growth	training
health	hygiene

The physiological needs and their cultural responses are stated in functional rather than scientific terms. Neither the needs nor their cultural responses represent discrete categories. Nor should any significance be attributed to the number of need and response categories. The redundancy in each of the categories is no more deniable than it is in life—some of the specifics related to the need for bodily comforts will surely appear in the need for safety and others will appear in the need for health. From the curriculum developers' perspective, these redundancies allow for flexibility in both the content of instruction and the emphasis and priority in instruction that is required by the scope and sequence of a comprehensive curriculum.

Cultural response categories are inclusive. Each category accommodates all of the ways for meeting the associated need that society has found useful and acceptable. For example, the category "commissariat" includes ways of meeting metabolic needs that range from specific foods and their sources to socially acceptable ways of disposing of wastes and surpluses and everything in between, from procuring, to storing, to preparing, to ingesting. Subcultural, religious, regional, and local factors can be accounted for within this category, as can those imparted to children and youth primarily by their families and other social institutions.

Establishing categories of cultural responses provides curriculum developers with a frame of reference and systematic procedures for organizing specific content areas of the curriculum. Thus, curriculum developers can address learner characteristics such as age, gender, and learning attributes because they have implications for the nature of content. This can be done within and across response categories. For example, instructional content for students with memory deficits can be organized so that teachers provide them with as many experiences as they need, over and above those usually prepared for less disabled students, in order to help them retain the facts and concepts important to their development.

As mentioned earlier, the list of physiological needs does not include the needs for love, belonging, self-esteem, and, ultimately, self-actualization. It is nearly impossible to achieve a consensus on the definition of these terms because they vary considerably from person to person and culture to culture (Hoffman, 1996; Markus & Kitayama, 1991). However one defines them, needs spring from psychological as well as biological sources, but, unlike physiological needs, they do not necessarily threaten survival of individuals, groups, and societies if they go unfulfilled. Goode (1959) asserted that "falling in love is a universal psychodynamic potential in the human being. Most human beings in all societies are capable of it" (p. 193). Linton (1936), on the other hand, states that love is a psychological abnormality that is about as common as epilepsy (p. 175). Accordingly, it would be appropriate to distinguish love, belonging, self-esteem, and self-actualization from the more basic physiological needs by identifying them as desires or wants, which are more often than not fulfilled by psychological rather than educational pursuits. The inclusive array of physiological needs and the cultural responses associated with them provide us with a format and the stability we need in order to develop a curriculum of the dimensions proposed here.

Identifying and Categorizing Cultural Responses

At this point in the curriculum development process, the task of determining the actual cultural responses and categorizing them appropriately looms large. If we followed the conventional practices in curriculum development for students with mild disabilities, we would do one of two things. We would assign to each physiological need and cultural response category the positive equivalent of the negative behaviors that have interfered with the social adaptation of students with mild disabilities and workers as reported in follow-up studies or by employers. Or we would fall back on our own values and experiences, arbitrarily assigning behavior categories based on our experiences and on what we personally believe are the behaviors that children with mild disabilities and youth need to acquire.

In keeping with our intent to develop a seamless, synergistic, and developmentally systematized curriculum for students with mild disabilities, we need to be prepared to offer students as broad a range of concepts, facts, and behaviors as their attainment of the goals of education requires. To this end, we need a reality-based determination of the content of the physiological needs and cultural response categories. As discussed earlier, while the need to eat is a biological fact, the kinds of foods, the ways in which we eat them, and the limitations on what we eat (whether religious, intuitive, or hygienic) are cultural, as are the rules regarding the quality and preparation of foods.

Thus, our interest in commissariat, for example, as a category of cultural response that meets the need for sustaining metabolism is not so much in the process by which metabolism makes energy available as much as it is in the large aggregation of information about nourishment that results in metabolic needs being fulfilled. This includes information on growing, obtaining, preparing, consuming, and disposing of food and metabolic wastes that is (a) normative for our society and our community, (b) specific to the immediate and projected needs of students in home, neighborhood, and community settings and beyond and (c) essential to the socialization of students with mild disabilities.

Knowing this, we can select information to be included in the curriculum that will provide a reasonable balance between what must be learned over the full span of students' schooling and the students' available learning time. This pattern is repeated when categorizing the knowledge and behaviors relevant to each cultural response.

By maintaining the relationship between physiological needs and cultural responses, curriculum developers can achieve greater stability in the curriculum's content. Physiological needs do not change over time as radically and dramatically as do the socially acceptable means for meeting those needs. Change in physiological needs is typically evolutionary, while change in cultural responses is more nearly revolutionary. The need for nourishment expressed by hunger, for example, remains far more constant than the ways and means that we have for alleviating it. How we express hunger, as well as the social and technological ways for satisfying it, can vary from simple to complex.

For example, advances in our knowledge of the effects of cholesterol on the vascular system and of its sources in the diet have changed the ways we select prepared foods. Shoppers who used to simply glance at labels to make sure that they had selected the desired item now carefully read the fine print on the label. Calories, cholesterol, fat, sodium, and many preservatives have become the subject matter of advertising and the basis for comparison shopping, sometimes supplanting cost and taste as critical variables. Because social and technological changes can occur rapidly, a curriculum for students with mild disabilities requires a built-in mechanism to keep it abreast of those changes and ensure that its content changes accordingly.

The Role of Psychological Needs

The absence of psychological needs as a factor in curriculum development must appear irresponsible, if not misguided, to many experienced educators of children and youth with mild disabilities. Under present conditions, this reaction is understandable. Because of our adherence to the medical model in special education, much of what now passes for instruction in the education of students with mild disabilities is influenced, if not guided, by psychological theory or eclecticism. For example, behavior management, in one form or another, is far more conspicuous than the content of instruction in a notable proportion of educational settings for students with mild disabilities. In fact, to the casual observer, it might seem that the primary purpose of academic instruction is to serve as a vehicle for behavior management. Because education, like nature, abhors a vacuum, this approach to education occurs by default in the absence of a body of teachable knowledge, that is, a curriculum.

Many individuals with mild disabilities exhibit more than their share of maladaptive behaviors. While many of these are likely psychogenic, research in genetics indicates that some behavioral propensities may be inherited. Other maladaptive behaviors are likely due to students misreading of the immediate activities, resulting in inappropriate and sometimes bizarre responses. Still others may result from gaps in the individual's response repertory that lead to immobilization or, at the other extreme, desperate flailing about for a response or a solution that is not readily available.

Reliably distinguishing one source of maladaptive behavior from another is typically a difficult, if not impossible, undertaking. From the standpoint of the educator, the most realistic inference that can be made about the basis for the observed maladaptive behavior is probably that it is the student's best estimate of the appropriate response for the situation. Because behavior is learned, educators can and for a century have been responding pedagogically to this state of affairs by offering instruction that provides the student with the ability to better understand problems as well as an expanded response repertory.

The Role of Psychological Theory

This is not to say that there is no place for psychological theory in educational settings for students with mild disabilities. The proposed curriculum for students with mild disabilities provides teachers and their students with a continuum of specific learning objectives to fulfill along with the content of instruction. This enables teachers to incorporate the contributions of educational psychology in their management of students' learning as well as in systematic ways of evaluating the results of instruction.

Educational psychology has made huge strides in research into methods of instruction and classroom management. Moreover, it will probably be easier to distinguish psychogenic behavior problems from other behavioral problems within the context of a purposeful, goal-oriented educational setting. This should be helpful to school and community mental health resources who provide treatment for these students.

Principles of teaching and learning are valuable adjuncts to the implementation of the curriculum, as are the contributions of child and adolescent psychology to the understanding and classroom management of children's behavior. Experience has shown that teachers' reactions to inferences about children's need for recognition, approbation, or belonging sometimes have what appear to be positive results and are often worth pursuing in teaching−learning transactions. Students' success in problem solving during the ordinary course of events does more than reinforce learning. It can also increase their self-esteem and sense of belonging. Clearly, although psychology does not and should not have the leading role in the management of the proposed educational program for learners with mild disabilities, it can and often does make important contributions to its implementation.

Conclusion

The social sciences concept of culture provides educators of students with mild disabilities with a systematic way of organizing the content of instruction. As Havighurst and Neugarten (1962) point out:

> By culture, we refer, in short, to the patterned way of life of a society. (The term society refers to the persons who share a given culture, and to the network of relationships that exists among the members of the group. A human society does not exist apart from a culture.) (p. 9)

The notion of a patterned way of life supports a concept of behavior that goes well beyond the almost exclusively psychological, stimulus−response, and affective views of behavior that have, to this point in time, characterized educational programs for students with mild disabilities. The pattern of life, in this case, is the dichotomy of physiological needs and cultural responses that characterizes normative behaviors and allows them to be categorized in ways that are consistent with each curriculum developer's design.

Within the context of curriculum development, categorized cultural responses take on a importance beyond that of a systematic way for comprehensively organizing normative behaviors. They can, at the same time, serve as the foundation of a model for curriculum development.

Chapter

Constructing a Curriculum Model

5

In the previous chapter, the point was made that cultural responses organized into categories provide curriculum developers with a frame of reference and systematic procedure for organizing the specific content areas of the curriculum, which would consist of the socially acceptable knowledge and behaviors that fulfill the needs subsumed in each cultural response category along with the related quantitative, literacy, and science-based problem-solving skills. For example, the cultural responses that fulfill the need for nourishment include the personal and interpersonal social skills relevant to shopping in a market as well as the literacy skills that facilitate the understanding of labels and the quantitative skills necessary to distinguish among amounts and costs. The specifics of the content are to be determined by each curriculum developer in accordance with the theme guiding the development of the curriculum.

Curriculum developers can draw the content for the categories of cultural responses from two sources. The first and most universal source is the body of knowledge imparted to children and youth by other social institutions: the family, the church, and community organizations. These institutions contribute the knowledge and behaviors that are basic to self-care, interpersonal activities, and communication—the same knowledge and behaviors that schools mediate, normalize, and expand and on which the school builds its distinctive contribution.

The second source of knowledge and behaviors is found in the socially acceptable activities that people of all ages perform as they make cultural responses that fulfill their needs or that serve society by fulfilling the needs of others. For example, particular knowledge and behaviors characterize the roles of people who occupy the status of shopper. Some knowledge and behavior is common to everyone regardless of their purpose for shopping, and some are very specific to the product or service being sought. At the same time, some knowledge and behaviors are typical of people who have achieved the status of sales associate or service provider. Their role requires knowledge and behavior that facilitates shoppers' efforts in accordance with the expectations of their employer.

Status and Role as Curriculum Constructs

Marshall (1994) discusses two views of social status: an individual's status or position in a social structure or organization, such as a parent or a bus driver, and the individual's status in a social stratification or a hierarchical ranking of people in accordance with what Weber (1922) refers to as social esteem: the status people achieve as a result of parentage, accumulation of wealth or property, or political activity. Both concepts of social status prove useful, each in its own way.

The concept of status as a position in a social structure is more useful as a factor in curriculum development than that of status in a social stratification. Status in a social stratification proves useful later as the curriculum model takes shape. This is not to say that the concept of status is as simplified in society at large as its use in curriculum development might imply. To the contrary, the concept permeates just about all aspects of social groups in many areas, including economic, political, and social pursuits.

Linton (1936) provides us with a useful discussion of status and role by making the distinction between achieved and ascribed statuses. Definitions of social status portray it as the place or, more realistically, the places that an individual achieves in society and the rights and duties associated with those places. Linton points out that achieved statuses are those positions in society, positive or negative, that individuals attain through their own efforts, misdirected efforts, or lack of effort. Thus, one can achieve the status of teacher by satisfying society's prerequisites for functioning in this status and, having done so, by securing a teaching position and fulfilling the role associated with the status to the satisfaction of the school's administration and the community. Through misdirection, one can achieve the negative social status of criminal by being apprehended for acting in ways that threaten society's tranquility and security and being convicted for violating certain societal laws. As a function of lack of effort, one can achieve the status of dependent or, in some cases, social misfit.

Ascribed statuses, on the other hand, are assigned by society by virtue of one's kinships and gender distinctions. For instance, a male offspring is ascribed the statuses of son and male and is expected to fulfill the associated roles in accordance with the customs and mores of his culture or subculture.

A social role consists of the behaviors associated with a status. According to Havighurst and Neugarten (1962):

> A social role may be defined as a coherent pattern of behavior common to all persons who fill the same position or place [status] and a pattern of behavior expected by other members of society. The pattern may be described without reference to the particular individuals who fill the role. (p. 78, emphasis added)

Thus, we expect teachers, for example, to act in certain ways in their classrooms but in other ways when we meet them as members of a community organization. In fact, our expectations for the behaviors of some people in certain statuses can be so exaggerated and fixed that they become stereotypical.

From the standpoint of the curriculum developer, both statuses and roles are dynamic. However, of the two, statuses tend to be more stable. They tend to persist as long as they appear to serve a purpose, actually contribute to society's well-being, or prove to be less trouble to endure than to discontinue. Roles, on the other hand, are characteristically more changeable because of their sensitivity to both social and technological change.

In considering the hierarchies we find in our schools, we find that the status of teachers, for instance, has changed little over the last decade. Teachers' roles, on the other hand, have changed dramatically. For example, the technological changes that brought computers into the classroom have expanded society's expectations of how teachers work with students. Another example is the social change effected by transformations in the typical family, such as the two-parent workforce and single-parent home, which has changed teachers' roles by requiring actions that were previously the province of others.

Differentiation by Status and Role: Status Ranking

Even though statuses in society are relatively stable in their relationships to each other, the people who occupy them are not nearly as static.

Vertical Movement in Status

Career ladders are examples of the opportunities people have to move vertically from one status to another. A worker, having achieved the status of mail clerk, can aspire to and possibly rise through the ranks to middle management and ultimately achieve the status of chief executive officer.

In this sense, each rung of the career ladder, or each status, represents a social stratum or ranking with its own social role. We expect that lifestyles of mail clerks and senior executives to differ because of the difference in their incomes—an obvious distinction in their vertical stratification.

A curriculum for students with mild disabilities has to take into account the fact that the ranking of statuses in the workplace involves properties that go well beyond income and its disposition. There is also the matter of the many skills and proficiencies that go into achieving and then maintaining each status. Education and an appropriate level of social sophistication are essential elements. That is, the mail clerk's high school education and the academic and social skills and proficiencies acquired in the process of earning a diploma are more likely to be in accord with the job description for that position than for the positions of comptroller or director of marketing.

The ranking of statuses is not limited to the workplace and related endeavors. Families, both immediate and extended, represent status hierarchies based on kinship in some instances and birth order in others. The importance of status rankings will become clear as the social sciences/based curriculum model for students with mild disabilities takes shape.

Horizontal Movement in a Status

In contrast with the potential for vertical movement in status, horizontal movement is rapid and, in some cases, unpredictable. The moment the mail clerk enters the lunchroom at noon, his status changes to diner and his observed behavior takes on the character of his new role to the extent that he has learned the behaviors appropriate to the company lunchroom as opposed to those appropriate to his home or to other places where people dine. On the way back to work, his status changes to son when he calls home and back to mail clerk when he returns to the office. With each change in status, the mail clerk must execute the necessary shift in role efficiently and unspectacularly. This means more than knowing how to behave in the status of the moment.

Why Understanding the Concept of Status is Important

A good understanding of the concept of status is basic to being able to anticipate and react suitably to the behaviors of people occupying related statuses such as the mail supervisor, the waiter or waitress, and so on throughout the day while at work, at home, and at play.

Like the rest of us, people with mild disabilities are judged on how well they make the transitions from status to status, horizontally or vertically, according to their ability to discontinue the behaviors associated with the role of the status just departed and to initiate behaviors appropriate to the immediate status without drawing untoward attention to themselves. This is the raw material of social adaptation. It is also the substance of the behavior that is foremost, functionally and psychometrically, in distinguishing children with mild disabilities and youth from others. Nevertheless, some persons with mild disabilities may blur, if not erase entirely, any distinctions in social functioning that set them apart from their peers if they participate in a curriculum that provides them with the knowledge and behaviors needed to negotiate the cultural response maze.

The impermanence of achieved statuses is a salient fact for educators. While one may achieve a status by meeting its prerequisites, sustaining that status is contingent on how well one fulfills the role associated with it. Those who cannot, for whatever the reason, fulfill expectations are sooner or later stripped of the status and assigned another in its place. Thus, a student who has been successful as a first grader and second grader but who falters in the third grade may, after prescribed procedures, be stripped of his status of third grader and, in the process, achieve in its place the status of student with mild disabilities. Even if he is subsequently mainstreamed in the third grade, the odds are good that his new status will persist if his performance remains unchanged. He will likely be known and referred to as a youngster with disabilities, not as a third grader.

In combination, cultural response categories, social statuses, and social roles provide us with a model for the development of curriculum as well as a systematic way of observing and assessing behavior. In curriculum development, each category of cultural responses provides a specific context within which individuals occupying social statuses (identifiable positions) fulfill their social role (solve problems) in ways that are consistent with both the required cultural response and the behaviors expected of someone in their status. The mail clerk, whose goal is to fulfill his need for nourishment, does and says all of the appropriate things as he navigates the cafeteria line, consumes his meal, and departs the cafeteria, thus solving this problem in a socially acceptable manner.

89

Accordingly, the curriculum developer, having ascertained the status of individuals coping with a specific problem, can identify the socially acceptable behaviors that lead to the solution of the problem and convert them into the content of instruction in whatever detail the development plans specify. That is, the developer can use the model to design a curriculum whose content can be generalized to (a) instructional settings for students with mild disabilities, leaving teachers to modify the content so that it will be consistent with the character of their community and/or (b) develop a curriculum whose content is indigenous to the school's community or region and/or (c) develop a curriculum whose content is in the vernacular, so to speak, of subcultures within our core culture. While this may seem to be a somewhat elaborate if not intricate approach to curriculum development, the detailed discussion of the social sciences–based model in the next chapter reveals that it is far from as complicated as the foregoing might suggest.

Essentials of a Social Science Basis
for Curriculum Development

Each society provides its members with its culture as the source for socially acceptable ways of dealing with their social, psychological, and physical environments. Defined operationally, the socially acceptable ways for fulfilling needs are the need-meeting behaviors, procedures, and technologies that do not threaten the tranquility and durability of the society.

Clearly, the nature of the responses that cultures provide vary with the differences in social organization (Murdock, 1981; Murdock & Provost, 1980). These differences are most pronounced at the extremes. That is, the cultures of technologically advanced societies are more likely to provide a greater array of responses for meeting any particular need than societies whose major activities are limited to hunting and gathering. Similarly, highly organized and ritualized societies, in which people's ways of life are governed by a large and elaborate system of codified and uncodified rules and by the bureaucracies that implement them, probably provide their members with more complex ways to fulfilling their needs than do less complicated societies. However, because our culture includes a notable array of subcultures, curriculum developers need to stay alert to the fact that some apparently uncomplicated cultures may offer their members involved ways to fulfill some of their needs. In some cultures, moieties and kinships are often uncodified and can be extremely convoluted (Levi-Straus, 1969).

This should not be construed as a suggestion that the curriculum for students with mild disabilities should conform to one of the more recent fads in education: the multicultural curriculum. To the contrary, Hoffman (1996) points out the superficiality of current programs in multicultural education and raises doubt about the wisdom of engaging children in activities that are popular but unproductive. She questions the ability of the schools to do much more than explore the superficial aspects of multiculturalism by decorating the classroom with posters, celebrating holidays, and sharing indigenous foods, dances, and songs. Furthermore, there is so much that children with mild disabilities need to learn and so little time in which to learn that the in-depth study of multiculturalism would likely be an unwarranted diversion.

A Model for a Curriculum Based on the Social Sciences

The three-dimensional social sciences construct on which the proposed curriculum for students with mild disabilities is based focuses on (a) the responses to physiological needs discussed earlier (Malinowski, 1944),

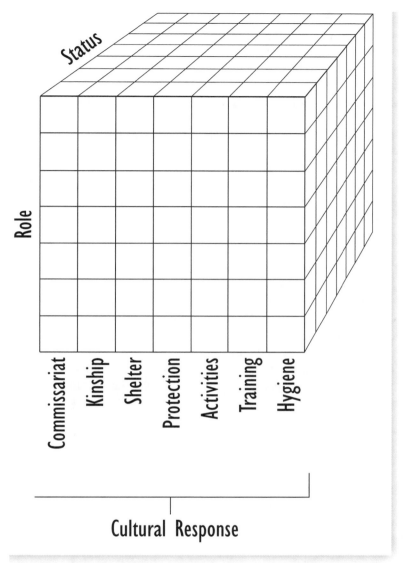

FIGURE 5.1. Curriculum development model.

(b) the statuses and (c) the roles of people active in fulfilling their own needs and the needs of others. This construct is portrayed in Figure 5.1.

Each need category provides the curriculum developer with the framework for the cultural responses that address that need. *Commissariat,* for example, includes cultural responses that address the needs required to sustain metabolic processes: the nutrients that support metabolism, their

Constructing a Curriculum Model

sources and derivation, their utilization, and, having served their purpose, their disposition. The range of responses in this category extends from the simple, such as drinking from a cup, to the complex, such as research in digestion and in the food sciences. This breadth of responses is characteristic of all cultural responses. The role of the curriculum developer is to identify the responses in each category that are important to the growth and development of students with mild disabilities.

Hygiene encompasses the cultural responses that deal with the need to maintain a level of health necessary to cope with and survive in one's physical, social, and psychological environments.

Kinship provides cultural responses that contribute to the need of groups in society to reproduce as an important process in sustaining survival through numbers as well as in uniting individuals into productive, socially approved relationships.

Shelter is responsive to peoples' need to protect themselves from the effects of extreme weather, weather-related phenomena, and long-term exposure to harmful temperatures and humidity.

Protection consists of the cultural responses designed to avert or fend off the potentially lethal effects of manmade devices and hazardous environmental conditions and the dangers of human and other predators.

Activities encompass the cultural responses that acknowledge not only the need to sustain a healthy level of individual physical mobility, but also the enterprises and occupations that draw people together into cooperative and collaborative groups as a means for achieving the kinds of balances in skills and proficiencies that contribute to survival.

Training provides the cultural responses that include formal and informal schooling and retraining as well as the child-rearing practices that lead, ultimately, to the maturation and the achievement of independence by the totally dependent infant that is so important to the survival of society. Societies also formalize training in order to inculcate in their young the values, attitudes, and beliefs that are consistent with maintaining the society's strength and durability.

Realities of the Social Sciences Construct

Certain facts about the social sciences construct, the concept of cultural responses, and need-meeting behaviors must be recognized before going further. First, the social sciences construct is neither fixed nor fully inclusive nor does it offer the convenience of anything as clearly delineated as the parameters of an equation. The categories of cultural responses, for example, are not mutually exclusive. Some cultural responses that fit nicely into hygiene are also relevant to commissariat or vice versa, and responses subsumed under shelter might also be suitable in protection.

Criteria for the Inclusion of Concepts and Facts in Curriculum

The issue is not where a fact or concept precisely belongs. What is important is that the curriculum developer identify facts and concepts which are normative in the society and critical to the maturation of children with mild disabilities and that they include these facts and concepts in the curriculum and place them in accordance with how the developer conceptualizes it, meaning that they are properly placed in the developmental sequence of teaching and learning. Toward this end, the discipline inherent in the continued attention to the curriculum project's commitment to the goals of education and to the objectives by which educational programs for students with mild disabilities attain them reins in tendencies on the part of curriculum developers to become overly inclusive or to be diverted by attractive but otherwise irrelevant content.

Furthermore, we need to take into account the tendency of schools to take on responsibilities abandoned by other social institutions. For example, as the family's contributions to the growth and development of children have changed with the increasingly frequent employment of both parents and increasing number of single-parent homes, many communities have turned to their public schools and to the school administrators to find the wherewithal to provide those aspects of the instruction, care, and shelter no longer provided by some families. It has become customary for schools to expand their curriculum, as well as their personnel and physical facilities, to include the added instruction and experiences in the school day. Without checks and balances in place, these additional responsibilities can inflate the curriculum to an unmanageable size with predictable, limited outcomes.

The social sciences construct does not have a built-in alarm system that alerts developers when content overload and meltdown is imminent. Continuing awareness of the goals of education, constraints on the time allocated to schooling, and the learning needs of students with mild disabilities provide educators with criteria for establishing the limits of the instructional content's inclusiveness. Limits serve to keep the curriculum from expanding into an unmanageable giant that soon perishes under its own weight, and they do so without restraining or dampening the creativity that curriculum development allows and encourages.

Some who have engaged in curriculum development or in the development of its poor relative, the curriculum guide, have learned that almost everyone who comes near the project does so as a self-appointed expert bearing a store of content that they are convinced needs to be included (Goldstein & Seigle, 1958). Accordingly, the onus is on the curriculum developer to establish the criteria that will govern the selection of what is to be imparted to students, irrespective of the source, and to monitor the implementation of the criteria throughout the life of the enterprise.

Status and Role as Dimensions of the Curriculum Model

As depicted in Figure 5.1, social status and social role constitute the remaining two dimensions of the curriculum model as they relate to its base of cultural responses. In practical terms, the social statuses and roles in each category of cultural responses represent people exhibiting behaviors that are appropriate to their position in society in the course of their fulfilling their needs or the needs of others. To put it another way, any cell in a cultural response column includes the status someone in that category occupies and the behaviors associated with that status. Thus, a cell in Figure 5.1 represents the behaviors expected of those occupying the status of commuter, someone who uses public transportation to get to work, in the category of activity. The role in this cell would consist of both the general and specific behaviors expected of someone using public transportation to get to work. For example, general behaviors, those expected of commuters irrespective of the locale, would include being able to act on the fact that there is a fare to be paid and that public transport runs on a fixed schedule along a fixed route. Specific behaviors would include knowing the amount of the bus fare in the rider's community. The next cell represents the status of bus driver, whose role would include mastery of the vehicle in traffic, the ability to adhere to the schedule, familiarity in dealing with travelers, and others.

After stating in detail what we can ascertain about the statuses and roles accessible to people in cultural response categories in a prescribed geography—neighborhood, community, or region—we can take the next step of ordering or ranking statuses and roles in each of the categories. The vertical arrangement of statuses and roles signifies a hierarchy based on the prerequisites for achieving the status and the competencies required to retain it. For instance, in the shelter category, the status of architect ranks above that of construction worker because of the educational and experiential prerequisites for licensing or certification as well as demonstrated mastery in the profession. These also influence the differences in lifestyle and quality of life that accompany differences in compensation.

An Objective Process for Ascertaining Social Contexts

From the standpoint of identifying what curricular content is most suitable for students with mild disabilities, the combination of cultural response, status, and role makes it possible to get an in-depth picture of the social context within which a school or a total school system functions. As mentioned earlier, Havighurst and Neugarten (1962) made the point that the pattern of behavior that characterizes a social role can be described without reference to the particular individuals who fulfill the role. Accordingly, by placing people in the background and bringing their behaviors, or cultural responses, into the foreground, we can study the customs of the neighborhood or the larger community independently of its members in order to discern conventional cultural responses and the statuses associated with them.

For example, by observing the work being done by department store sales associates in a number of typical settings, we can note in detail what behaviors people in the status of sales associate have in common irrespective of who they are, where they work, what we know about them, or what we know about their work setting. By augmenting our observations with the department store's job description for sales associates, we are able to ascertain the roles of sales people that are specific to their immediate setting. The same process can be applied wherever work is accomplished.

Furthermore, we can separate specific work skills and proficiencies from work-centered and work-related behavior as well as from interpersonal relationships associated with the customs and mores in the work settings, for example, the rituals of break time and how people relate to each other for that brief period. We are able, then, to identify employment patterns and opportunities in general. Having established this kind of base, we can (a) distinguish and separate out the untapped employment opportunities and statuses that people with mild disabilities may achieve and sustain successfully if they are educated appropriately and (b) use our observed and collected data as a basis for developing curriculum content.

We can also use this procedure to identify recreation opportunities, shopping sources, medical facilities, and others along with the general and specific behaviors necessary for their utilization. By focusing on the work people do rather than on people who are working, we reduce the probability of our observations being biased by what we know or think we know about the worker. Furthermore, we are less likely to be led astray by behaviors that are peculiar to a worker and not to the work itself, behaviors that might be inappropriate in another person's repertory. This is no small matter. Experience has shown that the clinical orientation of teaching fostered by the medical model often leads, consciously or not, to the development of instructional materials for the purpose of remedying a specific student's observable deficits. The relevance of these instructional materials to other students, their generalizability, is purely a matter of chance.

Having ascertained the roles that people fulfill in occupational, recreational, or family statuses, we can reverse the procedure by placing the individual occupying a status in the foreground and the cultural response matrix in the background. This is the first stage of curriculum-based assessment. The process allows for the observation of an individual's performance in a single cultural response area or any combination of them.

Using what we have learned about the norms or behavioral expectations for people occupying the same status, we can ascertain the strengths and weaknesses of the person being observed. The same process can be applied

Constructing a Curriculum Model

when assessing the relevance of the curriculum to these behaviors. This is discussed in greater detail later.

This process also provides us with a departure from conventional curriculum development practices that lead to a curriculum being fixed in place on printed pages and, therefore, very difficult and costly to update. Because there are no comprehensive curricula for students with mild disabilities and therefore no commitment to precedent, curriculum developers are free to explore ways for communicating the curriculum that are consistent with the nature and rate of social and technological change.

We now have technologies that allow the recording, storage, analysis, and dissemination of information in response to changes in the community— a database, in effect, that contains information about the community that has bearing on educational practices. This enables a curriculum development group or a school system to stay abreast of social and technological changes that can affect the statuses of students with mild disabilities in each cultural response area. These technologies make it possible to modify curriculum along with and sometimes in anticipation of changes in job descriptions and in the customs and mores of the neighborhood and community. For example, some food markets are presently testing a totally automated checkout device that is cashier free. A large monitor leads the customer through the steps, from scanning each item to feeding payment into a slot and receiving change. By systematically observing how shoppers react to the device, curriculum developers can determine what additions or modifications, if any, need to be made to the curriculum for students with mild disabilities.

Also, in the area of communication, most curricula provide instruction in the use of telephones and the social protocols for this form of communication. The instruction almost always assumes that another person will respond to the telephone call. However, given the changes in telephone technology, callers sometimes find themselves in communication with a computerized telephone system that requires them to respond to the computer's instructions as a condition for getting or imparting information. Having the capability to adapt quickly to such technological and social changes by making immediate alterations in the curriculum would certainly be advantageous for students with mild disabilities.

Ranking Social Status and Role

Social statuses and roles, or the positions individuals achieve in society and the behaviors or performance associated with those positions, often vary considerably with the age and gender of the individual. For example, while we expect all children occupying the status of student to be able to read and reckon, we recognize that the ages of the individuals who occupy the status affect their academic performance. Thus, we expect students to display a broader and deeper array of academic skills and proficiencies as they progress through the grades. These expectations carry over into adult life as well. We expect a greater array of skills and proficiencies from an artisan or professional than we do from his or her apprentice or intern. We attribute most of these differences to their educational experiences as students, to their occupational or professional preparation, and to their life experiences in their work.

For curriculum developers, having the facility to rank statuses and roles by prerequisite preparation and experience, as well as by the sensorimotor and cognitive skills and proficiencies important to success in role fulfillment, is a great asset. Ranked skills and proficiencies reveal to the teacher, school psychologist, evaluation professionals, and others the factors that distinguish between ranked statuses and roles in any one of or combination of the cultural response dimensions. This enables curriculum developers to sequence the content of instruction developmentally.

From the teachers' perspective, a detailed and well-defined analysis of students' preparation and experiences, along with the sensorimotor, cognitive, and other social adaptive skills and proficiencies that together constitute a role allows them to make more definitive decisions about what should be taught, when, and how. Furthermore, because the statuses and roles of schoolchildren represent a vertical continuum, the same analysis should reveal the knowledge, skills, and proficiencies prerequisite to the achievement of the next status in the continuum. This type of analysis is not limited to the vertical dimension of the curriculum model. As pointed out earlier, cultural response categories are not mutually exclusive; the behaviors that define or characterize a certain role in one cultural response category may have relevance in whole or in part to roles in other response categories. Thus, by plotting a profile of an individual's achieved statuses across the cultural response categories and studying the behaviors that are characteristic of the roles associated with each status, a number of assessment criteria are presented, such as the individual's ability to generalize and transfer skills used in one cultural response category to appropriate responses in other categories. Because such an assessment takes place within the format of cultural responses, the relationships between and within statuses and roles across responses can be ascertained.

Status and Role as the Framework for Curriculum Development

To this point, cultural response, status, and role have been discussed in the abstract as artifacts of theory. In order to bring these variables into the functional relationship required by curriculum development for students with mild disabilities, we need to observe the specifics of the individual's actual performance as an occupant of a status. To put it another way, a century of experiences with children and youth with mild disabilities in schools and with adults at work and in the community has provided special educators with a catalog of behaviors that need to be in the behavioral repertory of every individual with mild disabilities to serve as the basis of his or her socialization.

People with mild disabilities are expected to be responsive to time commitments, to be honest and reliable, and to maintain an acceptable level of personal hygiene, among other attributes. Accordingly, instructional materials for imparting these and analogous concepts and facts can be developed effectively without leaving the academic halls or public school building.

The fact that most students with mild disabilities are engaged in learning these socializing attributes but nevertheless fail to achieve many of the autonomies that the vast majority of adults do at their maturity indicates that there are other social and personal skills that must be identified and incorporated into curricula for students with mild disabilities. The only sure way of doing so is to observe individuals in action in order to get a reliable view of the demands of their social, physical, and psychological environments and the skills and proficiencies they need in order to respond effectively. Observing individuals who occupy similar statuses in different locales and/or conditions reveals the skills and proficiencies that are useful generally as well as those that are indigenous to their locale or region or peculiar to the conditions of their work or recreation.

On-the-scene observation provides the opportunity to note the customs established by employees, the "in" behaviors that characterize membership in the group. These are too often overlooked because of our preoccupation with more universal, work-related behaviors. In some instances, the expectations of peers can be a critical factor in job retention in subtle but nevertheless important ways. For example, counseling and teaching staff in a transition demonstration project (Goldstein, 1993) found that a significant number of students who had been placed in a number of competitive employment sites were isolated on the job and during coffee and lunch breaks.

After observing the workers in representative conditions during the workday, it was apparent that those who were isolated could be distinguished from those who became integrated members of the workforce on the basis of one factor—their inability to participate in the small talk that characterized break time and on-the-job chatting and banter. It turned out that the isolates knew practically nothing about the current performance of the Mets or Yankees, the "in" shops at the Garden State Mall, MTV hits, what rock band had just been or would soon be appearing at the Meadowlands, or the "in" basketball shoes. Not unexpectedly, they knew remarkably little about the sources of such information. Having nothing to contribute to this small talk, they soon were ignored and, in some instances, ridiculed. It was readily apparent that these were hurtful experiences. In a short time, these mildly disabled workers withdrew from their coworkers. During coffee breaks, some were observed sitting at a distance from the group. Their morale was sinking fast, as was their motivation to continue on the job. Quick action by the staff led to "small talk" sessions in the training program that were based on the staff's observations of the interests in current events expressed by the coworkers. This led to some remarkable changes in some of the workers with mild disabilities, not the least of these being a tendency toward garrulousness.

Small talk, "in" language, dress, and behaviors, and other peer-centered styles and fads appear to be as important to the social adaptation of children, youth, and adults with mild disabilities as the more normative aspects that catch our attention. Some are so unique to certain age groups or so overshadowed by normative role behaviors that they escape the notice of the curriculum developer. Clearly, these are important elements of the curriculum and are often the behaviors that contribute a great deal to sustaining statuses.

Parenthetically, curriculum developers may find it worth knowing that it was the project staff, not the employees, who characterized the workers' discourse as "small talk." To the employees being observed, the subject matter of their communication was far from small talk. The fact that they have interests and sources for their information that differ from those of their parents, teachers, and employers needs to be a guiding principle for curriculum developers. From the workers' point of view, the content of their conversations included vital current events and the conventional wisdom of the times and was of greater importance than finding ways to reduce the size of the national debt or resolve conflicts in foreign countries.

Conclusion

A curriculum for students with mild disabilities needs to equip them with the knowledge and behaviors that will facilitate their transition from school to the larger community. More often than not, their instruction focuses on the social and personal skills that are important for entry into relationships and interactions with others, for securing employment, and for managing their personal circumstances. While these are of paramount importance, the literature on transitions indicates that the mastery of them does not ensure lasting success (Ysseldike, Algozzine, & Thurlow, 1992).

The frequent need for job coaches indicates that there are conditions and expectations at work that call for specific knowledge and behaviors that may be more accurately perceived as customs than essentials. For example, the ability to engage in light and casual conversation, seemingly of minor importance compared with the knowledge and behaviors required of effective workers, is based on complex experiences, including sensitivity to one's peer culture and popular trends in entertainment, sports, and dress, along with the self-confidence to react to the statements of others and to voice one's opinion. These are learned behaviors, and it has yet to be established whether students with mild disabilities can learn them well enough to make a difference in their relationships with their peers. However, including them in curriculum is a necessary first step toward an assessment of their ability to do so.

The Content of a Synergistic Curriculum

■　　■　　■　　■　　■　　■　　■　　■　　■　　■　　■

This chapter deals with the scope and sequence of the content of a synergistic curriculum that is based on a social learning theme. As previously discussed, simplified versions of the general education curriculum are inappropriate for most students with mild disabilities. Typically, the content areas in general education are conceptually and temporally separate in the ordinary course of instruction because it is presumed that most individuals who learn how to read and reckon are able to bring these skills to bear as problem-solving tools in the course of daily events at work, in their households, for personal purposes, and in leisure activities.

We can presume that general education programs devote more effort and time to instruction in the acquisition of skills and proficiencies related to academic content than to instruction in problem solving because of the expectation that most general education students are able to generalize their academic skills to solve a wide variety of problems.

Given the learning problems of students with mild learning disabilities, however, there is no basis for presuming that most of them share this ability. In fact, there is support, albeit somewhat indirect, for the presumption that these students would be better served by a curriculum in which quantitative and literacy skills and proficiencies are learned within the same problem-solving context—that is, when they are synergistic (Rosenshine, 1997).

Conventional curriculum development strategies in which academic content areas are formulated independently of each other do not promote synergy. The challenge to those developing a curriculum for students with mild disabilities is to organize content and social learning specialists into collaborative teams within the common frame of reference provided by the social sciences concepts of cultural responses and the statuses and roles of individuals acting on them. How to meet this challenge is discussed in detail in Chapter 8.

Social Science Concepts as a Framework for a Synergistic Curriculum

Curriculum content that provides students with the knowledge and skills required to fulfill status and role expectations by employing cultural responses appropriately leads us to believe, with some degree of confidence, that students who achieve and retain the status of student and fulfill the role successfully throughout their school careers will one day be better qualified for the status of employee and other adult statuses than those who do not. We can help students meet the criteria for social adaptation at successive stages of maturation by implementing the curriculum at the age when students enter school in order to capitalize on their existing skills and proficiencies. We can do this by teaching, in a developmental progression, the facts, concepts, skills, proficiencies, and behaviors that are relevant to students' fulfillment of immediate status and role as students as well as the basic skills and proficiencies that are critical to achieving and sustaining many statuses characterized by responsible adults. Attributes such as promptness, responsibility, and trustworthiness are as relevant to first graders in their schools and neighborhoods as they are to adults in their homes, workplaces, and leisure activities.

Teaching Predictably Useful Knowledge and Behaviors

If curricular decisions and the timing of instruction are correct, the sequence of students' learning and experiences should culminate in the appropriate knowledge and skills being in place in students' response repertoires as they approach their transition to succeeding environments. The specific knowledge and behaviors relevant to work and work settings, for example, can be added to this foundation at the appropriate time for each student.

Teaching positive and constructive knowledge and behaviors in anticipation of their usefulness is likely to reduce the probability that students with mild disabilities will learn maladaptive behaviors by default. That is, anticipating future statuses and roles and teaching appropriate behaviors in a timely manner may reduce the probability of their inappropriate counterparts emerging in order to fill a void in the problem-solving process.

Attributes such as responsibility, promptness, courtesy, and honesty are good examples of knowledge and behaviors that can be taught in anticipation of their need. We can predict with confidence that students will act on these attributes in their roles as adults whether at work or in recreational pursuits. An educational analogy of the physical law that states that two objects cannot occupy the same space at the same time is appropriate; namely, one cannot be prompt and tardy or courteous and rude simultaneously. Thus, by teaching predictably useful behaviors, teachers and students are spared the tedious and time-consuming task of extinguishing maladaptive behaviors and replacing them with socially acceptable behaviors.

Escaping From Labels

Because of its synergy, a curriculum for students with mild disabilities should be able to offer as many relevant ways for solving a problem as each student can learn. In practical terms, the more satisfactory options that a student has for solving a problem, the lower the likelihood that unproductive and undesirable responses will be made and, through repetition, become fixed in the student's response repertory. In the final analysis, if the schools are successful in helping students to acquire an effective cultural response repertory, this should reduce the prevalence of maladaptive behavior in students with mild disabilities. As a result, we may find that a notable proportion of these students will no longer qualify for the disability status they had previously achieved.

This may seem to be a visionary goal to some. Nevertheless, we cannot ignore the fact that all of the follow-up studies of mildly disabled school-leavers report that some former special education students cannot be located in the community, accounted for in community records, or traced to other locations. Some argue that this is the result of faulty research design and poor record keeping. Others speculate that these former students have adapted to adult life so well that they have melted into the general population, leaving their labels behind. In other words, they no longer qualify for the status of mildly disabled that they achieved as students.

While few continue to endorse the once popular concept of the immutability of the IQ, there is, nevertheless, a discernible reluctance to give ground on the interchangeability of statuses. Many are prone to hold on to the view that while schools can make individuals with mild disabilities more acceptable to others, the likelihood of their ever escaping their label is remote, if not impossible.

Problem Solving as the Context for Instructional Content

The discontinuities in content areas that characterize general education curricula come about because these curricula are developed and then published independently of each other. Publishers of educational materials offer school systems one or more reading, arithmetic, music, and science series, for example. These are reviewed and selected by the local education agency's (LEA's) subject matter committees or specialists. Rarely is there anyone on these committees who can speak authoritatively to the educational needs of students with mild disabilities.

Once adopted, these texts and series become the instruments of instruction and their subject matter areas are, more often than not, scheduled and taught independently of each other during the course of the school day. The fact that this process has become the conventional approach to curriculum implementation in general education suggests that educators are optimistic that discontinuities in subject matter areas have little or no limiting effects on the problem-solving abilities of nondisabled children. That is, educators of nondisabled students appear to be confident that their students' abilities to assemble, combine, and synthesize concepts and facts from disparate sources will enable them to recognize the existence and nature of a problem, draw from their knowledge banks the principle or rule that is relevant to the solution of the problem, apply the necessary concepts and facts, assess the outcomes of their problem-solving strategy, and, given the outcomes, make any necessary adjustments.

Experience suggests that no such presumption about the synthesizing abilities of children with mild disabilities is warranted. On the contrary, literature on the learning characteristics of students with mild disabilities underscores the fact that the synthesis of disparate concepts and facts for the purpose of problem solving is not one of their strengths.

Nevertheless, the general education curriculum has implications for the education of children with mild disabilities for two reasons. First, as a consequence of the 1997 amendments to IDEA, the widespread mainstreaming of students with mild disabilities, the acceptance of the Inclusive School Movement (ISM) by many school systems, and the implementation of the No Child Left Behind (NCLB) legislation, more students with mild disabilities are participating in educational programs that use general education class curricula than ever before. Second, rather than developing curricula that are appropriate to the education of students with mild disabilities, experts are advising teachers of students with mild disabilities to adapt the general education curriculum to accommodate their learning characteristics (NECTAS, 1999; Orkis & McLane, 1998).

This leaves teachers of students with mild disabilities and some general education teachers with two options: they can take the advice of experts and shoulder the immense task of reshaping the general education curriculum to meet the needs of their students with mild disabilities, or they can continue to do what teachers of these students have been doing for the last century—draw on their experiences and intuition and assemble bits and pieces of subject matter into their best estimate of what is appropriate for the education of their students. In either case, the results have seriously limited the problem-solving abilities of students with mild disabilities. In practical terms, this means that it is highly probable that many school-leavers with mild disabilities will continue to enter an increasingly complex adult world poorly equipped to solve the ordinary problems of everyday life.

In addition, problem-solving strategies and tactics are probably not as comprehensive in general education curricula as they should be because most problems in life are either solved autonomically or automatically or by a combination of these two means. That is, the vast majority of problems are so easily solved that the appreciation of the strategies and tactics brought into play are minimized. For example, an increase in body temperature creates a biological imbalance that is autonomically countered by sweating. While sweating solves the biological problem, there is a constant reminder in our media that it can be offensive to others, thereby creating a social–personal problem. Most people are aware of this, so bathing and/or the application of a deodorant has become almost automatic for most of us.

This is only one of an array of problems that either abate quickly or are so easily solved that they provoke little more than enough temporary anxiety to promote awareness. Such problems are typically dealt with briefly, if at all, in the early stages of the curriculum for nondisabled children. At the same time, the impact of inadequate personal hygiene in social and occupational settings is well known, as are the implications of this problem for the adaptation of children and adults with mild disabilities, whose personal hygiene practices may be inadequate.

Problem solving comes into its own when the consequences for inadequately solving a problem introduce the possibility of disaster. There are few, if any, easy solutions to the numerous possible aftereffects of the derelict alarm clock or of the arrow on the gasoline gauge pointing to the big E in the dead of night. Of course, the prudent person knows that these and even more serious problems may be only a moment away, and they evolve all kinds of preventive measures, mnemonics, routines, and rituals to avoid them or to blunt their effects. For example, there are many people who never let their gasoline gauge drop below the halfway mark. In any case, these are the times when reasoning skills and a sizable repertory of solutions are at a premium.

Most nondisabled students and adults can learn life-saving and job-saving rules in the abstract, generalize them to real-world experiences, make the appropriate connection between problem and solution at the critical moment, and move on to the next problem. We cannot be as sanguine about the success of children and adults with mild disabilities who acquire their problem-solving skills in the same way that their nondisabled classmates do. Their experiences indicate that they need a curriculum that provides intensive and continuous practice in applying problem-solving strategies in abstract, vicarious, and actual situations. They need a curriculum in which the usual temporal and conceptual distinctions between conventional content areas are indiscernible because of their synergy.

Academic Content in a Synergistic Curriculum

Like a conventional curriculum, a synergistic curriculum provides content and experiences that lead to the acquisition of knowledge, skills, and proficiencies that are basic to effective problem solving. Unlike a conventional curriculum, however, the instructional content in a synergistic curriculum is seamless. Instead of each content area standing alone as part of a daily instructional schedule of discrete academic experiences, each is combined with other relevant areas in a problem-solving context. In this way, ordinarily discontinuous subject matter areas are unified as they combine to fulfill a common purpose. For example, consider a class project that entails a trip to a nursery where vegetable seedlings will be purchased for the class garden. The reading lesson would focus on plant availability and planting procedures; the vocabulary words would be drawn from this activity and from the science activity; the science content would deal with the implications of weather and the process of germination; and arithmetic topics would range from number recognition to pricing, temperature, and time.

All of the foregoing learning content can have relevance to the students in the class and, some day in the future, to former students who, as adults, opt to grow their own vegetables. The synergy in learning content that is represented in the curriculum has its origins in the synergy of the content and social learning specialists who collaborated in the development of the curriculum.

There is a difference between conventional and synergistic curricula in how subject matter areas are weighted. In conventional curricula, reading, arithmetic, and science have taken on lives of their own much more so than have social learning and the aesthetics. In fact, reading, arithmetic, and science achievement have become the standards for judging the quality of education on a national and international scale. Clearly, the intrinsic value of these content areas to students transcends their extrinsic value.

In contrast, because all subject matter areas in a synergistic curriculum are interactive, they are all seen as problem-solving tools. Their extrinsic value—the extent to which they are useful in solving real-life problems—exceeds their intrinsic value, represented by students' performance on achievement tests and in the classroom. To put it another way, there is no subject matter hierarchy in a synergistic curriculum. The importance of subject matter areas varies from problem to problem, with the criterion being its usefulness in solving the problem. In a practical sense, eliminating or reducing instruction in music and art when economic, facility, or time constraints arise would not be an issue if a synergistic curriculum were being followed. All subject matter areas, irrespective of how they are identified, need to be taught as intensively and effectively as possible, and students with mild disabilities need to become as competent as possible in reading and arithmetic as well as in music and sports.

As noted, a curriculum is synergistic when all of its subject areas are interactive in the instructional process. Subject matter areas can be interactive if they are (a) developed together within a common problem-solving context and (b) used in combination in the course of instruction. These criteria were implicit in the educational programs discussed by Farrell (1908–1909), Descoeudres (1928), Ingram (1935), Duncan (1943), Hungerford, DeProspo, and Rosenzweig (1952) and developed by Goldstein and Seigle (1958), Goldstein (1974, 1975), and Mayer (1975).

Similarly, many teachers of children with mild disabilities know intuitively that these students need a synergistic curriculum. Numerous articles in the *Journal of Psycho-Asthenics* dating back to the turn of the 20th century and, subsequently, in the *American Journal on Mental Deficiency* show that despite the absence of a comprehensive curriculum, teachers have attempted to integrate the academic aptitudes of their students with social experiences. For example, they organized the instruction of reading and arithmetic within the framework of solving very specific and immediate life problems.

Many teachers of students with mild disabilities have found that skills and proficiencies acquired in the course of real experiences contribute more to their students' ability to transfer and generalize classroom learning to problem-solving situations than those learned in vicarious or symbolic experiences. Accordingly, whenever possible, some teachers identify problem-solving areas that they feel are relevant to their students' developmental status. For example, a problem might involve tactics for meeting a need in commissariat, such as shopping for food. Together, they study the problem situation, first acquiring and then capitalizing on the applicable subject matter skills and proficiencies. When possible, teachers take their students on field trips to neighborhood and community settings where they assume the status of shopper or client and learn how to fulfill the appropriate role.

Unfortunately, these encounters with reality have become increasingly more complex and expensive due to the high cost of insurance and the possibility that the slightest mishap will lead to litigation. As a result, teachers of special classes for children with mild disabilities have had to compromise and provide vicarious experiences to the extent that space and funds permit. This makes the curriculum and the nature of classroom instruction that much more important to the growth and development of these students. The instruction must be so effective even in abstract and vicarious conditions that students can implement the knowledge acquired despite missing the real experiences provided by field trips.

It is a rare elementary special education classroom that does not have a small version of a supermarket, complete with canned goods, boxes, and cartons, in a corner where literacy, quantitative, and other relevant proficiencies can be exercised and their implementation evaluated. However, this is a constant reminder of the distance between technological change and schools' ability to match the pace of that change. Notable absent in classrooms are technologies that are now commonplace in all kinds of stores and shops: scanners that enter the cost of items into the cash registers, electronic scales that weigh and price items, and cash registers that inform the checkout clerk and the shopper of the total cost of the merchandise.

Nevertheless, when funds are available, many teachers purchase off-the-shelf packages of instructional aids that contain reading materials in the form of signs and labels along with price tags, weights and measure stickers, and other qualitative and quantitative materials that represent arithmetic experiences. Some teachers use the nutrition facts printed on food products along with concepts of balanced meals as the focus of classroom instruction in which literacy, quantitative thinking, science, and aesthetics are integrated. Within this context, the social-interpersonal transactions that characterize the status and role of shoppers and store staff are practiced through role playing and group discussion. Some sense of how limited teachers are when they lack the support and guidance of a curriculum can be obtained by considering the fact that all of the teaching efforts described above fit into one cell of the three-dimensional social sciences constructed discussed in Chapter 5: the status and role of consumer or shopper in the cultural response category of commissariat.

Clearly, without the support of a comprehensive curriculum, teachers are extremely limited in their ability to assemble and implement a synergistic curriculum. Teachers' experiences with students with mild disabilities indicate that they need a synergistic curriculum whose content is developmental in sequence and consistent with the goals of education. While teachers have not expressed their wish for such a curriculum in so many words, the way that they go about educating their students with mild disabilities speaks for them. The fact that the results of their efforts fall far short of their goals, as seen in the many follow-up studies of school-leavers with mild disabilities cited earlier, adds urgency to their need for curricular support.

Using a Problem-Solving Context to Achieve Synergy in Academic Content

The synergistic curriculum can be characterized as a body of knowledge in search of a problem. This is because synergy, the combined action of subject matter areas, is best achieved within a problem-solving context. This is not to suggest that all subject matter areas are relevant to the solution of any given problem at any given time. Rather, it is the conjunction of those that are instrumental in solving a given problem that provides the essence of the synergistic curriculum and its seamlessness. That is, instruction that leads to the acquisition of literacy, language, and quantitative skills is implemented within the same conceptual framework as instruction that provides students with basic cognitive and motor skills.

In a synergistic curriculum, vocabulary and spelling lists, for example, are not selected from published lists or workbooks intuitively or because some appear to deserve priority over others. Instead, new words to be integrated into the students' vocabulary are identified within the problem-solving matrix and become the objectives for skill building. Thus, students learn to recognize and spell the words they need to read in order to solve the problem at hand.

Furthermore, selecting content to provide the basis for skill development does not preclude teachers from capitalizing on proven instructional tactics and strategies that provide students with necessary practice and repetition. The conceptual framework provided by the problem is the major facilitating factor in this process because it provides disparate skills with a common foundation in a way that words selected from discrete vocabulary lists and arithmetic computation from workbooks cannot.

Because so many skills, proficiencies, and behaviors are common to many statuses and roles, it is possible to design a synergistic curriculum in which all elements of the content interact with each other within the context of cultural responses, statuses, and roles. In such a curriculum, instruction in conventional academic skills, in some instances, deals substantively with facts and concepts involving social skills. In other instructional interactions, social skills are practiced during the course of instruction in an academic subject matter area and its related skills and proficiencies.

For example, one version of a curriculum might choose to deal with the role of the shopper in a number of cultural response areas, such as shopping for food within the framework of commissariat and shopping for home supplies and clothing within the frameworks of shelter and protection, respectively. Our experiences tell us that there are similarities and differences in the behaviors associated with each role in accordance with the similarities and differences in settings, the customs peculiar to the type of shop, and how the merchandise or service is marketed. That is, while some of the ways in which shoppers interact with sales staff may be similar regardless of the nature of the setting, there are, nevertheless, differences that need to be understood.

In most supermarkets and large discount stores, for example, shoppers are expected to gather their selections and convey them to a cashier. At other sources of merchandise, such as conventional retail clothing stores, a sales associate deals directly with shoppers and responds to their preferences. In a practical sense, the consumer, while holding the same status, plays a different role in accordance with the customs. This calls for a level of social sophistication that many students with mild disabilities can acquire in the classroom.

To capitalize fully on the synergy in the proposed curriculum, the problem-solving matrix must incorporate the full school experience. It is left to the curriculum developer, however, to determine the theme and content of instruction and to ensure that it is consistent with his or her conception of the role of the curriculum as the central educational instrumentality in programs for students with mild disabilities.

In a manner somewhat less detailed than Malinowski's, Stratemeyer and her colleagues (1947) proposed a theme for a problem-solving matrix in a curriculum for nondisabled children that consisted of persisting life problems, a theme that is implicit in Ingram's (1935) earlier concept of a curriculum. Stratemeyer proposed that certain problems confront members of society without regard to their social class and other diversities. She claimed that by learning how to identify and solve these problems, students would acquire the skills and proficiencies that would contribute to the solution of these problems in the community and lead to achieving an effective level of participatory citizenship.

In contrast, Hungerford and his curriculum development team (Hungerford, DeProspo, & Rosenzweig, 1952) based their work on a theme that maintained that the goal of education for students with mild mental retardation was to provide them with the skills and proficiencies that would lead to getting and maintaining a remunerative job. Accordingly, their curricular theme encompassed concepts, facts, and behaviors that are directly as well as peripherally crucial to the occupational scene, a premise that had considerable merit 45 years ago.

Goldstein (1974, 1975) submitted that while getting and keeping a job was one of the most important outcomes of an effective educational program for students with mild disabilities, it could not be accomplished independently of learning socially acceptable ways for fulfilling their social, psychological, and physical needs. The curriculum that ensued was therefore based on a social learning theme, focusing on the knowledge, skills, and behaviors that are fundamental to the achievement of the autonomies that characterize a productive, participating citizen.

It is important to note that in the half-century that has elapsed since Hungerford's occupational education curriculum (Hungerford, DeProspo, & Rosenzweig, 1952), the nature and direction of social and technological change have been such that the prospects of people with mild disabilities securing and sustaining remunerative work in competitive settings are diminishing. This trend can be seen in the growing unemployment rate of adults with disabilities reported by advocacy agencies and services. Nevertheless, whether they are remuneratively employed, participating in government-supported work, or on one form of welfare or another, many individuals with mild disabilities still need to make the most of their lives in community settings. Some live independently, some reside with their families, and others live in community residences. They are not going to be sent off to institutions or in any other way live apart from society.

As controversial as community residences for people with disabilities may be in some communities, such residences must eventually take their place in society as a way of accommodating people with mild disabilities. How well these individuals become integrated as residents of their neighborhoods communities will be determined, in great part, by their social and personal skills. Thus, there is no foreseeable diminution in the role of education in the growth and development of children and youth with mild disabilities. In fact, the case can be made for an increasingly important role for our schools as everyday tasks become more complicated and our responses to environmental phenomena become more stressful.

Social Learning as a Curricular Theme

It might appear from the foregoing that differences in curricular themes make for differences in the content of instruction. This is not necessarily so. More often than not, differences are found in the emphasis placed on certain subject matter areas and, as a result, in the cadence of instruction. Most general education classes focus on reading, arithmetic, and science. These subjects comprise the tripod on which the total educational program rests. In contrast, in a synergistic curriculum with a social learning theme, academic subjects are taught as intensively as in other curricula, but the emphasis is on both their intrinsic and extrinsic values. As a result, they become the source of students' prestige and success while they are in school as well as efficient problem-solving tools in the larger world.

Figure 6.1 shows a conceptualization of the scope and sequence of the content of teaching and learning in a synergistic curriculum for students with mild disabilities. The model in Figure 6.1 represents a problem-

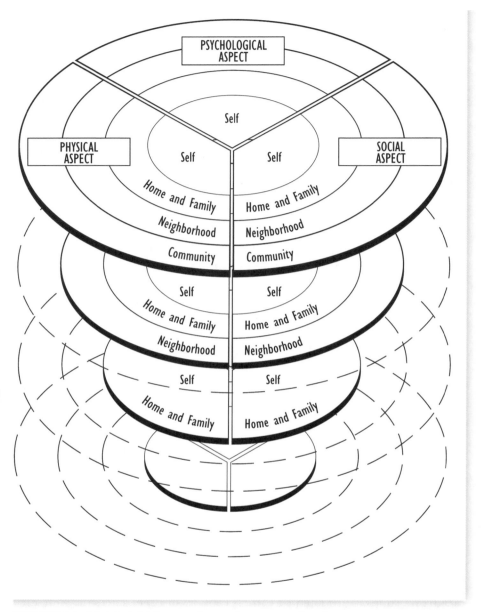

FIGURE 6.1. Model of child's expanding environment and environment components.

solving framework and, therefore, is a metaphor for the growth, maturation, and socialization of children from infancy through adulthood. Each disk, for example, represents one of the major successive, modal social environments through which maturing children pass on their way to adulthood. The broken circles surrounding each disc represent the fact that each environment is constantly within the larger context of ongoing life conditions. Furthermore, although the model suggests that life for students with mild disabilities is limited to the community, reality tells us that there is no upper limit to the model. Some life experiences extend well beyond the community.

The model also portrays the fact that as children mature and become more competent, their social environment expands. Thus, children of entering school first become students of their social, psychological, and physical selves. Although students are the immediate focus of instruction, the impact of occurrences in the larger environment around them is not excluded or ignored. As students' knowledge, skills, and proficiencies accumulate, they become increasingly able to deal with more people, things, and conditions and to ultimately make the transition into the next social environment.

Environment

Each environment depicted in Figure 6.1 has social, psychological, and physical aspects, which offer a systematic way for curriculum developers to classify the concepts, facts, skills, and proficiencies to be learned and to build them into the related academic learning as concrete counterparts to the abstractions that characterize the early stages of the curriculum.

The social aspects of the environment include the purposes, functions, and social organization of groups, the statuses and roles of people in the environment, and the customs and mores associated with the environment. Psychological aspects include people's attitudes, feelings, and motivations as well as the conventions for interpersonal activities and relationships. Physical aspects include things that people use, such as living and working space and the furnishings and tools in common use, as well as environmental conditions within which these interactions take place, including temperature, lighting, and natural phenomena such as weather. Children with mild disabilities need to learn how these aspects of their environment sometimes play a role in problem solving and at other times are elements of the problem.

While the environments in Figure 6.1 appear discrete, the synergistic curriculum that evolves from the model treats these environments as milestones on the road to maturity rather than as disconnected environments. That is, the content of instruction in the curriculum is continuous so that the actual study of a social environment initiates the learning that provides the wherewithal for transition to the next environment. Accordingly, children first engage in detailed study about themselves by way of discussions that are reinforced by literacy activities.

The Content of a Synergistic Curriculum

Self

An important characteristic to note in Figure 6.1 is that environments are cumulative. For example, at the "self" level, each child becomes the subject of self-study as an environment with social, physical, and psychological aspects. However, self-study cannot have meaning if it proceeds independently of the conditions and influences in students' surroundings. The dotted lines surrounding "self" indicate this and signify to the curriculum developer that events and conditions in surrounding environments, such as the family and neighborhood, impinge on each child's social, psychological, and physical aspects even though the focus of instruction and learning is on the child.

Family

As students learn important facts about themselves and integrate them into their cultural response repertoires, the learning activities begin to prepare students for their newly achieved statuses and roles as members of their families. To this end, the curriculum provides students with the knowledge to help them realize that reciprocity is an important aspect of family life, and they become able to take part in family activities and accept statuses whose roles include being responsible, being reliable, sharing, and other attributes that represent mastery of the hedonic tendencies that prevail in very young children.

Children's transition from the status of a dependent member of the family to that of a participating member begins as they acquire the knowledge and behaviors that are essential to achieving and maintaining statuses within the family. As seen in Figure 6.1, study of the self continues, but now it occurs within the context of the home and family. That is, children are ready to augment the hitherto hedonic question "what do my family members do for me?" with the more mature query "what do I need to do for members of my family?"

In order to sustain the gradual transition into family membership, children with mild disabilities need to understand and appreciate the statuses and roles of other family members, immediate and extended, along with the rights and privileges that accompany them. Very specifically, they need to understand how family members' statuses and roles interrelate with theirs and vice versa. In this process, the customs of the larger family, as well as its history and hierarchies, contribute to children's understanding. Comprehension and appreciation of the statuses and roles of family members increases the probability that students with mild disabilities will generalize this knowledge and behavior to the families of their friends and schoolmates.

The study of the home and family and their physical, social, and psychological aspects is rich with information that is characteristic of the expanding world of children with mild disabilities. So much of what nondisabled children learn incidentally and from the modeling of important people in their lives too often escapes the attention of children with mild disabilities and must, therefore, become part of their curriculum. Synergy in content areas provides students with novel repetitions of the same complex experiences that should help facilitate retention.

Establishing priorities so that solid foundations for learning can be laid is an important goal for curriculum developers. The ethnic diversity that characterizes most educational settings requires that the study of children's homes and families be comprehensive yet objective. They need to learn that ways of doing things, values, and beliefs can be different without necessarily being better or worse. This is not to say that children are not permitted to express their personal likes and dislikes. The curriculum should help children to learn that their preferences for certain foods over others, for example, can be a personal matter and may have little or nothing to do with the ethnicity of people who include such foods in their diets.

Expanding Instruction

Curriculum developers need to take into account the fact that students' vertical transition from one environmental level to the next is contingent on fulfilling the prerequisites for entry to and participation in the environment. Some prerequisites, such as age-appropriate behaviors, are probably universal to all cultures and subcultures and are brought to the attention of children in the form of cautionary reminders such as "act your age."

The curriculum for children with mild disabilities in particular needs to deal with the probability that they need intensive instruction and experiences in understanding the expectations of members of their family and others in their expanding environments if they are to learn to behave in ways appropriate with their maturation. To this end, the conventional concept of reading needs to be expanded to embrace the skills and understanding associated with "reading" one's social, physical, and psychological environments—that is, recognizing the subtle and often nonverbal clues and messages that can be helpful commentaries on one's behavior. These include understanding observable situational clues, such as frowns and smiles, and the activities of others. Children's ability to capitalize on these skills will help them to avoid conflict.

The Content of a Synergistic Curriculum

Behaviors and Their Consequences

A synergistic curriculum for students with mild disabilities should provide students with continuing experiences throughout their schooling in reading, or deciphering, the many kinds of messages in their social, physical, and psychological environments and in linking them to the appropriate cultural responses. The concept of consequences is the key to this aspect of curriculum: behaviors can have aftereffects. Those children with mild disabilities who are able to acquire this concept can then be taught to integrate it into their response repertory and to reflect on the consequences of their behavior in the ordinary course of events. Those who have difficulty understanding the relationship between behavior and consequences need to be taught very specific strategies to help them incorporate a respect for the inevitability of ramifications in their interactions with their environments.

The increase in the dimension of each succeeding social environment in Figure 6.1 represents the increase in the number and kinds of people, things, events, and conditions peculiar to that environment that each child is likely to experience as well as the cultural responses—the knowledge, skills, proficiencies, and behaviors—that effective interactions require. Each curriculum needs to take effective interaction into account. Children with mild disabilities, like all children, start life in a confined physical, social, and psychological space that expands with their maturation, and, in the process, makes increasing demands on their aptitudes.

Quantitative and Qualitative Change

The fact that the quantitative change in each child's experience is accompanied by qualitative change should help foster synergy in the group developing the curriculum's academic content. From the perspective of living in succeeding social environments, the addition of people, things, and events to those that have accumulated from earlier experiences means more than just an increase in the number of interactions. It also means that the children achieve additional statuses and roles as their activities expand to accommodate the new events and conditions. In addition to the status and role of student, achieved statuses in school and in the neighborhood include friend, playmate, competitor, and others. Furthermore, increased interaction with people, things, and occurrences often results in more stress, more opportunities to succeed or fail, and more concepts and facts to learn and use, in effect, a change in the quality of life.

Within this context, curriculum developers need to prepare instructional experiences that address the growing ethnic diversity in our schools. The increase in diversity raises the possibility that some children may find themselves caught up in a conflict between the school's customs and mores and those of their homes and neighborhoods. Some of the ways things are done in the school and the values they represent may be contrary to those held in high regard by the family. In some communities and neighborhoods, some highly esteemed characteristics such as the probity rewarded in the school can be hazardous to display outside the school.

Within the confines of the school, the behaviors and personality characteristics of children with mild disabilities radiate from the classroom to the school and playground, where they are dealt with in some way by other children. The emotional impact of many of these interactions is carried back to the classroom, where they can have effects—sometimes subtle, sometimes obvious—on children's behavior and learning.

The Self as a Curricular Environment

The view of a young child as the focus of intensive and extensive study represents a major difference between conventional curricula and synergistic curricula appropriate for students with mild disabilities. As they enter school, all children achieve the status of student as well as the onus of sustaining this new status. As students participate in the prescribed activities of the school, they find that some customs and mores of the school are unfamiliar, others bear a resemblance to activities in and around their homes, and still others are clearly in conflict with practices in their homes and neighborhoods. Furthermore, children find themselves subjected to an entirely new roster of formal and informal authority figures ranging from the principal to the playground bully. In combination, all of these novel experiences can make for a confusing and overwhelming time for many children. The efforts to survive in such a stressful situation are likely to draw on all the resources that some children with mild disabilities can muster.

Curriculum developers need to contend with more than the effects of novel school experience on students with mild disabilities. There is also the influence of the child's maturational level on the nature of the curriculum content to consider. Young children are noted for their self-centeredness. As Lipsitt (1988) points out, irrespective of theory, the hedonic factors so pronounced in infants are seen as essential for normal adjustment and development during early childhood when response patterns that can last a lifetime are acquired. This is likely to be more obvious in the behavior of children with mild disabilities and is a way of accounting for the reputation for immaturity imputed to them.

Even though parents play an important role in teaching their children to acquire skills in the self-regulation of their hedonism (Erikson, 1968), the fact that self-gratification behaviors are powerful and that they persist for a lifetime explains why teachers in preschool and primary general education programs devote so much time and effort to promoting sharing, taking turns, and delaying gratification in general. Teaching these behaviors effectively can help children learn ways to manage lifelong tendencies toward self-absorption and self-aggrandizement that others may find wearing or even intolerable. It also leads to greater tranquility in the classroom and school and, later in life, in the community and workplace.

Furthermore, if allowed to persist unchecked, hedonism can have an undesirable effect on an important array of attributes during and well beyond the school years. Self-centered people are not likely to be the best candidates for the give and take that characterizes collaborative and cooperative enterprises. Nor are their tendencies toward self-indulgence apt to make them very reliable when it comes to meeting time commitments in social-personal, financial, and occupational matters. It is worth noting that the data from many follow-up studies of school-leavers with mild mental retardation show significantly more serious deficits in social-personal behaviors than in occupational skills.

Because hedonistic tendencies persist throughout life, there is much to be said for a curriculum that gives young children with mild disabilities an opportunity to engage in an intensive self-study of how their attitudes and behaviors mesh with the norms in their school. This is an important component of their socialization. In the course of these explorations, they also have the opportunity to learn facts about themselves, individually and collectively, that could become personal standards or points of reference for making judgments and decisions about their relationship with people, things, and events.

Being conscious of their personal standards and their preferences in commonplace matters such as games, foods, and friends, as well as the conditions that make them feel happy, sad, and fearful, can have both an immediate and long-term impact on their lives. When children with mild disabilities have established a personal sense of values, they are more likely to be ready to apply what they have learned to an understanding and appreciation of their classmates' values and those of other people important in their lives.

It is possible that the development of feelings of empathy in students with mild disabilities begins with their awareness of the sense and sensibilities of others. To put it another way, understanding that they are not the only people with preferences and feelings is probably the basis for seeing the rationality of quid pro quo in self-gratification, thereby gaining some control over hedonistic tendencies.

Additionally, framing self-study and the appreciation of others within the context of status and role may facilitate the learning of what many nondisabled children seem to pick up incidentally—that they, like others, occupy certain statuses that engender behavioral expectations in others. The role confusion that often gets in the way of children's social adaptation can be reduced by a clear understanding of the relationship between status and role. Moreover, children may be able to associate the cultural responses learned during the school day that characterize such roles as playmate, student, and helper and generalize this knowledge to similar roles in activities and associations at home and in the neighborhood.

However, for young students with mild disabilities, the school day includes more than problems stemming from their entrance into school. In fact, as reflected in the problem-solving orientation of a synergistic curriculum, these problems underscore children's needs to acquire very powerful problem-solving tools such as the ability to think critically, along with quantitative, literacy, and perceptual-motor skills, if they are to solve these and succeeding problems effectively. From the discussions and role playing that help children with mild disabilities to clarify statuses, roles, and cultural response issues come the new words to be learned, measurements to be taken and recorded, thinking strategies to be learned and implemented, personal care concepts to learn and live by, and the appreciation and enjoyment of music and art as expressive outlets.

All of these need to be taught intensively, as facts in rote learning situations and concepts in rudimentary inductive reasoning processes, as a basis for developing skills in *both* critical and independent thinking. *Both* is emphasized because teachers of children with mild disabilities often are distressed by students who can think critically but not independently. These are reflective students who have a difficult time committing themselves to a response even though it is clear to the teacher that they possess the correct information. These are also the impulsive students who, despite teachers' admonishments to wait to be called on, blurt out answers regardless of their relevance. These behaviors do not serve people well at any age.

Finally, capitalizing on the social, psychological, and physical aspects of the school as the setting for children to learn important facts about themselves and each other has advantages that will facilitate the same kind of analyses later. Very young children coming together for the first time need whatever time is required to sort out the many new facts and concepts that suddenly surround them before they can learn them. School provides a stable environment for this kind of activity because change in the structure is minimal compared with shifts in the home, family, and neighborhood. That is, the school, its population, and its social organization change very little over the course of the school year. Also, changes in students' activities within the school are more nearly a matter of evolution than revolution because remarkably few objectives and goals have only immediate or short-term target dates.

Ordinarily, statuses in our schools are stable, and the amount, nature, and rate of change in the roles of adults and children occupying these statuses is minimal, uncomplicated, and slow. Once children become familiar with the customs and mores of the school, they find them, with few exceptions, predictable. Thus, children who might be bewildered by such a huge array of novel ways for doing things and the rewards and sanctions that accompany them become acclimated relatively quickly. Unaltered novelty soon becomes routine.

The decision of whether the self is a rational starting point for the school's educational program to socialize children with mild disabilities is up to the curriculum developer. In the final analysis, all features of the curriculum need to be consistent with the conceptualization of the curriculum and its goals and objectives as articulated by its author and designer. If, for example, one subscribed to the concept put forth by Ingram (1935) and Stratemeyer and her colleagues (1947) of a curriculum designed to address persisting life problems, the curriculum content would not include the child as the focus of intensive study. Instead, it would take the shape of a developmentally organized continuum of vignettes portraying individuals doing what is necessary to recognize and then solve each of the persisting life problems. The teacher would select the continuum and the place on the continuum where students would start.

These vignettes would portray individuals with whom students could identify so that each could assume the role of a person in the vignette and collaborate with their classmates to find a solution to the problem. If students' lack of certain skills holds up progress, the skills and proficiencies in each vignette can be isolated, studied independently and in selected combinations, and at the appropriate time, they can be integrated and the vignette reconstituted. If necessary, commonalities in language across content areas can be exploited in the same way as distinctively different uses of the same words. This procedure, one of many ways for implementing a synergistic curriculum, can be applied as often as is necessary to meet the instructional goal.

The Home, Family, and Beyond

When young students with mild disabilities learn important facts and concepts about themselves and their classmates and show signs of being able to act on this knowledge effectively, they are probably ready to move on to the next knowledge base, the home and family environment, and, subsequently, to the neighborhood and the community, where thinking and acting on the social and occupational skills learned in the school have an impact on quality of life.

Experience has shown that at about this time in the maturation of many children with mild disabilities (during the study of the home and family), the evidence of their developmental delay surfaces. This often takes the form of a discrepancy between their social–personal behaviors and the norms for children of their age. That is, as compared with nondisabled children of school-entering age, many children with mild disabilities have mastered little more than their ascribed statuses. For this reason, many are slow to achieve the statuses that accompany the autonomies expected by school personnel and families: responsibility for their self-care, the fulfillment of the chores and tasks relegated to them, and, not long after, adaptability to their neighborhoods and their community. These discrepancies become increasingly evident over time.

As discussed earlier, experience also has shown that due to the influence of the medical model, the first reaction to the evidence of developmental delay observed by teachers and others who impart curriculum is to narrow the focus of instruction to remedies for what each believes to be the student's more egregious behaviors. As a result, the educational program is almost immediately transformed into a clinical enterprise. The outcome of this digression from an otherwise productive curriculum development process is an array of treatments so specific to individual children that they defy generalization. In the long run, this is of relatively little use to teachers of children with mild disabilities. A more effective way of reducing the discrepancy between the social-personal growth of children with mild disabilities' and behavior age-norms is to provide teachers with a curriculum in which the content addresses as broad an array of cultural responses as possible along with an objective, systematic way for assessing children's curricular needs and setting priorities for instruction. This allows each teacher to select from the curriculum the content that is most appropriate to the learning needs of the child as well as relevant to the needs of groups. Given a useful array of options, teachers are in a far better position to match content with learner's needs than are curriculum developers.

As students with mild disabilities begin the study of the home and family, which is a critical stage in their growth and development, the accelerating expansion rate of their social, physical, and psychological environments is the factor that should guide decisions about the substance and organization of the curriculum. The expansion of their environments should be accounted for in the curriculum by the proliferation of important facts, concepts, skills, and behaviors that emerge from the increase in the numbers and kinds of people, places, and events as well as the changing conditions within which these variables interact. This is critical because important and timely aspects of their schooling are concerned with the roles that family members and others play—roles that students may have to assume someday and that will influence their employment as well as their activities and leisure pursuits in the neighborhood and community.

Similarly, the curriculum needs to take into account the variability of neighborhoods as well as the important similarities and differences. For example, some neighborhoods have been characterized as a family of families because of the relationships formed by residents. There are also communities where such concordance does not exist and anonymity often prevails.

The Content of a Synergistic Curriculum

Wherever they may be, children with mild disabilities and youth need to become familiar with the customs and mores that govern the actions of neighbors and of strangers. To simply generalize what they have learned about their home and family to the behavior of their friends and acquaintances in our diverse society may lead to misunderstandings and serious conflicts. Students do not need to know precisely how the families and neighborhoods of others differ so much as they need to know that they may find differences and have to deal with them.

This also applies to activities in public areas such as parks and other recreation facilities, shopping districts and malls, and on public transportation. The curriculum should help students learn to respect their neighbor's privacy, property, and grounds. They also need to learn about their responsibility to contribute to the physical, social, and psychological well-being of their neighborhood as well as to their community.

Once students with mild disabilities acquire the generalizations relevant to neighborhoods and communities, it is time for them to take the next step: learning how these generalizations apply to the specific nature of the social, physical, and psychological aspects of their neighborhood and community. The statuses and roles of people across all the cultural response categories and the specific places and conditions of their activities need to be studied intently and realistically with the practical application of this knowledge as a constant goal. Learning how to implement their knowledge about their neighborhoods and community is, in effect, the basis for their transition from school to community.

To accommodate children with mild disabilities' learning needs in environments that confront them with a large variety of concepts, facts, and skills that are important in their socialization, the curriculum needs to be both readily accessible and flexible. Teachers should find it easy to locate the content for instruction as they need it. They should also have access to the instructional tactics and strategies that engage the children most effectively.

More About the Role of Academic Content

It is worth repeating that no matter how the curriculum takes shape, the first step toward the construction of a synergistic curriculum is taken when curriculum developers accept that academic learning, like all other learning, is *one* of a number of means to the end of social adaptation and that the extrinsic value of literacy skills as problem-solving tools transcends their importance as school-based subject matter. This should end the confusion regarding the goals of education for students with mild disabilities and, in particular, the misconception that the major purpose for sending these children to school is to make them literate.

The next step, then, is to set aside the custom of confining arithmetic and reading instruction to separate books in separate series. A more lifelike alternative is, as described earlier, the incorporation of academic content in ways that lead to the acquisition of normative behaviors. The learning characteristics of students with mild disabilities indicate that they need to begin this process from the time they enter school through graduation.

Reconsidering the Selection and Deployment of Students

With a comprehensive curriculum in place, evaluation of the outcomes of instruction should make it obvious that what and how much students know and the extent to which they are able to act appropriately and independently are far more relevant to their educational classification and deployment than measures of their physical, intellectual, and/or emotional deficits. While these measures often help to account for deficiencies in children's knowledge or behavior, so do factors in the ecologies of children growing up in impoverished environments. Children whose families are constantly on the move, such as migrant agricultural workers, as well as an increasing number of children from dysfunctional families and those whose parents are substance abusers may have measurable intelligence well within the normal range but display the same deficits in social skills of children who are less well-endowed intellectually and are in special education settings.

A sizable proportion of these children, when they become adults, are likely to display the pattern of unemployment and lower quality of life frequently associated with people with mild disabilities, and for essentially the same reason—educational deprivation from an early age, resulting in inadequate social adaptive skills. This alone should make students from deprived circumstances eligible for participation in the proposed curriculum under the presumption that early and continuous engagement in an educational program that balances social and academic learning should mitigate, if not reverse, the effects of educational deprivation. There is the likelihood that many of these students will so accelerate their academic achievement that they will be able make the transition from the proposed curriculum to the conventional general education curriculum early in their school careers.

Goldstein, Moss, and Jordon (1965) found that a number of children placed in experimental special classes for students with mild mental retardation when they started school were progressing well ahead of the expected rate by the end of the first year. These were children whose performance on intelligence tests and screening criteria earned them the status of children with mild retardation and placement in a experimental special education class where they participated in an intensive synergistic curriculum.

By the end of the first year, their academic and social-adaptive achievements were outstanding. However, they remained in the special class for their second year, and their instruction was augmented with tutoring designed to prepare them for entry into a general education third-grade class at the beginning of their third school year. As a result, they made an uneventful transition to a general education in third grade.

It is worth noting that none of the control children in the general education first-grade classes exhibited a comparable acceleration in academic and social growth. A parsimonious accounting of this would allow that this may be because there were no false positives in the control group. On the other hand, there could have been false positives, but, lacking an appropriate curriculum, they fell short of the level of achievement they might have otherwise attained.

There is a pervasive notion that no matter how or why they get there, nondisabled children who are placed in programs for students with mild disabilities are destined to remain there for the duration of their schooling (Mercer, 1970). This concern motivated the establishment of many preschool educational programs for children who live in neighborhoods that contribute disproportionately to special classes for students with mild disabilities.

Whether there are data to support the claim that these students remain in special education is not an issue here. What is important is that children's education needs to be relevant to their developmental needs irrespective of how they are labeled or where they are educated. With the proposed curriculum in place, denying access to children whose limited social adaptive skills portend little improvement in life conditions simply because they dodged the IQ bullet is hardly an educationally responsible act. The practice of denying children access to a program on the grounds that, once admitted, they will remain in that program for the duration of their school experience may have had merit at one time. With the proposed curriculum in place, however, curriculum-based assessment will become a conventional aspect of the total program, revealing when it is time to change a student's educational placement.

Presently, discoveries about the dramatic impact of the sensory stimulation on the growth and development of neonates' central nervous systems not only support the theories of Locke, Itard, Seguin, and their sensationalist colleagues, but also point to the need for early and continuous stimulation regardless how children are or are not categorized. Furthermore, the results of sensory stimulation efforts help to explain why the preschool programs for at-risk children that engage them in a comprehensive curriculum achieve better results than those pursuing narrower goals (Skodak, 1968; Weikert et al., 1970; Wellman, 1932–1933; Wellman, 1934–1935).

Conclusion

A synergistic curriculum, by its very nature, encompasses comprehensive and purposeful sensory experiences that naturally flow into both social and academic learning. The emphasis on reasoning and problem solving and on the development of skills that lead to proficiencies may help to develop criteria for advancement that are more realistic than conventional achievement by grade levels. The educational model based on social sciences constructs provides the substantive framework for a continuum of instruction and experiences that could begin in each child's home, connect with and carry over into the school program, where it would be the basis for an appropriate education, and ultimately lead to students' transition to adult life and the realization of the goals of education.

The Attributes of the Cyber Curriculum

Conventional curricula can be outdated quickly by technological innovations and social change. Relevance of the content and the methods of instruction, then, depends on the ability of the curriculum development personnel to include ways of accommodating unanticipated change in the way things are done in society as well as innovations in the technological systems that help get them done. For example, immediately after Texas Instruments introduced the handheld calculator, the writers of curriculum on the use of slide rules had to discard everything they had prepared and quickly develop instructional content relevant to the use of the calculator. While those who develop curricula for students with mild disabilities are rarely confronted with such an abrupt and technologically complex cultural change as this, the fact of innovation and change is nevertheless a constant and both can have notable impact on the social adaptability of students with mild disabilities.

Ironically, while the content of a curriculum needs to be dynamic and contemporary to keep pace with social and technological change, the processes for its publication and dissemination are relatively static, cumbersome, and dated. The dynamic aspects of curriculum development and curriculum revision include the task of constantly mediating a complex, ever-changing culture; being responsive to the educational needs of students whose social, physical, and psychological environments are in a constant state of change; and managing the logistics and procedures for keeping all of these variables in a workable balance.

Experience has shown that the operational plans for a curriculum development project can readily accommodate any change in educational setting or condition and in society in general as rapidly as they are detected. In the late stages of a curriculum's development, substantial change is made in content and teaching aids based on the experiences reported by teachers and administrators in the course of field testing. Additional revisions are made based on the overall assessment of the field-test results.

In contrast, immediately after the completion of the development stage, the curriculum is turned over to the publisher's production staff, who perform the tasks of printing, packaging, and the dissemination of the curriculum. Thus, the delivery of the curriculum to the publisher marks the end of the development staff's ability to make changes in the curriculum for a period that can extend over a number of years because the printed curriculum, or any printed materials for that matter, cannot be changed without a total revision of the entire publication. Some have attempted to circumvent this limitation by printing the curriculum on loose-leaf pages and sending out updated pages to replace those that are obsolete. This has often been satisfactory for the in-house operations of organizations and businesses but futile for disparate and loosely connected organizations such as local school districts.

Clearly, the conventional, printed curriculum is too inflexible to be as responsive as it needs to be for the educational needs of students with mild disabilities. The alternative is a computer-based curriculum. Unlike printed curricula, the computer-based curriculum allows for instant revision and change. It also allows for many kinds of applications as the developers can conceive. These advantages are discussed in detail later.

Advantages of the Computer-Based Curriculum

Advances in word-processing programs, the networking of personal computers, desktop publishing programs, and peripherals such as scanners and CD-ROM drives and media have expedited the compilation and assembly of curricula. Compared with the development of conventional print curricula for students with mild disabilities discussed earlier (Goldstein, 1974; Mayer, 1975), the development of a computer-based curriculum promises to be notably more economical in every way—in time, personnel, material, and equipment costs. At the same time, the ease with which various media can be incorporated into the content of instruction reduces restrictions and constraints on the creativity of developers.

Options in the Configuration of the Curriculum

A cyber curriculum emerging from such an enterprise can, but need not, take the configuration of the conventional printed curriculum. With economies in time, production, and dissemination costs in mind, a curriculum on diskettes or CDs along with access to the curriculum's Web site makes far more sense. Furthermore, because the curriculum's text is not frozen on paper, updating curriculum can be done concurrently with social and technological change, whether the change is cultural, regional, or local. For example, if the local bus company increases or decreases fares, the activities in the curriculum that deal with the use of public transportation can be brought up to date immediately.

The cyber curriculum's ability to deal with social and technological change is unlimited. Equally important, the nature of word-processing programs and the amenability of the computer to networking means that curriculum developers and their evaluation coworkers need never be out of communication at any time over the course of its development, field testing, evaluation, and implementation, even after its dissemination.

Despite the absence of precedents for the development and implementation of a computer-based curriculum on the educational scene, there are helpful precedents in the form of computer formulations, networks, and satellites that are now commonplace in the business world, in every level of government, and in many universities. The rapid pace of computers and software development and the growing popularity of computers with teachers, students, researchers, and others indicate that it will only be a matter of time before comprehensive computer-based curricula become commonplace.

Teachers' Networks

The capacity to form computer networks is not limited to the curriculum development process. Teachers and others who implement the curriculum can also build their own networks with advantages hitherto denied teachers. For example, individual teachers in geographically isolated areas, having installed the curriculum software on their computers, could not only activate the curriculum but also, with the help of a modem, establish communication with the curriculum's Web site, other teachers, the curriculum center that developed the curriculum, relevant departments in colleges and universities, and curriculum centers in other public school systems. Teachers will soon find that their participation in the network will lead to many kinds of productive associations and problem solving that go well beyond the bounds of the curriculum.

Similarly, teachers of students with mild disabilities in large school systems, local or regional, might also install the curriculum on their classroom computer, or they might be a member of a network of teachers who are linked to a mainframe, or central computer. Their network could then include any number of classrooms and other educational settings.

Each teacher's cyber curriculum could also be cross-referenced with links to lists and locations of teaching aids and instructional materials. Instructional activities, organized in whatever ways field testing and evaluation indicate are most helpful to teachers and students, would be immediately available to other teachers and support staff. Teachers would have options for the form of the instructional materials, ranging from printouts of text and graphics to the computer screen and large-scale projections.

Capitalizing on the Internet

With the computer-based curriculum as the frame of reference, e-mail and the Internet would provide teachers with the ability to communicate throughout the system and literally with the world at large. Teachers would have access to the Web sites of professional organizations worldwide, to special interest projects, and to information resources. They would also have access to informal chat groups in which they could share experiences and problem-solving strategies. For the first time, teachers of students with mild disabilities who are physically distant from their teaching colleagues would be able to establish close and frequent contact with each other and with resources of unlimited scope.

The ever-increasing amount of memory in hard drives along with the storage capacity of CDs, DVDs, and other peripherals means that the total computer-based curriculum for students with mild disabilities could be installed in every classroom as easily as in a central computer. In practical terms, this means that for the first time, every teacher could have immediately available a comprehensive continuum of instruction for students with mild disabilities ranging from preschool through secondary school. In the course of day-to-day instruction, teachers would be able to ascertain the relationship between their immediate instructional plans and those that have preceded as well as those yet to come in the students' future school years.

In addition, teachers would be able to ascertain the relevance of their curriculum to conditions in the community. Using the curriculum as the reference point, statuses and roles, customs and mores, factors bearing on quality of life, and all factors in social and technological change that are related to the growth, development, and social adaptation of students with mild disabilities could be kept under constant scrutiny in a number of ways. For example, periodic scanning of the community by schools' counseling and occupational placement staff and others should detect changes in the community's social and occupational settings that have direct or indirect effects on the transition of students with mild disabilities from the school to the larger community.

On a broader scale, the counseling and placement staff would have access to Web sites provided by professional organizations such as the Council for Exceptional Children, to government organizations such as the Office of Special Education and Rehabilitation Services in the U.S. Department of Education, and to those of private and governmental advocacy groups. With the computer-based curriculum being immediately available to teachers and curriculum specialists in the schools, modifying the curriculum to bring its content in line with current and anticipated conditions could be accomplished without delay.

"Personalized" Curriculum for a School System

The focal point for all of the foregoing activity and more can be a Web site managed by the organization developing the curriculum, the organization disseminating the curriculum, or a management team who represents both. The advantages of a Web site are countless. It can store the entire curriculum along with any number of variations on the core theme so that curriculum developers can be responsive to demographic, ethnic, and language factors in participating school systems. At the same time, they can update the curriculum, instructional materials, and media as well as innovations in instructional methods. Chat rooms can be provided for students, teachers, administrators, and parents. In short, because the cyber curriculum for students with mild disabilities is, in the technical sense, a form of software, its Web site should be able to serve its clientele in much the same manner as those of the major software purveyors and information clearinghouses.

Curriculum-Based Evaluation

The availability of the computer-based curriculum underscores the importance of curriculum-based evaluation as an important innovation in special education (Deno & Fuchs, 1987; Fuchs & Fuchs, 1986; Marston, Deno, & Mirkin, 1984). The plan for assessing students' performance by ascertaining what they have learned and how well they have absorbed the knowledge and behaviors imparted to them in the course of their educational program is consistent with the goals of the education. It would also be responsive to the IDEA requirements for accountability.

As important as this concept of curriculum-based evaluation is, it pales alongside the fact that without a reliable means of curriculum-based evaluation, educational programs for students with disabilities are limited to the use of educationally irrelevant criteria for assigning students with disabilities to educational settings and for grouping them for instruction and assessing outcomes.

In contrast, the availability of curriculum-based assessment measures provide administrators of educational programs for students with mild disabilities with the means to identify students' commonalities in learning needs and to classify them accordingly. Furthermore, being able to classify students along educationally relevant lines makes it possible to then group children for instruction according to their immediate and specific learning needs. When this process becomes routine, special educators will finally erase the last educational distinction between special and general education. All students with and without disabilities will be in appropriate educational settings and, therefore, engaged in educational activities that are relevant to their growth and development.

However, because there is presently no comprehensive curriculum for students with mild disabilities, the notion of curriculum-based evaluation of their performance is more of a topic for discussion than a reality. As a result, their educational evaluation has been based almost exclusively on the results of academic achievement tests and either off-the-shelf or teacher-produced behavior checklists. Although limited in scope, these data are often generalized as being emblematic of an entire program. This has been the convention because the educational program for students with mild disabilities, particularly in the presecondary school experiences, has consisted mainly of intensive instruction in academic subjects and behavior management procedures.

More often than not, the usual practice in curriculum development is to assemble the content of instruction, teaching aids, and other support and to leave evaluation for measurement specialists. Some reading, arithmetic, science, and social studies series come with end-of-chapter, mid-semester, and semester-end tests. None of these procedures is useful in evaluating the outcomes of a synergistic curriculum because the proportion of discretely measurable skills and knowledge in the curriculum as a whole is very small and overshadowed by the conceptually linked content that leads to problem-solving activities. Teachers' planning and pedagogy depend on an accurate assessment of the condition of their students' literacy and computational skills, but they also need to know how well their students have learned the facts and concepts that are fundamental to learning the rules and principles of problem solving. These need to be assessed within the context of the statuses and roles that students are currently occupying so that projections can be made of their social-adaptive needs when they reach maturity.

Evaluation Specialists as Members of the Curriculum Development Team

Evaluation experts need to devise systematic, curriculum-based measures that go beyond subject matter achievement tests and observer-based behavior checklists. In addition, they need to devise objective measures of students' knowledge of cultural responses and their ability to apply them in problem-solving experiences associated with the statuses and roles they occupy.

Because there is no precedent to guide the development of evaluation procedures that are appropriate to a synergistic cyber curriculum for students with mild disabilities, it is advisable to have the evaluation experts join and work with the development team from the start, including participation in the explication of the philosophic orientation and goals of the curriculum as well as in the strategies and tactics selected to attain its goals.

Synergy in the deployment of the professional staff means that all concerned are active in the basic planning. This provides for a common conceptual base to which the evaluation expert can contribute a measurement point of view. That is, while development and evaluation specialists both look at the content of instruction from the standpoint of instruction, the evaluation specialist also views it within the framework of test construction and measurement procedures. Thus, as the development staff state each of the objectives of instruction and put forth in detail the substantive and procedural means that lead to their attainment, the measurement staff can help them express both the content and methods of instruction in language that is consistent with measurement principles and procedures. At the same time, measurement specialists should design the screening procedure for ascertaining the priorities of the learning objectives for students as well as evaluation procedures for verifying the extent to which students have met the objectives of instruction.

These activities are particularly important in the aspects of the curriculum in which the synergy of subject matter areas in problem-solving contexts blurs the familiar distinctions between reading, arithmetic, science, and social studies and incorporates the factors of statuses, roles, and cultural responses into the evaluation process. Thus, as the synergistic cyber curriculum begins to take shape, the contribution of the evaluation specialist helps the developers configure and sequence content in ways that facilitate both instruction and evaluation.

This approach to curriculum development is designed to produce a computer program that includes (a) a comprehensive, developmentally organized, synergistic curriculum for students with mild disabilities, (b) a multimedia configuration of the teaching aids that support the curriculum, (c) an assessment or screening procedure for ascertaining the state of each student's knowledge and behaviors and, as a result, the student's specific position in the curriculum with respect to what he or she has learned and retained, knows presently, and needs to learn next, and (d) an evaluation procedure that not only evokes immediate reports of the efficacy of instruction, but also compiles and stores data so that long-term evaluation and post-school follow-up studies are possible.

Implementation of the Cyber Curriculum

From a practical perspective, a systematic procedure for assessing students' progress in the curriculum would make it a simple matter for teachers to keep data on each student's performance current. They could close each day with input to the computer detailing each student's accomplishments. Documentation of students' work could be scanned directly into their individual files or in archives designed for this purpose. This information would simultaneously alter students' profiles, thereby providing a current record as well as adding to the history of their performance in the various skills and proficiencies that characterize the curriculum.

The kinds of data to be stored in the computer and the purposes they serve are limited only by curriculum developers' preferences and their abilities to identify useful data and work with their programming colleagues to design ways of collecting and retrieving the data. The curriculum developer would have the option of expanding this capability to include other important data such as descriptors of students' manifest behavior and changes in their learning characteristics. In addition, the computer can be instructed to maintain the record of each student's performance in computer-aided instruction (CAI), computer-managed instruction (CMI), and interactive TV, including a record of the errors, error counts, response times, and other variables in accordance with what the curriculum specialists and teachers see as important information. Also, apart from confidential information, all stored data could be made available to researchers. For the first time, many kinds of short- and long-term efficacy and follow-up studies would become possible because the data reflecting each child's performance would be cumulative from the first of day of school.

Student Data as a Basis for Pedagogy

With accurate, relevant, and up-to-the-minute information readily available to teachers, one can see the best combination of the art and the science of teaching beginning to take shape. The data stored in the curriculum program, together with teachers' reports based on their knowledge of students' learning styles, motivation, and social sophistication, would provide a starting point for making decisions on the nature and rate of instruction. Being able to form groups that are homogeneous in terms of attributes that are pedagogically relevant would make instruction more effective. Furthermore, because rate of learning is a variable used in assigning students to groups, those whose rate of learning accelerates beyond that of the group will surface in the data immediately, introducing the possibility of their reassignment.

Experienced teachers develop, over time, a repertory of teaching strategies and tactics and a sense of students' learning characteristics that help them make the necessary match between the learning characteristics and the teaching strategy that is likely to be the most responsive. The ability to form groups that enable teachers to narrow the focus of the content of instruction and the strategies used to impart the content would enable teachers to intensify their efforts and manage instruction with greater efficiency. This is one aspect of the art of teaching that can be enriched by providing teachers with a way to augment their subjective assessment with objectively derived data such as students' learning history, including their positions in elements of the curriculum, and data that quantify variables such as their rate of learning, skills, and aptitudes.

The Configuration of Curricula
for Students with Mild Disabilities

Computer-based curricula, no matter what their configuration, will probably capitalize on a number of databases with the content of instruction at the epicenter. Logically, the content of instruction should evolve directly from data that describes the statuses that children with mild disabilities, youth, and adults should, could, or have achieved in each of the cultural response areas seen in Figure 5.1.

The content of instruction should consist of developmentally organized teaching and learning activities—the academic, social, and aesthetic experiences—that prepare students to achieve and sustain statuses in all of the cultural response areas as a function of their social adaptive skills and proficiencies. How these activities take shape depends on the preferences of the developers. There are no precedents to influence development, so some may opt for the conventional lessons typical of general education classes, while others may prefer some variation on the theme of topical modules. Some will surely breach tradition with innovative styles.

Because the content of instruction needs to be comprehensive and because literacy skills and proficiencies can be as much means to the end of social adaptation as behavioral attributes, synergy should prevail and all subject matter areas should be integrated in the instructional elements. That is,

The Attributes of the Cyber Curriculum

rather than taking the form of discrete reading and arithmetic series as they do presently, they will be integrated into learning activities where they play a role in problem solving. For example, students who are learning how to care for and conserve their belongings will gain more if, in the same time span, they talk, read, work on science projects, reckon, sing songs, draw pictures, and play games about the facts and concepts important to conservation as they pursue their learning about the things they own and are responsible for and why conservation makes good sense. In such combined and contiguous activities, the social learning aspects of the activity, the literacy, and the other skills are synergistic and mutually reinforcing as a function of sharing the same concepts, facts, vocabulary, time, and place.

In this type of curriculum, synergy is not confined to one instructional bit at a time nor is it unidirectional. Instruction is free to move horizontally across cultural responses as well as vertically within a single response category. Thus, principles of conservation can be linked with problem solving in the categories of food, shelter, hygiene, and others. If programmed to do so, the computer can show the developer as well as the teacher a mosaic of how concepts fit together and support each other in solving of any array of problems.

By adding a search capability, the computer can examine the "problem library or catalog" appropriate to each cultural response and display the location of the selected concepts in each element of the mosaic. Because the teacher has access to the curriculum program, indigenous problems can be added to those already in the computer. This would facilitate the teacher's implementation of the curriculum in accordance with the growth and development of the children. Of equal importance is the fact that this application of the curriculum is not restricted to students with mild disabilities.

Instructional Alternatives

Teachers need as many options for implementing curriculum elements as possible. These options need to be specified in the curriculum to help teachers see the relationship between the content of instruction and the alternatives available to them as means for imparting the content to their students. Instruction should capitalize on technologies such as CAI, CMI, interactive TV, Expert Systems, and so on. Interactive TV is one of the few technologies presently available to teachers that helps bridge the gap between abstract experiences and real-life situations because of its capacity to provide students with vicarious experiences.

In practical terms, classroom discussions of certain customs in supermarket shopping, for example, may be all that is available to students because trips to the supermarket and actual practice in shopping may be logistically impossible. An interactive videotape that shows people shopping in a super-market can display the behavioral options open to shoppers and the end results of their behaviors. The teacher can involve students in the shopping process by having them take the roles of the people they are observing. The discussions that evolve from these interactions can be a constructive alter-native to actually visiting a supermarket. Having the opportunity to assume the role of others and witness the results of their experiments with the deci-sions and actions they will likely experience can be good practice and the basis for real experiences.

The larger the array of teaching alternatives that developers incorporate in the computer-based curriculum, the more accurately teachers can match the style of their instruction to the learning characteristics of their students. If, for example, the learning activity is new to the students, the teacher may choose the option that gives initial management of the instructional activity to the teacher. In this instance, the teacher would introduce and control the pace and duration of instruction. If an activity is somewhat familiar to stu-dents, the teacher may prefer to alternate teacher-managed instruction with interactive TV. Later, the teacher may want to reinforce students' learning by presenting certain aspects of the same activity in the form of computer-managed instruction (CMI). They can select from the total activity only those elements of learning that need reinforcing and then write the short and temporary programs, by means of teacher authoring techniques, to fit the specific learning needs of individual students. Ultimately, the results of field testing will provide developers with the most reliable information as to the relationship between the content of instruction, options for instruc-tional styles, and teachers' preferences.

Advantages of the Cyber Curriculum

Earlier, the point was made that our culture consists of an infinite array of concepts and facts that constitute the knowledge and behaviors that distin-guish it from other cultures. Within this context, it was proposed that a key role of educators is to separate from this encyclopedic array the knowledge and behaviors that programs for students with mild disabilities are commit-ted to impart as education fulfills its role as a social institution. The curricula that evolve from this process reflect the philosophy of the curriculum devel-opers as well as their view of the configuration of the curriculum content.

The particularity of the curriculum's configuration has considerable bearing on the range of its utility within the total instructional setting. That is, a curriculum can be remarkably useful in the school's pursuit of the goals and objectives of education even though its configuration and content limit its application to the barest essentials of teaching and learning. On the other hand, they can, if configured to do so, be effective in both teaching and learning enterprises as well as in important related activities such as assessment of students' aptitudes and behaviors and evaluation of many facets of the educational program.

Status and Role as a Basis for Curriculum Configuration

Basing the curriculum's configuration on the statuses and roles subsumed in cultural response categories, for example, makes the facts, concepts, skills, and behaviors that form the curriculum available as a database which describes (a) what behaviors show up in roles associated with statuses across and within cultural response categories and (b) the skills and proficiencies that are components of specific behaviors.

To illustrate this point, in the clusters of behaviors that represent the roles of people occupying the statuses of nurses and of nurses aides in the cultural response category of hygiene, some of the listed knowledge and behaviors are common to both while some are not. For example, the professional preparation of nurses equips them to assume responsibilities and provide services and treatment that are well beyond the capabilities of nurse's aides. On the other hand, there are other behaviors that nurses and nurses' aides share; for example, both often engage in the care and feeding of patients. Similarly, looking across the categories, the behaviors comprising the roles of coaches and athletic trainers in the activities category include some that are typical of nurses and ward attendants, particularly the treatment of the injuries, fatigue, and health problems of athletes. In fact, it is likely that an inventory of behaviors associated with various roles would show that they have in common a huge body of knowledge and hitherto uncountable or uncounted skills and proficiencies.

Implications for Individualized Education Programs

With a computer-based curriculum, committees that develop individualized education programs (IEPs), which are limited presently to a statement of teaching–learning objectives based on each student's achievement test results and teachers' observations, would have not only the student's profile based on his or her performance in statuses and roles addressed by the synergistic curriculum, but also a reference to the specific knowledge, skills, and behaviors associated with each status and role. By using the concept, skill, or behavior as the keyword in the computer's search or find function, committee members can have the computer display its location within and across cultural response categories and statuses. Accordingly, they will be able to formulate individual plans from the entire scope and sequence of the curriculum.

Rare and subtle behaviors will be identified by the computer as readily as high-intensity, high-frequency behaviors. This will enable teachers and support staff to go beyond speculation when accounting for a student's successes and failures in each cultural response area. By giving the computer the student's coded designation as, let us say, a mainstreamed member of the third grade or of a self-contained classroom, the student would first appear in the listing of statuses in the cultural response category entitled training. His or her performance in each of the behaviors that comprise the role associated with his classroom assignment, having been cross-referenced with all of his other statuses in all seven cultural responses, would display a profile of his performance in each response. His strengths and weaknesses would be revealed by the discrepancies between his or her performance and the norms, formal or informal, for each role in the profile.

One of the many advantages of this arrangement is the ease with which teachers, members of IEP committees, and others can determine how and where shortfalls in students' skills and proficiencies create behavioral deficits or inappropriate behaviors and how these impede a student's progress. Furthermore, this database should help allay the concerns held by many regarding the deceleration of an able student's progress as a function of his being restricted, for whatever the reason, to the achievement norms of the special class. The data should highlight both the student whose placement in a special education setting has outlived its usefulness and the shining light in the classroom who has been assigned to an inordinate amount of time tutoring less able classmates at the expense of his or her own progress.

The immediate availability of data for each student and the computer's capacity to portray and then extrapolate each student's achievement while highlighting unusual configurations in profiles reduces the probability that changes in behavior and unusual performance will go unobserved. The computer can be programmed to call immediate attention to any student profile that surpasses or falls short of the norms, however the school states them, for any curriculum element or combination of elements.

Implications for the Assessment of Student Performance

The second database within this context can help create a bridge between the implementation of the curriculum and the curriculum-based assessment that contributes to its effectiveness. It should contain the results of an analysis of the skills and proficiencies that underlie the behaviors and aptitudes that, in combination, represent roles. This database will emerge from observations and studies describing the statuses that children, youth, and adults with mild disabilities should, could, or have already achieved. In practical terms, this means performing a task analysis on each behavior. We have a precedent for this in achievement testing, behavior inventories and checklists, diagnostic procedures for students with learning disabilities, and behaviorally oriented curricula for students with moderate and severe disabilities. Having the computerized behavior database as a point of departure for the analysis of skills and proficiencies that underlie behaviors is an important first step in developing the computerized evaluation program.

The behavior database provides a starting point for exploring behaviors in ways that yield information that allow us to focus on hitherto unattainable teaching targets. Until now, we have been limited to speculation about the structure of abstractions such as aptitudes. We can argue interminably, for example, about punctuality and what comes first—the concept or the behavior. What, for example, are the constituent parts of punctuality as a concept and as a behavior? They range, of course, from basic perceptual skills such as number recognition through exceedingly complex cognitive-affective abstractions such as empathy—knowing what it feels like to be kept waiting. However, with a behavior database categorized by cultural responses, the arguments become moot because the elements of an aptitude can be tracked through all of the statuses and roles in which they are important. Categorizing the behavioral manifestations of aptitudes needs to be done within the framework of their implication for social adaptation. Beyond the question of what does one need to know or be able to do to be punctual, there are the collateral questions (a) what actions are called for if there are indications that one *might* be late and (b) what does one need to do if it becomes clear that one *is* going to be late? Also, there are absolutes such as being able to tell time and alternatives such as having the presence of mind to inquire about the time if a clock isn't in view. With these behavioral details identified and installed in the computer supplementary to the curriculum, greater precision in specifying and addressing instructional objectives can be achieved.

There is no question that cataloging behaviors and their component parts is a major task. However, as discussed earlier, there are conditions to facilitate the work. For one, we would start the data gathering, actual construction of the curriculum, and all related activities from square one. There are no precedents to restrict or confound the conceptualization of the content, the configuration, or the parameters of the curriculum. Nor are there established customs and mores to deal with in all or part of the status quo. Although we emphasize that sustaining the viability of a curriculum is a never-ending task, by recording the curriculum and its collateral programs in a computer rather than on the conventional printed page, we reduce the constraints imposed by the fear of making errors of omission and commission. That is, the ease with which mistakes can be corrected, redundancies eliminated, gaps filled, and awkward sentences deleted and replaced makes experimenting with ways of expressing ideas an anxiety-free activity.

At the same time, the precedents that are already established in areas related to the development and implementation of the curriculum—particularly in test construction, measurement, task analysis, and methods of teaching and learning—will facilitate the development of a synergistic curriculum. Due to the seamlessness of the subject matter in this type of curriculum, precise measurement of students' achievement alone will not provide enough data to present an accurate profile of students' aptitudes. The procedures for measuring students' performance in reading and arithmetic and for identifying learning problems must include ways for ascertaining how effectively they apply the knowledge and skills of the subject matter as well as their social skills in problem solving and conflict resolution. Similarly, interviewing and survey techniques must be adapted to include information about the active statuses and roles of children, youth, and adults with mild disabilities.

Conclusion

When we examine the curricular and instructional needs of children and youth with mild disabilities and their underachieving peers, it appears that computers were invented specifically to facilitate the development and implementation of their educational programs. That is, in combination, the nature and rate of social change and the learning styles and characteristics of students call for maneuverability and flexibility in the development and implementation of curriculum that only computer systems can provide. Because the curriculum is irrevocably a part of social change, there will always be innovations and alterations in instruction and in the conditions of curriculum development and implementation, irrespective of their conceptual foundations and form.

Thus, if properly equipped, local education agencies (LEAs) will not have to rely entirely on external sources such as publishers and curriculum developers to provide updated content and teaching aids. Instead, each technologically equipped LEA will be able to manage changes in its version of the curriculum in both general and locally relevant terms. Similarly, as increasingly user-friendly technologies become available, their use in implementing, modifying, and evaluating of curriculum will help LEAs to keep the curriculum for students with mild disabilities timely and germane.

Experience suggests that, in the immediate future, there will be some resistance to the use of computer-based curriculum in educational settings for students with mild disabilities in particular and in LEAs in general. Opponents will argue that the curriculum comes between teachers and their students, thereby blunting teachers' sensitivities and, as a result, their creativity, judgment, and artistry. Some will see the computer as emblematic of the mechanization and depersonalization of education. Others will admit, candidly, that their objections stem from their lack of understanding and competence in the use of computers and their conviction that it is too late to change their ways.

However, there are indications that the current generation of new teachers and administrators are more comfortable and competent with computers. They have grown up with computers in their homes and schools, their professional preparation includes the personal and professional use of computers, and they arrive in their classroom expecting to find computers as standard equipment and technical assistance as a part of the total support system for teachers. Accordingly, teachers of students with mild disabilities will find that a computer-based curriculum and their competence in augmenting its programs with their authoring skills will fit into their plans nicely.

First Steps in the Development of a Synergistic Curriculum

Chapter

8

■　　■　　■　　■　　■　　■　　■　　■　　■　　■

While the prospect of developing a synergistic curriculum for students with mild disabilities and their underachieving counterparts that is consonant with the goals of education has unlimited horizons, it is also fraught with challenges and mysteries. However, those few who were successful in developing limited versions of such a curriculum in the late 1960s and early 1970s would be quick to attest to the likelihood for success.

Two publications are devoted to procedures for the development of curriculum specifically for students with mild and moderate retardation: *Planning Curriculum Development* (Mayer, 1975) and *Curriculum Development for Exceptional Children* (Goldstein, H., 1981). The first describes in detail the procedures, from data collecting through field testing and revision, employed by five federally funded curriculum development projects of sizable proportions: two for students with mild mental retardation and three for students with mild disabilities. The second presents the development process for a curriculum for students with mild mental retardation. These works are the products of the first and only generation of major curriculum developers of programs for students with mild disabilities since the rise and fall of the *Occupational Education Curriculum* (Hungerford, 1948; Hungerford, DeProspo, and Rosenzweig, 1952). The challenge to current and future generations is clear.

The Curriculum Development Team

The first step toward the development of the proposed curriculum is to assemble a team of content specialists, social learning experts, and technological support staff whose collective working styles are as synergistic as the teaching and learning content they create for the curriculum. This is no small task given the long history of the development of discrete content areas along with the implicit hierarchy that the competency test movement has provoked—reading is the belle of the ball, and arithmetic and science are not far behind. The humanities, aesthetics, and health areas bring up the rear. Social learning is left to the judgment and competencies of interested parties, if any exist. Fortunately, there are explorers and innovators in education who are intrigued by an opportunity to express ideas and ways of organizing content that transcends the conventional.

Characteristics of an Effective Development Team

The conditions that make a productive synergistic development team can vary considerably. However, certain factors are critical to the success of such projects. First, this author's experience indicates that leadership by committee or consensus does not work. The project's leadership needs to be the responsibility of one person who articulates a thorough and clearly stated commitment to the goals of education and who has the ability to explicate these goals to the development staff in both abstract and concrete terms. These goals should be related to curriculum theory as well as to the conceptualization of the metamorphosis of well-educated students with mild disabilities and their unclassified counterparts into competent adults.

The statement of goals should be the framework for the selection of staff and the basis of their development efforts. That is to say, while technical and professional skills are of great importance, the team will be confined to conventional procedures if they do not possess creativity and vision. In addition, the experiences of curriculum developers further indicate that the leader of a curriculum development project is well advised to appoint an advisory board or committee to act as a sounding board and problem-solving resource.

Second, if synergy is to be achieved, the development staff needs to recognize that narrow loyalties or commitments to content areas and specialties must be held in check and that the work of all members of the team, including development, evaluation, media, computer programming, and others, takes place within a collaborative, social learning frame of reference. In practical terms, the development staff must think of its collaboration as a means for realizing a curriculum whose purpose is the socialization of all children and youth who are at risk of failing to attain an active and productive role in society.

Developers who have been specialists in reading, arithmetic, or science, for example, must set aside the conventional notion of the uniqueness and intrinsic value of their content in the educational scene and view it, instead, as a very powerful problem-solving tool that is useful in coping with conditions in one's social, physical, and psychological environments. Accordingly, reading, arithmetic and science specialists must design the skill-acquisition content in terms of readiness to implement the skill and knowledge in problem-solving settings. Their work must take place within the framework of the social learning problems designed by the social learning specialists.

The key question for each content specialist is "what skills and proficiencies in my area of content specialization does someone need in order to effectively fulfill a given cultural response?" In a practical sense, content specialists must analyze each social learning objective to ascertain:

1. the basic sensorimotor, language, and quantitative skills that students need to acquire as prerequisites to engaging in the social learning activity and
2. the language, literacy, and quantitative aptitudes that they need to acquire in order to fulfill the social learning objectives.

Specialists in music, art, dance, health, and related content areas need to adopt the same approach in designing their contributions to the curriculum.

Third, nothing in these conditions suggests a blind devotion to and unquestioning acceptance of the proposed development plan. The master plan for the development of the curriculum is, at best, a working plan, the best estimate of a strategy for getting the job done. At all times, rational change has to be a real possibility. For the development project to succeed, it requires the contribution of the best and most daring thinking of every member of the staff, their rigorous self-assessment, and their ability to accept the assessment of others. The staff need to possess the conceptual integrity and flexibility to surrender, if necessary, long-held ways of doing things if they prove to be irrelevant to the process of designing and evolving an educational program. In its initial form and thereafter, the development plan will be an exercise in pragmatism.

Fourth, given the nature of the proposed curriculum, the social learning specialists should lead the way. Irrespective of the model guiding the development of the synergistic curriculum, the basic content must consist

First Steps in the Development of a Synergistic Curriculum

of the facts, concepts, and behaviors found within the framework of cultural responses that students need to learn if they are to fulfill the roles associated with their achieved statuses of child, student, playmate, collaborator, etc., as well as their ascribed statuses of son or daughter and family member. The content specialists need this content as the basis for identifying the literacy, quantitative, language, and sensorimotor skills that children must acquire in order to function in expected ways as they interact with people, things, and events in their environments.

The Roles of Content Specialists and Technical Support Staff

The goal of content specialists, including music, art, movement, and play experts, should be to shape the content of instruction in ways that provide teachers with motivating and introductory activities, with practice and otherwise reinforcing experiences, and with culminating activities important to the students' acquisition of knowledge and behaviors. To this end, teachers of students with mild disabilities often need a multitude of ways to teach and reteach the same concept or fact. Working together, content specialists can provide them with helpful ways of reinforcing learning without mind-numbing repetition. As the instructional content begins to take shape, the work of the content specialists is then seamlessly integrated into the content of instruction and turned over to the media specialists who, in consultation with the content and social learning specialists, design the necessary audio-visual instructional aids.

Because the proposed curriculum is computer-based, its synergy must go well beyond the content of instruction. Accordingly, the development team needs two additional full-time members—a computer programming expert and an evaluation expert. The former is there to advise the content, media, and evaluation specialists on the best way to structure their products so that they are consistently user friendly. Many special educators are much more at home with conventional publication processes than with computers. They know how books and other print materials and associated media are manufactured, and they turn to audiotapes, slides, photos, and videotapes as teaching aids. Constructing a curriculum that is programmed for use via computers requires production tactics that are often beyond their experiences.

One of the key contributions of the computer specialist will be orienting the development staff to the techniques necessary for the computerization of the curriculum and educating them about the ways of the cyber world so that they can exploit the advantages of this means for communication. The evaluation specialist is present to work with members of the development team in identifying the kinds of screening, assessment, and evaluation procedures that teachers need in order to make decisions about the objectives of instruction and attaining an effective level of instruction. In an important sense, then, both the computer programming and evaluation specialists are leavening forces in the development process. They each provide rationales for assembling the content in ways that enhance teachers' decisions and their work with students.

Developing a Teacher-Friendly Curriculum

Teachers of students with mild disabilities are at their best when they are making preparations for teaching, when they are teaching, and when they are examining the bases for their successes and failures as a means to improve their teaching skills. The less time that teachers spend making, finding, or shopping for teaching aids, pictures, and other media that support instruction, the more time and energy they have to devote to their students. Curriculum developers need to take this fact into account by relieving teachers of as many tasks subordinate to teaching as they can.

Experiences in the development of the social learning curriculum (H. Goldstein, 1974, 1975, 1981) indicate that a curriculum can provide teachers with everything they need to make teaching and learning as effective as possible. One of the goals of field testing is to obtain teachers' assessment of the completeness or thoroughness of the instructional content, teaching aids, and evaluation procedures. The computer-based curriculum should provide the teacher with everything from the basis for planning instruction, including the indicated teaching–learning activity, to the evaluation instrument used to assess the effectiveness of instruction.

The centerpiece of this sequence, the teaching–learning activity, should be accompanied by the materials that support and enhance instruction. For example, for instruction designed to advance children's language development, literacy, or computational skills, the computer-generated teaching–learning activity should be accompanied by a full array of relevant stimulus cards, printed in color and illustrated if the teacher desires. The teacher could select those needed by each child as indicated by the child's computer-generated profile. If the curriculum development team overlooked or omitted a stimulus card, the teacher can create the card on the computer and print it. Alternatively, the teacher could program students' computers to engage them in exercises and games that exploit the same language and quantitative stimuli as the cards.

First Steps in the Development of a Synergistic Curriculum

A Curriculum That Supports Instruction

Curriculum developers need to keep in mind the fact that "educationese" is a derivative jargon that draws freely from the behavioral and social sciences and, more recently, from commercial and industrial sources as well. Accordingly, the likelihood of misperception increases as many popularly defined terms begin to acquire multiple, often unrelated meanings. Unless curriculum developers take measures to reduce confusion in communication with teachers, the possibility that their educational goals for students with mild disabilities will not be realized increases.

Developers have a surefire method for reducing the potential for misinterpretation and misdirection. They can state all instructional procedures in a form that indicates desired outcomes, in this case educational objectives and sub-objectives. Along with clearly stated objectives and sub-objectives, they can provide teachers with guidelines in the form of a model script or scenario for each social learning activity that forms the framework for direct social and academic instruction.

Procedures for attaining social learning goals are more likely to be misunderstood and misdirected than those pertaining to academic goals (M.T. Goldstein, 1976, 1981). The probability that the intent of educational objectives will be misconstrued can be reduced if they are always expressed in the form of performance outcomes that are observable and measurable behaviors, such as "the student will be able to write his or her name."

It is important to recognize that stating instructional objectives is more complicated for a synergistic curriculum than for a more conventional curriculum. For example, stating that the child should be able to write his or her name is a sub-objective under the central objective of self-identification, which states "the student should be able to identify himself or herself by stating and writing his or her name, sex, age, address, and telephone number." The sub-objective presupposes that children have mastered writing skills well enough to write their names. This assumes that students have had instruction and practice in writing and have acquired writing skills at sometime prior to the implementation of the instruction designed to attain the sub-objective. To put it within the framework of curriculum development, the graphomotor skills and proficiencies that are needed to attain the sub-objective must be incorporated into the curriculum prior to the emergence of the sub-objective so that they can be called into play at the appropriate time.

Clearly, the challenge to the developers of a teacher-friendly synergistic curriculum for students with mild disabilities is to invent a curriculum layout or format that, given a sub-objective, brings all of the content areas that are relevant to the attainment of that sub-objective together in such a way that the teacher can select and order the instructional activities to conform with students' aptitudes.

The Computer as a Medium of Instruction

The content specialists and computer programmer work with the social learning experts to identify the learning activities within their spheres of expertise that serve the teacher's instructional purpose to introduce or reinforce learning. The computer's search capabilities can assemble these for the teacher. When the teacher calls up the targeted sub-objective, the computer can display the sub-objective, the core instructional activity, and the collateral instruction in literacy and quantitative thinking, as well as the games, music, movement, and other relevant instructional areas together with the elements of the sub-objective that they support. This information can help the teacher anticipate outcomes and assess the merits of collateral activities and the need for their revision.

If teachers are concerned that some of the collateral activities might be too immature for some students or too advanced for others, they can extend their view of the sub-objective forward or backward in the curriculum to succeeding or preceding levels in the model (see Figure 6.1) and select more age-appropriate collateral activities. Having done so, teachers can then instruct the computer to install the activity on specific students' networked computers or have the computer produce seatwork or collaborative work to be accomplished by groups. In either case, the computer should be instructed to record the results of students' work in their individual profiles, including the code for the specially selected collateral activities.

With the rapid and dramatic technological advances in computers and their programming strategies, the capabilities for micromanaging important aspects of instruction are limitless. For example, the computer makes it possible to cross-reference concepts and facts and allows teachers to use such cross-referencing as a thesaurus for instructional objectives and sub-objectives. By searching horizontally across the appropriate level in the expanding environment model (see Figure 6.1), teachers can find concepts and facts to augment those already familiar to some students, teach them as paired associates, and enrich their instruction accordingly. Clearly, the extent to which pedagogy can be managed and focused is limited only by the creativity and technological competency of educators.

Developing Teaching Scripts and Scenarios

Developer bias is a constant in curriculum development. The content of a curriculum represents the developers' selection, from the totality of information in our culture, of those concepts and facts that appear relevant to students' attainment of the goals of education. Many developer biases implicit in this enterprise arise from experiences in the education of children and youth with mild disabilities. Within this context, the folklore about students with mild disabilities stands out. In particular, beliefs that spring from the long-term influence of the medical model on educational decisions that direct attention exclusively to the learning "inabilities" of students with mild disabilities, in particular, their inability to learn abstractions, concepts, and ideas. Many are convinced that these "inabilities" become additive and ultimately contribute to deficits in students' long-term memory.

This conflict between the positive nature of the curriculum, consisting of things to be learned and done, and the clinical, remedial mindset of educators of students with mild disabilities calls for resolution. All things considered, social adaptation in a democratic society rests on the ability of individuals to think critically and act independently. Critical thinking, defined operationally, is the ability to select from one's knowledge bank a certain accumulation of social concepts and facts and to use them within a systematic problem-solving frame of reference in order to bring about solutions.

Acting independently is defined operationally as an individual's ability to act on the results of critical thinking, to assess the outcomes, and to make any necessary adjustment. Thus, critical thinking is based on knowledge, while acting independently is based on process, which consists of the strategies to put knowledge to work effectively. Fortunately, the literature on how to foster reasoning in children has increased dramatically (Resnick, 1987; Valett, 1978; Whimbey, 1991).

Rote instruction combined with drill and memorization, if used as the primary teaching strategy in the instruction of students with mild disabilities, can stand directly in the way of their achieving these aptitudes. Memorizing rules for behaving does not generate the reasoning skills that make behaviors rational. In fact, it precludes any need to think critically. This needs to be communicated to teachers who, lacking a comprehensive curriculum, may turn to rote instruction strategies as the means of indoctrinating students with mild disabilities with as many rules underlying socially acceptable behavior as time allows.

While curriculum developers are rarely able to communicate directly with the teachers using their curriculum, they are able to convey information to them through the curriculum content and the way it is organized. Typically, developers provide a preface to instructional content that offers suggestions for implementing the curriculum. In addition, they can configure the content of instruction in the form of a teaching script or scenario that takes the teacher through a sequence of instructional activities and spells out the teaching strategy for the content to be imparted.

To this end, the teaching content can be organized in the form of a logical sequence of questions leading to answers that signify the attainment of the instructional objective. For example, to realize an objective associated with maintaining one's health whose goal is to have students understand the importance of actively avoiding infection, the curriculum content may confront students with of a series of questions designed to get them thinking within the boundaries of the objective: the merits of being careful, clean, and prepared to deal with infectious conditions.

Teachers have considerable latitude to edit or augment the questions and activities they want to introduce within the framework of the stated objective (Dillon, 1988a; Hyman, 1979). This way of configuring instructional content does not override teachers' judgment as to when to abandon the reasoning approach because too much time is being consumed with too few results. When it becomes clear that the amount of time spent in the reasoning process far exceeds results, the teacher can turn to rote instruction, emphasizing the memorization of rules and when to act on them.

Alternatively, curriculum developers can present teaching activities in the form of a fully prepared script that contains dialogue for the teacher and indicates the desired responses from students. Teachers are urged to view such prepared instructional activities as a model that they can (a) use as an example of a way to impart the content that they can adopt or (b) use as a guideline for a strategy that they wish to implement in their own way. In this author's experience in field testing a curriculum constructed in this way, it was clear that while some teachers and administrators bridle at the suggestion of putting words into teachers' and students' mouths under any conditions, the vast majority grasped the developers' rationale for organizing teaching content in this way and concurred with their intent.

What follows is an example of a script or scenario to manage instruction for the attainment of an objective at the self level. The ultimate desired outcome is the attainment of the following objectives: (a) students know their full names, addresses, and telephone numbers, and (b) they are able to use this information in problem-solving situations ranging from introducing themselves to others to providing the information to inform others on how to help them find their way home. In fact, the immediate sub-objective focuses on this latter theme, with the goal that the student is able to state his or her address. The following scenario is a teaching activity created by the curriculum development team.

Task #1: Provide Teachers with Information Relevant to the Attainment of This Sub-Objective

Sub-Objective
The purpose of this lesson is to help students understand that there are situations in which they need to be able to state their names and addresses, such as if they become lost.

Teacher Information

You are provided with a story in the Teaching Strategies about someone who is lost. You may want to substitute or add another story, or you may want to make up a story that is more in harmony with the nature of your community. In any case, take into account your school setting (rural, urban, or suburban), and use the provided story as a model for the necessary content.

In the course of relating the story to your students, help them develop good listening habits and skills by stopping briefly at key points to ask questions such as "Who can tell me what has happened so far?" or "What do you think will happen next?" It is sometimes necessary to briefly summarize the story periodically before continuing. As the story unfolds, do not overemphasize the aspect of being lost.

If your students live in a rural area, you might want to shift the emphasis from city addresses to the custom for identifying residences in your area.

Task #2: Develop Computer-Based Teaching Materials and Cross-Referenced Programming for Children's Computers

Task #3: List in Detail the Teacher's Preparation for this Teaching Activity

For example, for this lesson, having students' home addresses at hand is helpful.

Task #4: Guide the Teacher in Structuring the Activity

Seat the students in a semicircle around you and read the following story or a similar story of your preference.

Terry Has a Problem

> On his way home from school, Terry saw some boys and girls who were skipping rope. Terry stopped to watch the children. He wished that he could play with them. Then one of the boys who were swinging the rope saw Terry. "Hey, come and play with us," said the boy. He handed Terry one end of the rope and showed him how to twirl it. Everybody was happy and laughing.
>
> Soon the boy who had invited Terry to play said, "Let's all go to my house." All of the children followed him to his house and played in his yard. The boy's mother came out of the house and said, "Eric, it's time to come in now."

Suddenly, Terry remembered that he should be going home. He looked around, but everything on the street looked strange. Terry said to himself, "I don't know my way home. I'm lost. What am I going to do now?"

Teacher Activity

After you read the story, guide a discussion with questions such as the following. Feel free to add questions that you feel will help students attain the lesson objective.

Discussion Questions

What has happened to Terry at the end of the story? (This type of question will give you an indication of how well students attended to the story and understood it.)

What does it mean to be lost?

If a person is lost, how can he get home?

What can Terry do to get home?

Do you think that Terry can get home by himself, or does he need someone to help him?

Whom should Terry ask for help? (Help students recall Eric's mother with questions such as "Who was the grownup who called to Eric that it was time to come in?")

How can Eric's mother or anyone else help him? Can anyone help Terry without knowing where he lives?

What will Terry have to tell Eric's mother so that she can help him?

What information tells other people where you live?

If you were lost, as Terry is, could you tell someone your address?

Have each student state his or her address. If the student does not know the address, tell the student his or her address and have the student repeat it. Note students who need extra practice and provide it via computer-aided (CAI) or computer-managed (CMI) instruction.

Have students role-play pretending that they are lost. Have each student report to a classmate that he is lost, ask for help, and give the other student his or her address.

Task #5: Provide Teachers with Additional Activities

Play a game with children that emphasizes their address, such as asking, "Will someone who lives at 192 Right St. come up here and select a cookie?" Be sure to reinforce the connection between name and address before ending each transaction.

153

Have students state their addresses before departing for home. Have students role-play situations in which telling someone their address is important, for example, inviting someone to their home to play or to have dinner.

This teaching strategy is structured, but it is not inflexible. The teacher has the option to use it as is, to modify it to suit their notion of how to best attain the sub-objective, or to ignore it and tackle the sub-objective as they see fit.

Experience has shown that some novice teachers and some of modest competence welcome the structure and direction offered by a prepared teaching script. As their confidence mounts, the tendency to assert their own ideas about how to use the script increases. Experience has also shown that some creative and expert teachers may assess the script's merit as a means of attaining the sub-objective and devise a lesson that is more consistent with their perception of their students' needs.

In the early stages of children's development, learning is concerned mainly with the acquisition of facts—the who, what, when, where, and often why of people, places, and things that are important in their lives. The preceding example illustrates this fact. Other than feeling anxious, Terry had no way of dealing with the concept of being lost without the facts associated with who he is, where he lives, and who can help him. Like all children, as those with mild disabilities mature, the facts they have learned become raw materials for the concepts that they must learn and use (Inhelder, 1968).

Accordingly, the content of teaching scripts or scenarios must take a form that accounts for this shift in emphasis from facts to concepts. Furthermore, because the extrinsic value of concepts and their function in problem-solving is primary, offering them to the teacher in a problem-solving context is more helpful than simply presenting a list of concepts to be taught.

Promoting Reasoning as a Problem-Solving Strategy

Organizing curriculum content into problem-solving activities that are consistent with both children's developmental needs and the goals of education conveys the curriculum developers intent and, at the same time, structures the teachers' actions to the extent that they need or want structure. While advocates of problem-solving strategies often differ in their recommended ways of imparting these aptitudes to children (Kaufman, 1975; Scandura, 1977), they agree that the end product of this type of instruction should be (a) knowledge of how to solve the problem being studied and (b) knowledge of the principle that governs the class or category of problems it represents.

Furthermore, they contend that the ability to devise problem-solving tactics based on the appropriate principle is the mark of those who are effective in thinking critically and independently (Goldstein & Goldstein, 1980; Krulik & Rudnik, 1995; Resnick, 1987). Parenthetically, the literature cited here represents a minuscule proportion of the texts, monographs, and journal articles that discuss children's reasoning and problem-solving strategies from a number of educational perspectives. While painfully few have direct reference to children with mild disabilities, they nevertheless offer curriculum developers and teachers theoretical and practical information of considerable value.

Scripting Teachers' Roles in Promoting Students' Reasoning Abilities

Developing a teaching script or scenario within a problem-solving context that accommodates the shift in emphasis from facts to concepts also anticipates a shift in the roles of teachers and students. In the script described earlier, the teacher directs students' activities by means of a questioning procedure. Developers need to construct scripts so that concept formation will begin to take shape in instructional settings. By so doing, they encourage teacher-student interaction as collaborators in problem-solving enterprises. This allows students to play a larger role in evaluating their responses and those of their peers and in monitoring the problem-solving process in general. In this way, developers increase the probability that reasoning can emerge as a mitigating force when students identify and solve problems.

Curriculum developers are not limited to a single script or scenario format. The literature on teaching within a problem-solving framework offers many helpful designs. No matter which format or formats the developer selects, all should have in common certain properties that communicate the intent of the curriculum developer and facilitate teachers' implementation of the activity.

First, a problem-solving activity in the curriculum must be a group enterprise that deals with a problem common to all the children so that they are able to participate in accordance with their individual conceptualizations of the problem. Second, the group should be homogeneous in their need to solve the problem and in their readiness to engage in the activity, as determined by the level of their achievement in the curriculum. Third, the activity should be structured so that there is an opportunity for each student to recognize in his or her own way that there is a problem. In other words, the language in the beginning of the script should be so clear that even if children do not detect the problem immediately, a simple question or two from the teacher will help them see it.

For example, let us say that in a curriculum element whose objective is learning how to use available public transportation, there is a sub-objective that involves planning to visit a local place of interest that is easiest to get to via the bus system. The teacher in a mid-elementary school level class has reached the point in instruction where he or she (a) has elicited from the children what they know or could find out at home about places of interest in their community and, through adroit questioning guided by the script, (b) has had them agree on a place to visit that the teacher has, unknown to them, already selected.

This is the logical point for one or more of the children to raise the question, How do we get there? Logical though it may be, sometimes this question is not asked. Experience suggests that this early in children's maturation, they rarely have to deal with this question because one adult or another in their environment usually makes this type of decision for them. Thus, odds are that they expect the teacher to tell them the plan for getting to their destination.

The script should advise the teacher to confront the children with the question if it is not asked. In this way, they become party to the problem-solving enterprise and sensitized to the fact that the teacher not only expects them to include travel plans in their deliberations, but also tacitly expresses confidence in their ability to solve the problem.

At this point in the discussion, it is clear that the synergy in this curriculum goes well beyond the involvement of social learning and content specialists, evaluation specialists and computer programmers. It also encompasses faculty in teacher education programs, particularly in curriculum and methods courses, in which strategies and tactics in addition to those contained in the curriculum can be imparted to teacher candidates. The fact is, in the foregoing interaction between teacher and students, there are many alternatives open to the teacher for involving students in the problem-solving process. Time and personnel constraints being what they are, curriculum developers cannot be overly inclusive in the substance of the curriculum if they are to offer teachers a manageable program. Faculty in institutions of higher education, on the other hand, can elaborate on the curriculum's themes and introduce teachers to their views on strategies for its implementation.

If curriculum developers settle on more than one problem-solving format or structure for the teaching scripts or scenarios, they need to take into account the fact that problem-solving formats can become children's problem-solving styles as an outcome of their repeated exposure to the format in instructional settings. In other words, having been repeatedly successful in solving problems during the course of instructional activities, some children may adopt that format, consciously or not, as their own process for solving problems in the ordinary course of events. Developers should alert teachers to the desirability of this outcome by reminding them that when they acknowledge children's success in solving a problem, they may be, at the same time, reinforcing their use of the format.

A Prototype of a Five-Step Problem-Solving Format

A variation on the theme of Dewey's "scientific method" for problem solving is a good example of one problem-solving format that could be well within the capability of students with mild disabilities. This format is a five-step inductive procedure that begins after the problem has been identified. It consists of the following steps:

Labeling—identifying elements of the problem that play a role in its solution

Detailing—identifying descriptors of the identified elements that contribute to the solution of the problem

Inferring—stating possible solutions (hypotheses) based on the data gathered in the preceding steps

Verifying—committing to a strategy for solving the problem, solving it, and assessing the results

Generalizing—identifying the rule or principle that governs the means of solving this class or type of problem

The labeling and detailing stages are critical. Children need to learn to distinguish elements of a problem and their descriptors that are important in its solution from those that are irrelevant. Confusion can arise from the fact that the same variables and descriptors may appear in any number of unrelated problems. In some, they figure into the solution. In others, they do not. Students with mild disabilities need a lot of practice in discovering this fact and capitalizing on it.

A teaching activity with the sub-objective of learning how to use public transportation but somewhat more advanced than the one discussed earlier can illustrate how this problem-solving format serves as a framework for curriculum content. As in the earlier activity, the curriculum's goal and, therefore, the teacher's primary objective, is to have the children learn the facts and concepts necessary to use public transportation effectively. Accordingly, the teacher, aided by the teaching script, must see to it that all discussions and actions culminate in the children agreeing that the public bus is the best solution to this problem.

Having asked students to discuss with their parents interesting sites in or near their community that merit a visit, the teacher must elicit a number of options and narrow them down to one that all agree is the place to visit. The teacher then confronts the class with the question, "How do we get to our destination?" Here the script provides questions that lead to the children naming (labeling) the various means of transportation that are available, including public transportation, parents' vehicles, taxicabs, and school buses. Next, they are asked to discuss the logistics (detailing) associated with each, such as availability, the number of parents who would have to provide vehicles, the cost of taxicabs, the availability and cost of a school bus, the cost of riding the public bus, and so on. The children are then encouraged to narrow down the possibilities to two (inferring)—most likely a school bus and the public bus—and, having investigated and found that a school bus is not available or too costly or both, they agree that riding the public bus is the best alternative.

Then they spend as much time as necessary listing the logistics of using the bus, including cost, schedules, and time en route and comparing them with analogous factors in other travel options (verifying). This leads to the conclusion that the class should travel via public bus, and they arrive at the point when all that remains to be done is set a date for the trip. Experience has shown that an instructional script that helps the teacher review information important to the success of the visit well in advance of the departure date allows for planning that can forestall a lot of problems. For example, the location of toilets and eating facilities are primary.

When the trip has been completed and the class gathers to review the efficacy of decisions made during the verifying step, the stage is set to elicit the rule or principle (the "whenever I need to. . ." generalization) that will enable them to independently assess the rationale for singling out the "best" option available.

The teaching script and the teacher's judgment as to the readiness of students to engage in this difficult and abstract task should help the teacher manage this complex activity. The curriculum should alert teachers to as many observable variables as possible. In implementing the activity, however, it is likely to be the teacher's observations of children's aptitudes for the kind of inductive reasoning that guide the development of generalizations.

Teacher authoring skills in combination with the capability of the computer to locate cross-referenced concepts and facts are helpful when designing reinforcing activities to enhance students' readiness to engage in the construction of generalizations. The chat rooms provided on the curriculum's Web site could be a resource for teachers who want to know their colleagues' thoughts on their plans or who need help in implementing the instruction.

The Underpinning of Instruction

Confusing the foregoing instructional activity with the conventional teaching unit often implemented in self-contained classes for students with mild disabilities would be a mistake. It is better visualized as one in a long series of instructional experiences with its source in the activities category of the cultural response model (Figure 5.1) and its position in the curriculum just prior to or early in the children's study of the home environment in the curriculum development model (Figure 6.1).

The synergy of content and social learning specialists leads to the development of curriculum elements that enable children with mild disabilities to bring the necessary language, literacy, and quantitative skills and proficiencies to their involvement in solving problems. In other words, instead of learning their academic skills and proficiencies as discrete elements of knowledge with the hope that they will be meaningful some day, academic and other skills and proficiencies relevant to the problem's resolution are prepared and taught early in their schooling. Thus, they are a part of the students' established knowledge bank and relevant to their participation in the class's problem-solving activities and, in particular, to their understanding of scheduling and the implications of distance, time, cost, and other concepts on travel plans.

Similarly, evaluation specialists can devise instrumentation and procedures for capturing and classifying students' performance data that are then made available to teachers in ways that facilitate decision making on the content to be taught and the most efficacious way of imparting it to students. This type of curriculum-based evaluation of student performance leads to ways of grouping students so that the best instructional focus can be realized. At the same time, the efficacy of grouping or placement decisions can be measured continuously, making it likely that the outcomes of the formation of instructional groups and the placement of individual students will be reviewed frequently and thereby reducing the probability that they will become static.

In summary, if a computer-based, synergistic curriculum for students with mild disabilities is to be teacher friendly, curriculum developers need to capitalize on the speed and flexibility of computers by organizing the content of instruction in as many ways as are needed to maximize the effectiveness of instruction. The content of a computer-based curriculum need not be limited to the customary scope and sequence that typifies the conventional, paper-and-ink curriculum. Categories for content areas should have three properties. First, they should appear as part of the instructional sequence, as illustrated in the teaching scripts earlier. That is, the arithmetic skills needed to deal with time and distance in the activity designed to meet the objective of using public transportation should be integrated with the literacy, social learning, and other related aspects of the activity.

Second, it should be possible to separate out each content area from the total curriculum so that teachers can see its developmental sequence, from beginning to end, independently of other content areas. For example, the flexibility of the computer offers curriculum developers a number of options for displaying arithmetic content. Skills can be laid out in a developmental sequence, or they can be associated with the proficiencies they support. This enables the teacher to look back or ahead in the curriculum to verify the relevance of their immediate decisions.

Finally, all concepts important to the attainment of instructional objectives need to be cross-referenced across content areas. This is a particularly important aspect of a curriculum for students with mild disabilities because it gives teachers a variety of settings for teaching and reinforcing any concept that needs repetition. Furthermore, this "library" of concepts is an important resource for teachers who wish to author instructional activities to augment the curriculum.

Validating the Curriculum

A curriculum's validity can be substantiated only in representative educational settings. The first version of a curriculum is, at best, a carefully crafted but tentative estimate by the development staff of what the appropriate content of instruction should be. The refinement and transformation of the first version into its final form depends almost entirely on the reactions of teachers in the course of its implementation, the reports of their experiences, and their recommendations for improvement.

Field Testing

Field testing the curriculum is the pivotal enterprise in the total development effort. On one hand, it is the proving ground for all of the work accomplished by the development team. On the other hand, it closes the gap between the abstractions of academe and the actualities of teacher–student interactions and the culture of the school. In closing this gap, field testing can be the medium for transmitting the understanding and appreciation of everyone involved.

Criteria for Field-Test Sites
Field testing a synergistic, computer-based curriculum is a complex process because many variables must be accounted for. Although slight variations can occur in the number of children in classrooms, the length of the school day, and the amount of technological support, very little leeway is allowed in the representativeness of field-test sites and in the availability of computers in field-test educational settings.

If the curriculum is to have relevance for students in urban, suburban, and rural communities that may range from very poor to very wealthy, it must prove its teachability and effectiveness in the course of field testing in classes and educational programs that comprise a cross section of educational programs for students with disabilities throughout the country. Similarly, if teachers are to capitalize on the fact that the curriculum is based in a computer program, they must have a computer in their classrooms.

To achieve representativeness, field-test sites need to be recruited in typical demographic areas with attention given to the ways that the programs are organized. With cost effectiveness in mind, it is advisable to target sites as close to the development scene as possible. This simplifies the logistics of maintaining contact with them. Experience has made it very clear that teachers and other professionals in field-test sites need a lot of immediate help and continuing support in a novel enterprise such as this.

Support for Teachers in Field-Test Sites

Field testing in special education settings is almost always a new experience for curriculum developers as well as most teachers and public school administrators. It is likely, then, that some unanticipated problems will arise even though teachers have been instructed in strategies for implementing the curriculum. Realistically, teachers cannot put their class on hold while they wait for a solution to a problem. Early curriculum development projects found that teachers who are kept waiting for a solution are likely to withdraw from the field-test plan and return to their usual instructional program.

Being able to contact the development staff by e-mail and having access to updated listings of frequently asked questions (FAQs) on the curriculum's Web site can be helpful, provided that the teachers know that they need help, can express their problem, and are seeking a solution to a common problem. The development project's administrator, who is coordinating the field-test settings at the field-test site, should be aware of the kinds of problems that could confront teachers and be able to help them identify and express their needs. If a teacher's problem is unique, immediate telephone contact with a knowledgeable professional on the development staff is necessary.

Evaluating the Curriculum in Field-Test Sites

Teachers who are field testing the curriculum are the source of data that enable development staff to establish the validity and reliability of the data-gathering instruments and to elicit teachers' assessment of the curriculum's relevance and teachability. These data are the basis for revising and refining the field-tested curriculum and, ultimately, for converting it into a final version that can be disseminated to educational settings for students with mild disabilities. (For an example of a detailed field-test model and its implementation, see M.T. Goldstein, 1976, 1979, 1981.)

Some important questions need to be answered before the validity of the curriculum can be ascertained. These include questions concerning:

1. the teachability of the curriculum,
2. the relevance of the content of instruction to the maturational needs of students with mild disabilities,
3. the concordance of the content with students' learning characteristics,
4. the efficacy of the teaching aids and other instructional supports,
5. the reliability of the evaluation instruments used to ascertain the efficacy of the teaching aids, technologies, and students' progress, and
6. how clearly suggestions and instructions to teachers are communicated.

Experience indicates that the design of methods for collecting data to answer these questions needs to be a collaborative effort on the part of development and evaluation personnel. Development personnel must specify to their evaluation colleagues the kinds of information that are helpful so that the evaluation questions can be framed in ways that make responses relevant. Evaluation staff must follow the conventions of test construction to ensure that the results obtained from teachers are valid, reliable, and useful (Bepko, 1981).

Also, evaluation staff need to resist the inclination to collect as much data as they can. Experience has shown that teachers who are field testing a new curriculum can be overwhelmed by long and complex questionnaires, checklists, and rating scales that are overly time-consuming. Questions should be clear and precise so that teachers do not have to interpret the intent of questions. The challenge to the evaluation staff is to devise a lean and parsimonious evaluation procedure that elicits important information without being burdensome to teachers. There should also be a procedure in place for immediately communicating results of the evaluation to the appropriate development staff as well as a feedback system for teachers.

The fact that the proposed curriculum is essentially a computer program facilitates the field-test and evaluation stages. Unlike the communication methods used in field-test procedures for conventional curricula, such as the mail and telephones, communication between field-test teachers and the evaluation staff for a computer-based curriculum can be accomplished on a real-time basis through e-mail and the curriculum's Web site. Teachers can transmit data (collected by their computers) directly to the evaluation group over the Internet. This not only saves time, but also eliminates the substantial postage, paper, and printing costs entailed in supplying field-test teachers with the printed curriculum, evaluation materials, and correspondence.

The Role of Computer Experts

The computer experts on the proposed curriculum's development team must be involved in the project planning from the onset. They need to guide all of the production efforts, the writing of instructional materials, the design and preparation of teaching aids, and the construction of evaluation procedures and instruments. Furthermore, they need to set up the curriculum's Web site, debug its inevitable problems, and modify and improve its role as a conduit to and from field-test sites and, ultimately, wherever the curriculum is implemented.

Preparing Teachers to Field Test the Curriculum

Preparing teachers to implement the curriculum is the keystone of successful field testing. Experience has shown that the success of field testing depends almost entirely on the willingness of the teachers to set aside whatever instructional content they have been using, with all the familiarity and security that it entails, to replace it with an entirely technologically novel curriculum, and to commit themselves to the additional work that daily evaluation and reporting creates. To this end, the development staff is well advised to provide the teachers and their supervisors with (a) intensive in-service training and (b) a full-time coordinator who can also act as the link between teachers and the development, evaluation, and computer experts.

In-Service Preparation of Field-Test Teachers

Only rarely do special education teacher preparation programs, undergraduate or graduate, offer their students more than a one-semester course in curriculum and methods of instruction for students with mild disabilities. This suggests that special education faculty in institutions of higher education (IHEs) and administrators in public schools presume that if instructional materials are made available to teachers, they will somehow discover the principles underlying the development of the content and implement the materials as the developers intended. However, this is not the case. Teachers of students with mild disabilities are no different from general education teachers. Without thorough preparation to apply instructional materials, it is almost certain that their implementation will fall short of intended outcomes. Equally important, experience shows that instructional materials that do not meet teachers' expectations or are difficult to implement are quickly shelved.

Given the complexity of the proposed curriculum, its evaluation process, and the novelty of its computerization, conventional after-school and weekend in-service training sessions cannot provide adequate preparation for its implementation. The curriculum developers need to have the undivided attention of the teachers and adequate time to prepare them to implement the new curriculum. Similarly, they need the time and attention of the administrative personnel who will supervise and coordinate the teachers' implementation of the curriculum.

Considering the in-service preparation of teachers and supervisors as the equivalent of a graduate course in curriculum and methods is a worthwhile endeavor. In fact, the establishment of regional in-service summer sessions for teachers and their supervisors is suggested. The first of these should immediately precede the first field-test semester. Subsequently, summer seminars can be offered as the field testing continues into succeeding semesters.

Preparing field-test teachers over the summer provides time for the computer specialists to program their classroom computers, install the curriculum, enter the necessary student data, establish networks, and debug the classroom end of the curriculum program. When teachers return to their classrooms, it is important that they be able to manage all of the usual school start-up activities without being distracted by malfunctions in the curriculum process.

Coordination of Field-Test Sites

No matter how effective the summer preparation of teachers and their supervisors is, many will start the fall semester with feelings of insecurity. For teachers, implementing the field-test version of the curriculum means setting aside all of their familiar teaching activities and engaging in new instructional content and, in some cases, new teaching methods. Knowing that there is a contact person at the curriculum's source (the field-test coordinator, whose sole mission is to be responsive to their needs) can reduce their anxiety considerably. The coordinator must participate in the recruitment of teachers and in their preparation to implement the curriculum.

When field-test teachers need help, it is important that they get it immediately. It is possible that on the first day of field testing, problems that could not be anticipated will arise. Teachers cannot put their classroom activities on hold while a response to their call for help is pending. If they do not get a rapid response, most will discontinue the field testing and revert to their original program as a matter of survival. Thus, establishing a simple and rapid system of communication between the development center and the teachers and their supervisors well before field testing commences is crucial to the success of field testing. Teachers and supervisors should have one telephone number to call and one e-mail address as their links to the development center. Logically, the person at that contact point should be the coordinator of field testing who can direct the teacher's problem to the appropriate member of the development team. It is very important for the coordinator to collect as much information as possible about each of the field-test sites and to establish a protected database. Teacher and student information that is important to the curriculum development and the evaluation effort should be encrypted to ensure confidentiality. These data can also be provided selectively to researchers who wish to use the data in their research. This is, of course, a sensitive area and must be managed carefully. LEAs participating in the field test and the students' parents should be confident that information about their school personnel and students is totally secure.

In summary, field testing is the curriculum's first step toward generalization to schools at large. In many ways, it is analogous to the clinical testing of pharmaceutical products whose manufacturers are seeking approval by the FDA. If, after a thorough effort, most teachers conclude that the curriculum cannot be implemented effectively, the likelihood that there will be further steps is very remote. The key to success, then, is in the development of a curriculum for students with mild disabilities and their nonclassified counterparts whose content is relevant to their attainment of the goals of education and is, at the same time, teachable.

Conclusion

The development of a synergistic curriculum is a complex undertaking with many challenges. The curriculum's development should be accomplished by a team of content specialists, social learning experts, and technical support staff all working in ways that respect their areas of expertise yet remain flexible to creative approaches and nontraditional visions. The curriculum developers need to relieve teachers of as many tasks subordinate to teaching as they can and provide materials that support and enhance instruction. At the same time, teachers must have the flexibility to select and order the instructional activities to conform to their students' aptitudes. This synergy of content and social learning specialists leads to the development of the curriculum elements that enable children to bring language, literacy, and quantitative skills and proficiencies to the task of solving problems.

The synergistic curriculum should be computer based and should take advantage of the speed and flexibility of computers by organizing the content of instruction in as many ways as are necessary to maximize the effectiveness of the instruction. Categories of content should be available as parts of the teaching sequence, as content areas separated from the total curriculum, and as materials that are cross-referenced across content areas.

Evaluation specialists should devise instrumentation and procedures for capturing and classifying students' performance data, which are then made available to teachers in ways that facilitate decision making about the content to be taught and the most efficacious way of imparting it to students. This type of curriculum-based evaluation of student performance leads to ways of grouping students so that the best instructional focus can be realized.

The curriculum's validity must be substantiated in representative educational settings through a system of field testing that adequately supports the teachers and leads to evaluation data that are valid, reliable, and useful. With the successful coordination of these efforts, the results will be a synergistic curriculum that is relevant to the educational needs of students with mild disabilities and their nonclassified counterparts.

Subsequent Steps

The focus of this book has been the invention of educational programs for students with mild learning disabilities and their unclassified counterparts in general education and, toward this end, the procedures for the development of a synergistic curriculum to serve as the foundation for these programs. However, when the curriculum becomes available, the only educators who will be competent to implement it will be the teachers, administrators, and support staff whose in-service preparation to implement the curriculum preceded their participation in the field testing and who profited from their experiences in the course of field testing.

There is no reason to believe that while the proposed curriculum is being field tested, there will be changes in the conventional professional preparation of teachers, administrators, and support staff going on in institutions of higher learning that will make teachers and other education professionals who did not participate in the field testing as competent to implement the proposed, technologically complex curriculum as those who did. This could result in a paradox: the availability of a valid and reliable curriculum for students who are at risk for a difficult transition from school to adult society that cannot be implemented because educators are unable to apply it.

Because these educators will establish criteria and procedures for selecting the students for whom the curriculum is designed, imparting to them the body of knowledge the curriculum represents and evaluating the effects of their decisions and actions, steps need to be taken to ensure that the curriculum will play an effective role in their professional preparation. Accordingly, teacher preparation programs, the professional preparation of administrators, research goals, the student body, and transition programs must be reinvented.

Reinventing Teacher Preparation Programs

The present framework for the professional preparation of teachers—pre-service for undergraduates and in-service for experienced teachers—will accommodate most of the changes in substance and practice that the effective implementation of the curriculum will require. Major changes will be required in the content of courses and seminars. Practicums will have to be designed to capitalize on the experiences reported by teachers, administrators, and support staff who participated in field testing the curriculum.

The proposed curriculum will open new directions for research and evaluation, as will procedures for identifying the students to whom the curriculum is best suited. As students fulfill their experiences with the curriculum, new methods for facilitating their transition from school to adult society will need to be designed.

Pre-Service Teacher Preparation

It is important to engage prospective teachers of students with disabilities in pre-service professional preparation that meets current certification or licensing requirements but that goes beyond conventional coursework to include knowledge and skills important to the implementation and evaluation of the proposed curriculum. Their professional preparation program should have, as a conceptual base, the role of education as a social institution and how it goes about fulfilling society's expectation that students will become productive and participating adults. This will provide teachers with a frame of reference for making decisions about the education and classroom management of their students that will take into account both the immediate and the long-term goals of education—achievement in academic and other learning content in the school and the successes that lead to autonomy in their adult careers.

Thus, when confronted with alternatives in educational practices, teachers who understand the role of education in society and their part in attaining education's goals will use as a criterion for accepting or rejecting instructional alternatives the extent to which the outcomes of each decision facilitates the achievement of these goals. Developing in teachers an understanding of education's philosophic and conceptual basis increases the likelihood that they will emerge from their professional preparation more a teacher, in a pedagogic sense, than a technician.

Teachers need to become thoroughly grounded in the curriculum, its structure, and how variations on curricular themes make it possible for schools' to respond to a diverse student population. They also need extensive instruction in the management of a computer in instructional settings, including experiences with the computer-based curriculum and the technology that makes its implementation effective. Their practicum experiences should include the implementation of the proposed curriculum and the assessment of its outcomes.

It would be a mistake to delay work on restructuring the teacher preparation program until the proposed curriculum is completed. Field testing the newly developed curriculum should begin with the development of the first complete instructional package designed to attain the first set of teaching–learning objectives. Because curriculum development is an ongoing effort, by the time this package, with all of its teaching aids and evaluation procedures, has passed through the field-test teachers' in-service training period and reached implementation, the development staff will be well along the road of preparing materials for succeeding learning objectives.

Shortly after the first instructional package is activated, the cycling of field-tested materials will begin as data that reflect teachers' and students' experiences are analyzed and reported as feedback to the development staff. The development staff will use this information to refine and modify its work. While this process continues, faculty in the various professional preparation programs in institutions of higher education (IHEs) can plan the training that would-be teachers need to acquire the competencies required to provide an appropriate education for students with mild disabilities and their counterparts presently in general education.

In-Service Teacher Preparation

Teachers of students with mild disabilities who have completed their professional preparation will need extensive in-service training to become competent implementers of the curriculum. Beyond becoming thoroughly familiar with the curriculum's content, these teachers will need to master the strategies for working with a computer-based curriculum as well as the new techniques that computers offer them for capitalizing on their own creativity. Many teachers will have had experiences that can be converted into content formulations and instructional strategies to enrich the curriculum.

The conditions of in-service preparation need to be consistent with its goals. The time devoted to teacher preparation needs to be sufficient to accommodate teachers' learning and practice. It should be scheduled so that conflicts with daily commitments are held to a minimum. This effectively rules out the conventional three-hour after-school sessions and intensive weekend seminars.

There is a precedent in the professional preparation of teachers that can serve as an alternative to conventional, relatively short-term in-service training. Schools and IHEs can collaborate by cosponsoring summer programs for teachers, their support staff, administrators, and technical staff that focus on the knowledge and skills required for effective implementation of the proposed curriculum. Because of their relevance to pedagogy, these programs could be offered as graduate study.

The Role of Colleges and Universities

The structure and content of reinvented pre-service and in-service teacher preparation programs is the province of the appropriate faculties in IHEs. The teacher education faculty participating in the development of the curriculum are the logical people to activate this process. One way to accomplish this is to recruit faculty members who are offering the curriculum course in their own and other IHEs. The recruitment of faculty members in other IHEs can be facilitated by having a member of the development team provide the necessary instruction as an adjunct to the general education faculty. In this way, participants in teacher preparation programs will get the instruction they need under the tutelage of faculty that are experts in the theoretical and practical aspects of curriculum and in the role of the computer as the key element of the system that imparts the curriculum.

The supervised pre-teaching experiences in educational settings for teachers engaged in pre-service preparation will provide them with the practice they need to become competent professionals and will serve as a transition from the theoretical and didactic college setting to the practical classroom environment. Teachers, administrators, and support staff receiving in-service training will be able to introduce the curriculum in their classrooms with the help of the IHE faculty providing the instruction.

Reinventing the Professional Preparation of Administrators

Earlier, the role of special education administrators described during the field-test phase of the social learning curriculum was marginal. When confronted with the decision about whether to have teachers of children with disabilities adopt and implement the field-test version of the curriculum, the large majority abdicated their authority to accept or reject the curriculum by leaving the decision to their teachers.

The most frequently voiced reason for their indecision was their conviction that their teachers knew better than anyone else what their needs were and would therefore be better able to make the decision. The fact that they were managing by the consensus of the managed escaped them. Fortunately for the curriculum development staff, teachers who believed that they and their students would stand to gain more by participating in the field testing outnumbered their more disinclined colleagues.

Who made the decision to participate did not matter to the field-test and evaluation staff as long as there were enough students with mild disabilities and teachers involved to ensure a reliable test of the curriculum's teachability. Within the larger context of special education, however, the fact that administrators could not make a key decision about the curriculum for students with mild disabilities suggests that, unlike their counterparts in general education, special education administrators did not assign curriculum a high priority in educational programs for these students. Equally important, their inability to make the decision to accept or reject the novel curriculum perpetuated a leadership void that assured that curriculum would never attain the role in their special education program that it does in all other viable educational enterprises.

Priorities in the Professional Preparation of Administrators

Professional preparation programs for administrators should provide administrators with a thorough understanding of the role of education in society as a context for their leadership. Their commitment to the goals of education will serve as a basis for the implementation of the policies and decisions that ensure that their students acquire the knowledge and behaviors that will prepare them for productive and participatory citizenship.

A thorough understanding by administrators of education's role will lead to a realization of their role in school operations. That is, knowing that society expects the schools to provide students with both general and specific knowledge important to citizenship should make administrators aware of the critical role that they play in the education of students with mild disabilities. It will become clear that educational leadership requires them, not teachers or others, to be the ones (a) to oversee and validate the selection the curriculum and (b) to provide the personnel, practices, and places that will make the implementation of the curriculum productive and cost effective.

Their decisions about curriculum and instructional procedures will necessarily take into account the fact that the schooling of students with mild disabilities takes place during a fixed number of school years—a time span that makes little or no concession to their learning characteristics.

Furthermore, students with mild disabilities, like all students, have a one-time opportunity to capitalize on schooling—an opportunity that has no provisions for replacing learning time lost because of administrative and instructional decisions that do not contribute to the attainment of the goals of education. Decisions that take curriculum into account will provide a much-needed consistency in the substance and process in the schooling of students with mild disabilities.

The professional preparation of administrators should equip them with the knowledge and skills that will enable them to provide the leadership that these programs require. While mastery of school law, fiscal management, and personnel practices are important, they are nevertheless a means to the end of the school fulfilling its commitment to society. Teachers and their support staff expect their administrators to explicate the goals of their program; provide them with the curriculum that is consistent with the goals; supervise, evaluate, and coordinate their activities; and provide them with the facilities and materials that expedite their contribution.

The implementation of the proposed curriculum will challenge administrators' leadership ability. Their orchestration of the contributions that result from the professional staff's efforts will range from the selection and assignment of students to their pedagogy and on to a continuing assessment of the outcomes of the program. Administrators' commitment to the goals of education, the configuration of an appropriate education, and their knowledge of curriculum and the technology that supports its implementation will be the glue that holds their programs together.

Reinventing Research Goals

The development of one or more prototypes of a computer-based, synergistic, social adaptive curriculum will require trial and error in almost every aspect of the development process, from initial design to summative evaluation. In order to arrive at that point in the development of curriculum at which reliable, data-based knowledge will minimize speculation and trial and error while maximizing productivity and cost effectiveness, we must engage in research that will lead to knowledge about a sizable and diverse array of factors and conditions important to the development process.

This is an area of research hitherto neglected in education but of great importance in industry and commerce, where competition and stockholders demand growth and cost effectiveness. Because curriculum development is both labor intensive and reliant on a broad spectrum of production equipment, the most effective deployment of staff and facilities are important, researchable issues.

Research on the Interactivity of Teachers, Technology, and Students

Curriculum that is in electronic form rather than printed opens a broad and detailed area of research in the interactive roles of teachers, computers, and students in the educational technology setting and particularly in teachers' use of computers in the management and assessment of learning. We need to learn how to bring students, teachers, administrators, parents, and ancillary staff into the most productive interactions with the curriculum.

There will be questions about the hardware and software required for effective deployment of computers and related technologies such as interactive TV and the many computer peripherals. There will also be innovations in all aspects of curriculum development, implementation, and evaluation that will sustain research and demonstration projects as dynamic aspects of the total process.

Research on the Identification of Students to Participate in the Curriculum

Ranking high among the challenges to researchers will be the establishment of educationally relevant ways for bringing a diverse array of students into conjunction with the proposed curriculum. Conventional procedures for the classification of students with mild disabilities suggest that it would be pure sophistry to argue for limiting participation in the proposed curriculum to children who can demonstrate that their learning problems and behavior disorders are the basis for their maladaptive behavior. The results of studies of the efficacy of preschool programs for at-risk children and those in Head Start programs justify making the curriculum available to all children whose performance and experiences indicate the probability of their social–occupational inadequacy on the way to and at maturity.

Research on Alternative Programs

Once there is an available curriculum that is responsive to the educational needs of children whose social adaptability is presently or predictably substandard for whatever the reason, the challenge to the entire educational establishment will be to design instructional environments that are responsive to students' long-term developmental needs and, at the same time, sensitive and responsive to changes in their instructional requirements.

The capacity to identify change in students' rates and levels of achievement quickly and accurately and to accommodate them in settings that are more in harmony with their aptitudes will be an important element in such programs. Instead of resorting to trial and error, as in the past, it will be important to study the effectiveness of as many educationally appropriate alternatives as the diversities in the experiences and learning characteristics of children require.

The proposed curriculum allows for alterations in educational programs for children and youth that are free of the constraints and conventions imposed by the medical model. The nature and number of these alterations will be limited only by the creativity and insight of educators and their colleagues and by the accountability that accompanies the common-sense considerations of immediate and long-term cost effectiveness. With an educational model in place and a curriculum whose goals and objectives are clearly stated, we will be able to strike a rational balance between the intrinsic and the extrinsic values of schooling.

In particular, the focal point for decisions and actions of professionals and parents will be the conviction that everything children learn and do in school is a means to the end of their acquiring those social, physical, and psychological skills and proficiencies that lead to a quality of life consistent with constructive, productive, and participatory citizenship as children, youth, and adults. This concept of schooling applies as much to the education of children with disabilities and other at-risk children and youth as it does to their general education counterparts.

Research on the Effectiveness of Educational Programs

Research on the effectiveness of educational programs for students with disabilities has been limited to occasional follow-up studies of school-leavers. These studies compare the employment rate of adults with disabilities with the rate for the population as a whole. Some studies look for data on the quality of life as well. Other studies make note of the reported causes for failure to get or hold a job.

Unfortunately, the conventional research design of follow-up studies has confounded efforts to collect useful data. A meta-analysis of the data is out of the question because all that the studies had in common were the actuarial data used to describe school-leavers, typically IQs, age, and gender. Some studies included academic achievement test scores. Critical variables such as the content of their instruction and family and community demographics were not reported.

With the curriculum in place and curriculum-based assessment an integral part of schooling, data on students' performance in all aspects of their school experiences can be collected and stored. In years subsequent to graduation, their data will serve as a basis for comparing their school performance with their accomplishment as adults. In fact, with the computer-based curriculum as a frame of reference, school districts will be able to track students continuously and report their performance in the community in ways that will be helpful to curriculum developers, teachers, work placement services, and advocacy organizations. For the first time, educators will be able to respond with reliable data to charges that educational programs for students with mild disabilities are both overly expensive and ineffective.

Finally, if and when most of what needs to be researched and developed begins to materialize, we will be able, for the first time, to provide all children with an appropriate education. In the process, we will have obliterated some unnecessary and often onerous distinctions between children. There will no longer be a requirement to distinguish children on the basis of central nervous system deficits or disabilities.

Reinventing the Student Body

A paradox in special education nomenclature is becoming increasingly evident in the literature. While compliance with IDEA requires that differentiations be made between students with mild mental retardation, behavior disorders, and learning disabilities, researchers are acknowledging that these distinctions are, if not irrelevant, so limiting as to obscure important areas for research. In fact, the National Institute on Disability and Rehabilitation Research (NIDRR) in the U.S. Department of Education's Office of Special Education and Rehabilitation Services acknowledges this in its recent policy statement on research strategies for the future, which can be found at www.ncddr.org.

The policy, designed to guide research, discusses disability as an outcome of the interaction between individuals' characteristics—their conditions or impairments, functional capabilities, or personal and social qualities—and the characteristics of their natural, contrived, cultural, and social environments. That is, disability falls somewhere between enablement and disablement. Within this context, personal characteristics as well as the nature of the environment may be enabling or disabling, with the relative degree of disability often determined by conditions, time, and setting.

This concept of disability replaces the view of disability given in NIDRR's prior policy—that it is limited to medical conditions. This view portrayed disability as the result of a deficit in an individual that prevented the individual from performing certain functions or activities. As discussed earlier, this concept of disability is subscribed to in special education when categories of

175

students with disabilities are based on the severity of deficits associated with central nervous system disorders or physical defects or both. NIDRR states that the way that it now defines disability changes ways in which research is conducted.

Upgrading the Definition of Disability

It is worth noting that research with students with disabilities that is conforming, at least in part, with NIDRR's concept of disability is appearing in the literature (Gresham & MacMillan, 1997). While these studies are limited to students with mild disabilities currently in special education, they do not invoke the distinctions between students except by variables in the data analysis. This is also true in school-based enterprises such as occupational education and transition programs in which students with mild disabilities are provided with instruction and services independently of their categories.

Having already taken this progressive step, educators will have completed the first stage for reinventing the constituency of the student body when they adopt NIDRR's concept of disability and the array of students that the concept embraces—students whose functional status, social and personal qualities, and social environments require their participation in the proposed curriculum.

Presently, the locus of the reinvention of educational programs for students with mild disabilities is mainly in IHEs. When the time comes to make decisions about which members of the student body should participate in the proposed curriculum, the scene will shift to the schools. Unlike the reinvention of professional preparation programs, in which augmentation to and alteration of some existing courses are needed, identifying the students who need the curriculum, designing instructional settings that will ensure the most pedagogically relevant concentration of students, and devising a system for assigning students to these locations means abandoning old and familiar practices and designing new and appropriate ones. This will be necessary because, with few exceptions, the instrumentation and procedures designed to identify and classify students according to the severity of their central nervous system disorders have almost no relevance to an educationally oriented, curriculum-based program.

If there is any doubt as to the qualifications of these students to participate in the proposed curriculum, we need only recall the studies of adolescents in juvenile detention discussed earlier. It is difficult to find a better example of maladaptive behavior than that which leads to arrest, adjudication, and confinement in a juvenile corrections institution. As mentioned, a study of the juvenile corrections population reported that 70% had been diagnosed as youth with mild mental retardation, behavior disorders, or learning disorders. This left 30% undiagnosed and excluded from special education even though they shared intellectual characteristics similar to those of students with learning disabilities and many of the behavioral characteristics of students classified as having emotional disorders.

This is too large a proportion of a burgeoning population in corrections institutions to be ignored. It could be argued that the issue is immaterial because special education would most likely have no more impact on the unclassified students than it did on those who were classified. This claim remains pure speculation until students with disabilities are provided with an appropriate education and the outcomes are evaluated.

Criteria for Restructuring the Student Body

Designing a screening and assignment process requires that two factors be taken into account: students' learning needs and learning characteristics. The goal should be to bring about a teachable homogeneity by grouping students who are similar in their achievement in the curriculum as well as in their learning characteristics and, particularly, their rate of learning. This is contrary to the present emphasis in special education on individualized instruction, which makes for a tutorial atmosphere—one that limits the interactions of groups of students in instructional enterprises and the social learning experiences that enrich them.

The fact is, the development of a system for identifying students who could benefit from the curriculum should start early in the total curriculum development process. The strategies for doing so are well established in the measurement literature and easily converted to computer applications. An early start in the field-test process will facilitate the identification of students' statuses and roles in their school and family settings and will provide measurement staff with a stable student population that will facilitate long-term study. An early start will also provide measurement and computer staff with time to refine their instrumentation and to begin establishing the validity and reliability that will encourage their use when the curriculum becomes available.

Strategies for Assigning Students to Educational Settings

From the teacher's perspective, it will be important to have screening and placement data available in the computer in a teacher-friendly configuration. Students must be evaluated periodically so that teachers can assess students' progress as it reflects the effectiveness of their decisions and instructional methods. It is predictable that teachers will report some students' learning characteristics, and therefore their rate of learning, as changing over time as a function of their maturation and their educational experiences. Accordingly, administrators coordinating the program will need to consider a change in the placement of some students in order to maintain the most effective levels of homogeneity.

The policies for the placement of students cannot emerge until the instrumentation and procedures for screening and assigning students and the necessary computer formulations have been established as valid and reliable. These policies must include the configuration of educational settings. Schools are not limited to present procedures. Certainly, the conventional concept of the special education class as a locus of instruction will have lost its meaning. There are no special classes in other elements of public school education, nor are there hierarchies of importance. Vocational-technical programs are as valued as college prep. The transfer of students from one program to the other is seen as a lateral change in status. Accordingly, the educational program based on a comprehensive, synergistic, socially oriented curriculum should take its place alongside existing programs as their peer.

Outcomes of Reinvented Programs

It is axiomatic that the extent to which advocacy organizations and agencies are successful is determined, in great part, by the aptitudes of those whom they serve. That is, an agency or organization may have superior counseling and placement services and a roster of ideal, available work placement settings, but if its clientele has only marginal personal, social, and occupational abilities, odds are that descriptors such as excellent and superior will rarely appear, if at all, in the agencies' annual reports of the outcomes of their advocacy. This helps to account for the disparity between the huge costs and the limited outcomes of the many and varied transition programs designed to facilitate the passage of students with disabilities from school to adult society. It also helps to account for the limited impact of self-advocacy and self-determination programs.

The Need for Relevant Educational Programs

Despite their participation in secondary school occupational preparation programs, the majority of school-leavers with mild disabilities are unsuccessful in getting and retaining jobs even when they are provided with on-the-job support and guidance. It is becoming evident that secondary school programs designed to inculcate in these students the ability to represent themselves and express their preferences in decisions that are important to their quality of life are restricted to a small proportion of eligible students. The reason for the limited results gained by these programs can be traced directly to the fact that individuals with mild disabilities do not come to decision-making situations at work and in social-personal life situations with the necessary repertoire of knowledge and skills.

There is speculation that life conditions in industrial societies have reached such a state that the demands of the available jobs and the procedures and technologies for managing one's personal affairs are beyond the aptitudes of all but a few individuals with mild disabilities. This is based on the unwarranted presumption that these people come to work and decision-making scenes as well educated and prepared as they can be.

If educators and advocates become convinced that there is no longer a place for people with mild disabilities in our increasingly technological, global economy, the large majority will never realize their potential to act on the knowledge and skills they would acquire if their education were as effective as that of their nondisabled counterparts. The reinvention of educational programs for students with mild disabilities and for their counterparts in general education who share their need for a comprehensive, social adaptive curriculum will provide an alternative to present practices and opinions. By engaging students in a comprehensive curriculum that spans their public school years, the dissociation between their academically oriented elementary school years and the occupational education emphasis in their secondary school experiences will be resolved. The synergy of the proposed curriculum will bring academic and social learning together into a functional, teachable whole.

179

Conclusion

The goal of reinventing educational programs for students with mild disabilities is to provide them with the knowledge and skills to speak convincingly for themselves and to play a leading role in determining the nature and quality of their lives. For those who cannot achieve the autonomies that accompany remunerative work, there will be the opportunity to acquire the knowledge and skills that will enable them to contribute to society in other ways. Some may participate in projects designed and supported by local, regional, state, and federal government agencies. Whatever they choose to do, they can live with dignity, responsibility, and self-respect as citizens with the competencies to participate, if they so choose, in community affairs and activities.

There is irony in the fact that some of the technologies that presently militate against their successful employment can play an important role in their education. By making the curriculum, curriculum profiles, and evaluation procedures available in electronic form, teachers will be able to manage every aspect of their programs quickly and efficiently. The student's computer can become an effective instructional medium by way of computer-managed and computer-assisted instruction. While computer-managed instruction must await the installation of a comprehensive curriculum, computer-assisted instruction has already proven its value as an instructional tool. Furthermore, the access that the computer provides to the curriculum's Web site and to colleagues worldwide can lead to the enrichment of teachers' instructional and other educational experiences.

Challenges

It is ironic that P.L. 94-142, the legislation that was welcomed as the bill of rights for students with disabilities, will likely be the largest obstacle to be overcome if curricula that are foundations for an appropriate education are to be implemented in our schools. This legislation is an excellent example of the workings of the law of unintended consequences. P.L. 94-142 was successful in opening the public schools to all children and in providing order and regulation to special education. Unfortunately, it also enshrined and crystallized the medical model and, in particular, the rules for classifying students for educational purposes. These outcomes were perpetuated by IDEA.

Amending IDEA or replacing it with legislation that will ensure students an appropriate education free of demeaning and irrelevant labels will be a prodigious feat. Yet there are many precedents for the repeal of legislation that has not fulfilled its intentions or has outlived its usefulness. Beyond legislative action, there is a history of the successful implementation of innovative and experimental educational practices that were not included in enabling legislation but were nevertheless considered important enough to merit a waiver of restrictions.

Before becoming overwhelmed by the magnitude of the work entailed in installing the proposed curriculum, there is the matter of bringing it to life and, as an outcome, reinventing the lives of students with mild disabilities and their unclassified counterparts. For the vast majority of non-disabled students, schooling is a jumping-off point for entry to the adult world—directly into the world of work in occupations of their choice or into additional education and careers of their choice. The most important outcome of their education is the wherewithal to make choices from the options available to them.

To students with mild disabilities and their unclassified counterparts, schooling is more than a jumping-off point. It is the foundation of a productive and dignified life. For many, the choices are limited. Regardless of their abilities in self-advocacy and self-determination, even the most knowledgeable and skilled students may be limited in their career options and in the quality of life that they can achieve. These differences in educational outcomes underscore how critical the role of an appropriate education is in the lives of these students.

Undoing the results of a century of inappropriate educational practices for students with mild disabilities will take time and effort. For those who are overwhelmed by the work and time entailed, an old anecdote may hold a message. A septuagenarian returned from a shopping trip to a nursery with a number of plants and shrubs, which he handed to his gardener. Pointing to an attractive plant, the gardener remarked, "But sir, this variety blooms only once every hundred years." "That being the case," said the old gentleman, "let's not lose any time planting it."

References

Alexander, K. L., Entwistle, D. R., & Kabbani, N. (2001). The dropout process in life course perspective: Early risk factors at home and school. *Teachers College Record, 103(5)*, 760–822.

Alpers, T. G. (1978). *Individual Education Plans: How Well Do They Work?* Hayward: California State University, Department of Educational Psychology.

Barr, M. W. (1904). *Mental Defective: Their History, Treatment, and Training.* Philadelphia: Blakeston's Son and Co.

Bennett, A. (1932). *A Comparative Study of Subnormal Children in the Elementary Grades.* New York: Teachers College, Columbia University, Bureau of Publications.

Bepko, R. (1981). The role of evaluation in the development of curriculum. In H. Goldstein (Ed.), *Curriculum Development for Exceptional Children.* San Francisco: Jossey-Bass.

Billingsley, F. F. (1984). Where are the generalized outcomes? (An examination of instructional objectives). *Journal of the Association for Persons With Severe Handicaps, 9*, 186–192.

Blackorby, J., & Wagner, M. (1996). Longitudinal post-school outcomes of youth with disabilities: Findings from the National Longitudinal Transition Study. *Exceptional Children, 62*, 399–413.

Boggs, E. (1954). Day classes for severely retarded children. *American Journal of Mental Deficiency, 58*, 357–370.

Brown, R. (1989). Introduction. In *Programming for Mentally Retarded and Learning Disabled Inmates: A Guide for Correctional Administrators.* Washington, DC: U.S. Department of Justice, National Institute of Corrections.

Bryan, T., Pearl, R., & Herzog, A. (1989). Learning disabled adolescents vulnerability to crime: Attitudes, anxieties, and experiences. *Learning Disability Research, 5*, 51–60.

Bullock, L. M., & McArthur, P. (1994, August). Correctional special education: Disability prevalence estimates and teacher preparation programs. *Education and Treatment of Children, 17(3)*, 347–355.

Carrell, H. D., Kayser, J., Mason, C., & Haring, N. (1987). *The Concurrence between IEPs and Classroom Activities.* Unpublished manuscript. University of Washington, Seattle.

Carson, R. R., Sitlington, P. L., & Frank, A. R. (1995). Young adulthood for individuals with behavioral disorders. What does it hold? *Behavioral Disorders, 20*, 127–135.

Casey, P., & Keilitz, I. (1990). Estimating the prevalence of learning disabled and mentally retarded juvenile offenders: A meta-analysis. In Peter Leone (Ed.), *Understanding troubled and troubling youth* (pp. 80–101). Newbury Park, CA: Sage.

Chadsey-Rusch, J., Rusch, F., & O'Reilly, M. (1991). Transition from school to integrated communities. *Remedial and Special Education, 12,* 23–33.

Chambers, J. G., Parrish, T. B., & Hart, J. (2002). *What Are We Spending on Special Education Services in the United States?* Report 02-01. Arlington, VA: American Institutes for Research.

Clark, G. M. (1979). *Career Education for the Handicapped Child in the Elementary Classroom.* Denver: Love.

Clark, G. M. (1980). Career preparation for handicapped adolescents: A matter of appropriate education. *Exceptional Education Quarterly, 1(2),* 11–17.

Clark, G. M., Carlson, B. C., Fisher, S., Cook, I. D., & D'Alonzo, B. J. (1991). Career development for students in elementary schools: A position statement of the Division of Career Development. *Career Development for Exceptional Individuals, 14,* 109–120.

Cohen, R. (1985). *Legal issues and the mentally disordered inmate.* Sourcebook of the Mentally Disordered Prisoner. Washington, DC: U.S. Department of Justice, National Institute of Corrections.

Cone, J. D. (1987). Intervention planning using adaptive behavior instruments. *The Journal of Special Education, 21,* 127–148.

Connors, D. (1989). *Rival concepts of mental retardation in the evolution of special classes for students who are educable mentally retarded.* Unpublished doctoral dissertation. Teachers College, Columbia University, New York.

Cronin, M. E., & Patton, J. R. (1993). *Life skills instruction for all students with special needs: A practical guide for integrating real-life content into the curriculum.* Austin, TX: PRO-ED.

Deno, S. L., and Fuchs, L. S. (1987). Developing curriculum-based measurement systems for special education problem solving. *Focus on Exceptional Children, 19(8),* 1–16.

Descoeudres, A. (1928). *The Education of Mentally Defective Children: Psychological Observations and Practical Suggestions.* Boston: D.C. Heath and Co.

Dillon, J. T. (1988a). *Questioning and Discussion: A Multidisciplinary Study.* Norwood, NJ: Ablex Publishing Corporation.

Dillon, J. T. (1988b). *Questioning and Teaching: A Manual of Practice.* New York: Teachers College Press.

Dix, D. L. (1904). Memorial to the legislature of Massachusetts—1843. *Old South Leaflets, vol. 6, no. 148.*

Doll, E. (1921). Classification of delinquent defectives. *Journal of Psycho-Asthenics, 26,* 91–100.

Dugdale, R. L. (1877). *The Jukes.* New York: Putnam Sons.

Duncan, J. (1943). *The Education of the Ordinary Child: Lankhills Methods (With Schemes of Work).* New York: Ronald Press.

Durkheim, E. (1972). In A. Giddens (Ed.), *Selected Writings.* Cambridge: Cambridge University Press.

Edwards, W. J., & Reynolds, L. A. (1997, summer). Defending and advocating on behalf of individuals with "mild" retardation in the criminal justice system. *Impact, 10, 2.*

Erikson, E. H. (1968). Life Cycle. In D. Sills (Ed.), *International Encyclopedia of the Social Sciences.* New York: Crowell Collier & Macmillan.

Estabrook, A. H. (1915). *The Jukes in 1915.* Washington, DC: The Carnegie Institute.

Farrell, E. E. (1908, Sept., to 1909, June). Special classes in the New York City Schools. *Journal of Psycho-Asthenics, 13,* 91–96.

Fernald, W. E. (1912). The burden of feeble-mindedness. *Journal of Psycho-Asthenics, 17,* 87–111.

Fernald, W. E. (1919, Nov. 5). After-care study of the patients discharged from Waverly for a period of 25 years. *Ungraded, no. 2.*

References

Fink, C. (1990). Special education students at risk. In P. Leone (Ed.), *Understanding Troubled and Troubling Youth*. Newbury Park, CA: Sage.

Fitch, W. L. (1989). Mental retardation and criminal responsibility. In R. W. Conley, R. Luckasson, & G. N. Bouthilet (Eds.), *The Criminal Justice System and Mental Retardation* (pp. 121–136). Baltimore: Brookes.

Forness, S., & Knitzer, J. (1992). A new proposed definition and terminology to replace "serious emotional disturbance" in the Individuals with Disabilities Education Act. *School Psychology Review, 21,* 12–20.

Fuchs, L. S., and Fuchs, D. (1986). Curriculum-based assessment of progress toward long- and short-term goals. *Journal of Special Education, 20,* 69–82.

Gallagher, J., and Desimone, L. (1995). Lessons learned from implementation of the IEP: Applications to the IFSP. *Topics in Early Childhood Special Education, 15(3),* 353–378.

Gersten, R. (1998). Recent advances in instructional research for students with learning disabilities: An overview. *Learning Disabilities Research and Practice, 13,* 162–170.

Goddard, H. H. (1910). Heredity of feeble-mindedness. *American Breeders Magazine, 1,* 165–178.

Goddard, H. H. (1913). *Sterilization and Segregation*. New York: Russell Sage Foundation, Department of Child Helping.

Goddard, H. H. (1914). A brief report on two cases of criminal imbecility. *Journal of Psycho-Asthenics, 19,* 31–35.

Goddard, H. H. (1920). *Feeble-mindedness: Its Causes and Consequences*. New York: Macmillan.

Goldberg, I. (1959). The school's responsibility for "trainable" mentally retarded children. *Phi Delta Kappan, 40,* 373–376.

Goldstein, H. (1964). Social and occupational adjustment. In H. A. Stevens & R. Heber (Eds.), *Mental Retardation: A Review of Research*. Chicago: University of Chicago Press.

Goldstein, H. (1974). *The Social Learning Curriculum, Phases 1–10*. Columbus, OH: Merrill / Prentice Hall.

Goldstein, H. (1975). *The Social Learning Curriculum, Phases 11–16*. Columbus, OH: Merrill / Prentice Hall.

Goldstein, H. (Ed.). (1981). *Curriculum Development for Exceptional Children*. San Francisco: Jossey-Bass Inc.

Goldstein, H., & Alter, M. (1980). *The Social Learning Curriculum—Perceptual Motor Play*. Dallas: Melton Peninsula.

Goldstein, H., & Goldstein, M. (1980). *Reasoning Ability of Mildly Retarded Learners*. Reston, VA: Council for Exceptional Children.

Goldstein, H., Moss, J. W., & Jordan, L. J. (1965). *The Efficacy of Special Class Training on the Development of Mentally Retarded Children*. Urbana, Institute for Research on Exceptional Children, University of Illinois.

Goldstein, H., & Seigle, D. M. (1958). *The Illinois Plan for Special Education of Exceptional Children: A Curriculum Guide for Teachers of the Educable Mentally Handicapped*. Circular Series B-3, No.12. Office of the Superintendent of Public Instruction, Illinois.

Goldstein, M. T. (1976). *Field Testing: A Model and Its Applications*. New York: Curriculum Research and Development Center in Mental Retardation, Yeshiva University. (ERIC Document No. ED157223)

Goldstein, M. T. (1979). *Diffusion Tactics Influencing Implementation of a Curriculum Innovation*. Unpublished doctoral dissertation. Yeshiva University, New York.

Goldstein, M.T. (1981). Implementing a Curriculum Field-Test Model. In H. Goldstein (Ed.), *Curriculum Development for Exceptional Children*. San Francisco: Jossey-Bass.

References

Goldstein, M. T. (1993). LINK: A campus based transition program for non-college bound youth with mild disabilities. *Career Development for Exceptional Individuals, 16(1),* 75–85.

Goode, W. J. (1959). The sociology of the family: Horizons in family theory. In R. K. Merton, L. Broom, & L. S. Cottrell Jr. (Eds.), *Sociology Today: Problems and Prospects.* New York: Basic Books.

Goodman, H., Gottlieb, J., & Harrison, R. H. (1972). Social acceptance of EMRs integrated into a non-graded elementary school. *American Journal of Mental Deficiency, 76,* 412–417.

Gottlieb, J. (1975). Public, peer, and professional attitudes toward mentally retarded persons. In M. J. Begab & S. A. Richardson (Eds.), *The Mentally Retarded and Society: A Social Science Perspective* (pp. 99–126). Baltimore: University Park Press.

Gottlieb, J., & Corman, L. (1985). Attitudes toward mentally retarded children. In R. L. Jones (Ed.), *Attitude and Attitude Change in Special Education.* Reston, Va.: Council for Exceptional Children.

Gresham, F. M. (1992). Social skills and learning disabilities: Causal, concomitant, or correlational. *School Psychology Review. 21,* 348–360.

Gresham, F. M., & MacMillan, D. L. (1997). Social competence and affective characteristics of students with mild disabilities. *Review of Educational Research, 67,* 377–415.

Gresham, F. M., Sugai, G., & Horner, R. H. (2001). Interpreting outcomes of social skills training for students with high-incidence disabilities. *Exceptional Children, 67, 3,* 331–344.

Griffin, B. W. (2002). Academic disidentification, race, and high school dropouts. *High School Journal, 85(4),* 71–81.

Hall, J. N. (1989). Correctional services for inmates who are mentally retarded: Challenge or catastrophe? In R. W. Conley, R. Luckasson, & G. N. Bouthilet, (Eds.), *The Criminal Justice System and Mental Retardation* (pp. 167–190). Baltimore: Brookes.

Halpern, A. S., Close, D. W., & Nelson, D. J. (1986). *On My Own.* Baltimore: Brookes.

Hasazi, S., Gordon, L., Roe, C., Hull, M., Finck, K., and Salembier, G. (1985). A statewide follow-up on post high school employment and residential status of students labeled "mentally retarded." *Education and Training of the Mentally Retarded, 20,* 222–234.

Havighurst, R. J., and Neugarten, B. L. (1962). *Society and Education.* Boston: Allyn & Bacon.

Hay, W. (1952). *Association of Parents of Mental Retardates.* Vol. 2. Arlington, TX: National Association for Mentally Retarded Citizens.

Hendricks, I., and MacMillan, D. (1989). Selecting children for special education in New York City: William Maxwell, Elizabeth Farrell, and the development of ungraded classes, 1900–1920. *Journal of Special Education, 22, 4,* 395–417.

Hilleboe, G. L. (1930). *Finding and Teaching Atypical Children.* New York: Teachers College Press, Columbia University.

Hocutt, A. M., Martin, E. W., & McKinney, J. D. (1991). Historical and legal context of mainstreaming. In J. W. Lloyd, N. N. Singh, & A. C. Repp (Eds.), *The General Education Education Initiative: Alternative Perspectives on Concepts, Issues, and Models.* Sycamore, IL: Sycamore Publishing Company.

Hoffman, D. M. (1996). Culture and self in multicultural education: Reflections on discourse, text, and practice. *American Educational Research Journal, 33, 3,* 545–569.

Howe, S. (1849). The condition and capacities of idiots in Massachusetts. *American Journal of Insanity, 5,* 374–37.

Hungerford, R. H. (1948). Philosophy of occupational education. Reprints from *Occupational Education, 46.*

References

Hungerford, R. H., DeProspo, C. J., and Rosenzweig, L. E. (1952, Oct.). Education of the mentally handicapped in childhood and adolescence. *American Journal of Mental Deficiency*, 214–228.

Hyman, R. T. (1979). *Strategic questioning*. Englewood Cliffs, NJ: Merrill / Prentice Hall.

Ingram, C. P. (1935). *Education of the Slow-Learning Child*. New York: Ronald Press.

Inhelder, B. (1968). *The Diagnosis of Reasoning in the Mentally Retarded*. New York: John Day.

Ireland, W. (1877). *On Idiocy and Imbecility*. London: J. & A. Churchill.

Itard, J. G. (1894). *Rapports et memoires sur le savage de l'Aveyron, i'idiote et la surdi-mutite*. Paris: Bureau de Progres Medical.

Johnson, D. R., & Sharpe, M. N. (2000). Results of a national survey on the implementation of transitions service requirements of IDEA. *Journal of Special Education Leadership, 13*, 15–26.

Kauffman, J. M. (2001). *Characteristics of Emotional and Behavioral Disorders of Children and Youth* (7th ed.). Columbus, OH: Merrill / Prentice Hall.

Kaufman, R. A. (1975). *Need Assessment: A Focus for Curriculum Development*. Washington, DC: Association for Supervision and Curriculum Development.

Kavale, K., & Forness, S. (1999). Effectiveness of Special Education. In C. Reynolds & T. Gutkin (Eds.), *Handbook of School Psychology* (3rd ed., pp. 984–1024). New York: Wiley.

Keilitz, L., & Dunivant, N. (1986). The relationship between learning disabilities and juvenile delinquency: Current state of knowledge. *Remedial and Special Education, 7*, 18–26.

Kendall, J. S., & Marzano, R. J. (1997). Content knowledge: A compendium of standards and benchmarks for K–12 education (2nd ed.). Aurora, CO: Midcontinental Regional Educational Laboratory and the Association for Supervision and Curriculum.

Kerlin, I. (1887). Moral imbecility. *Proceedings of the Association of Medical Officers of American Institutions for Idiotic and Feebleminded Persons*, 32–37.

Kohler, P. D. (1993). Best practices in transition: Substantiated or implied? *Career Development for Exceptional Individuals, 16*, 107–121.

Kohler, P. D., & Chapman S. (1999). *Literature Review on School-to-Work Transition*. Urbana-Champaign: Transition Research Institute, University of Illinois.

Krulik, S., and Rudnik, J. A. (1995). *The New Source Book for Teaching Reasoning and Problem-Solving in Elementary Schools*. Boston: Allyn & Bacon.

LaGreca, A., & Stone, W. (1990). Children with learning disabilities: The role of achievement in social, personal, and behavioral functioning. In H. L. Swanson & B. Keogh (Eds.), *Learning Disabilities: Theoretical and Research Issues* (pp. 333–352). Hillsdale, NJ: Erlbaum.

Levi-Strauss, C. (1969). *The Elementary Structures of Kinship*. Boston: Beacon Press.

Linton, R. (1936). *The Study of Man*. New York: Appleton Century.

Lipsitt, L. P. (1988). Hedonic processes in infants. In E. D. Hibbs (Ed.), *Children and Families*. Madison, WI: International Universities Press.

Malinowski, B. (1944). *A Scientific Theory of Culture*. Chapel Hill: University of North Carolina Press.

Markus, H. R., & Kitayama, S. (1991). Culture and the self: Implications for cognition, emotion, and motivation. *Psychological Review, 98(2)*, 224–253.

Marshall, G. (1994). *The Concise Oxford Dictionary of Sociology*. Oxford: Oxford University Press.

Marston, D., Deno, S., and Mirkin, P. (1984). Curriculum-based measurement: An alternative to traditional screening, referral, and identification. *Journal of Special Education, 18(2)*, 109–117.

References

Maslow, A. H. (1970). *Motivation and Personality*. New York: Harper & Row.

Mayer, W. V. (Ed.). (1975). *Planning Curriculum Development*. Boulder, CO: Biological Sciences Curriculum Study.

Mercer, J. (1970). Sociological perspectives on mild mental retardation. In H. C. Haywood (Ed.), *Socio-Cultural Aspects of Mental Retardation*. New York: Appleton Century Crofts.

Mithaug, D. E., Horiuchi, C. N., & Fanning, P. N. (1984). A report on the Colorado statewide follow-up survey of special education students. *Exceptional Children, 51(6)*, 397–404.

Mithaug, D. E., Martin, J. E., Agran, M., & Rusch, F. R. (1988). *Why Special Education Graduates Fail: How to Teach Them to Succeed*. Colorado Springs, CO: Ascent Publications.

Mort, P. (1928). *The Individual Pupil in the Management of the Class and School*. New York: Teachers College Press, Columbia University.

Murdock, G. P. (1981). *Atlas of World Cultures*. Pittsburgh, PA: University of Pittsburgh Press.

Murdock, G. P, & Provost, C. (1980). *Measurement of Cultural Complexity*. In H. Barry & A. Schlegel (Eds.), *Cross-Cultural Samples and Codes* (pp. 147–160). Pittsburgh, PA: University of Pittsburgh Press.

National Council on Disability. (2000). *Back to School on Civil Rights*. Washington, DC: Author.

National Early Childhood Technical Assistance System (NECTAS). (1999). Programs for young children with disabilities under IDEA: Excerpts from the 21st annual report to Congress on the implementation of the Individuals with Disabilities Education Act. Chapel Hill, NC: Author.

Norley, D. (1997, summer). Being there: The role of advocates. *Impact, 10, 2*.

Orkis, R., & McLane, K. (1998). *A Curriculum Every Student Can Use: Design Principles for Student Access*. Reston, VA: Council for Exceptional Children.

Osborne, A. (1894). President's annual address. *Proceedings of the Association of American Institutions for Idiotic and Feebleminded Persons*, 386–399.

Patton, J. R., & Dunn, C. (1998). *Transition From School to Young Adulthood*. Austin, TX: PRO-ED.

Pennsylvania Association for Retarded Children (PARC) v. Commonwealth of Pennsylvania. 334 F. Supp.1257 (E.D. Pa. 1971).

Pertsch, C. F. (1936). *A Comparative Study of the Progress of Subnormal Pupils in the Grades and in Special Classes*. New York: Teachers College, Columbia University.

Postman, N., & Weingartner, C. (1969). *Teaching as a Subversive Activity*. New York: Dell Publishing.

President's Commission on Excellence in Special Education. (2002). *A New Era: Revitalizing Special Education for Children and Their Families*. U.S. Department of Education.

Ransom, B. E., & Chimarusti, J. (1997, summer). The education of juveniles in the criminal justice system: A mandate. *Impact, 10, 2*.

Ray, I. (1831). *A Treatise on the Medical Jurisprudence of Insanity*. Boston: Little, Brown.

Resnick, L. B. (1987). *Education and Learning to Think*. Washington, DC: National Academy Press.

Richards, L. (1935). *Samuel Gridley Howe*. New York: Appleton, Century, Crofts.

Rosenshine, B. (1997). Advances in research on instruction. In J. N. Lloyd, E. J. Kameenui, & D. Chard (Eds.), *Issues in Educating Students With Disabilities* (pp. 197–221). Mahwah, NJ: Erlbaum.

Rowan, B. (1976). Mentally retarded citizens in correctional institutions. In M. Kindred (Ed.), *The Mentally Retarded Citizen and the Law* (pp. 63–71). New York: Free Press.

References

Santamour, M. B. (1989). *The Mentally Retarded Offender and Corrections.* Washington DC: American Correctional Association.

Santamour, M. B., & West, B. (1977). *The Mentally Retarded Offender and Corrections.* Washington, DC: Law Enforcement Assistance Administration.

Scandura, J. M. (1977). *Problem-Solving: A Structural/Process Approach with Instructional Implications.* New York: Academic Press.

Scheerenberger, R. C. (1983). *A History of Mental Retardation.* Baltimore: Brookes.

Schwartz, G., & Koch, C. (1992). U.S. Department of Education correctional education initiatives. *Issues in Teacher Education, 1(2),* 100–108.

Segerstedt, T. T. (1966). *The Nature of Social Reality.* New York: Teachers College, Columbia University.

Seguin, E. (1841). *Theory and Practice of the Education of Idiots.* Paris: L'Hospice de Incurables.

Seguin, E. (1846). *Traitement Moral, Hygiène et Education des Idiots et des Autres Enfants Arrières.* Paris: J. B. Bailliere.

Seguin, E. (1907). *Idiocy: Its Treatment by the Physiological Method.* New York: Teachers College, Columbia University.

Siperstein, G. N., Leffert, J. S., & Wenz-Gros, M. (1997). The quality of friendships between children with and without learning problems. *American Journal on Mental Retardation, 102, (2),* 55–70.

Sitlington, P., Frank, A., & Carson, R. (1993). Adult adjustment among graduates with mild disabilities. *Exceptional Children, 59,* 221–233.

Skiba, R., & Grizzle, K. (1991). The social maladjustment exclusion: Issues of definition and assessment. *School Psychology Review, 20,* 217–230.

Skodak, M. (1968). Adult status of individuals who experienced early intervention. In B. W. Richards (Ed.), *Proceedings: First Congress of the Association for the Scientific Study of Mental Deficiency* (pp. 11–18). London: Michael Jackson.

Snarr, R. W., & Wolford, B. I. (1985). *Introduction to Corrections.* Dubuque, IA: William C. Brown.

Steelman, D. (1987). *The Mentally Impaired in New York's Prisons: Problems and Solutions.* New York: Correctional Association of New York.

Steward, J. H. (1963). *Theory of Cultural Change.* Urbana: University of Illinois Press.

Stodden, R. A., Galloway, L. M., & Stodden, N. J. (2003). Secondary school curricula issues: Impact on postsecondary students with disabilities. *Exceptional Children, 70, 1,* 9–25.

Stratemeyer, F. B., Forkner, H. L., & McKim, M. G. (1947). *Developing a Curriculum for Modern Living.* New York: Teachers College, Columbia University, Bureau of Publications.

Talbot, M. E. (1964). *Edouard Seguin: A Study of an Educational Approach to the Treatment of Mentally Defective Children.* New York: Teachers College Press.

Tylor, E. B. (1913). *Primitive Culture: Researches Into the Development of Mythology, Religion, Language, Art, and Custom.* London: Murray.

Tylor, P. L., & Bell, L. V. (1984). *Caring for the Developmentally Delayed in America.* Westport, CT: Greenwood Press.

U.S. Census Bureau. (2002, July). *The Big Payoff: Educational Attainment and Synthetic Estimates of Work-Life Earnings.* Washington, DC: U.S. Department of Commerce, Economics, and Statistics Administration.

Valett, R. F. (1978). *Developing Cognitive Abilities: Teaching Children to Think.* St. Louis, MO: Mosby.

Wagner, M., Newman, L., D'Amico, R., Jay, E., Butler-Nalin, P., Marder, C., et al. (1991). Youth with disabilities: How are they doing? The first comprehensive report from the

National Longitudinal Transition Study of Special Education Students. Menlo Park, CA: SRI International.

Wagner, M., & Shaver, D. M. (1989). Education programs and achievements of secondary special education students. Findings from the National Longitudinal Transition Study. Menlo Park, CA: SRI International.

Walker, H. M., & Bullis, M. (1991). Behavior disorders and the social context of general education class integration: A conceptual dilemma. In J. Lloyd, N. N. Singh, & A. C. Repp (Eds.), *The Regular Education Initiative: Alternative Perspectives on Concepts, Issues, and Models*. Sycamore, IL: Sycamore Publishing Company.

Weber, M. (1922). In M. Rheinstein (Ed.), *Max Weber on Law, Economy, and Society*. Cambridge: Cambridge University Press.

Weikert, D., Deloria, D., Lawser, S., & Wiegerink, K. (1970). Longitudinal results of the Ypsilanti Perry preschool project. Monographs of the High/Scope Educational Research Foundation, No. 1. Ypsilanti, MI: High/Scope.

Weisenfeld, R. B. (1987). Functionality in the IEPs of children with Down's syndrome. *Mental Retardation, 25*, 281–286.

Wellman, B. L. (1932–1933). The effect of preschool attendance upon the IQ. *Journal of Experimental Education, 1*, 48–49.

Wellman, B. L. (1934–1935). Growth in intelligence under differing school environments. *Journal of Experimental Education, 3*, 59–83.

Welton, J. (1981). *Individualized educational program evaluation model: Development and field study*. San Jose, CA: Santa Clara County Superintendent of Schools and California State Department of Education, Sacramento Division of Special Education.

Whimbey, A. (1991). *Problem-solving and Comprehension*. Hillsdale, NJ: Erlbaum.

Wolford, B. I. (1987). Correctional education: Training and educational opportunities for delinquent and criminal offenders. In C. M. Nelson, R. B. Rutherford, & B. I. Wolford (Eds.), *Special education in the criminal justice system*. Columbus, OH: Merrill / Prentice Hall.

Ysseldyke, J. E., Algozzine, B., & Mitchell, J. (1982). Special education team decision making: An analysis of current practice. *Personnel and Guidance Journal, 60(50)*, 308–313.

Ysseldyke, J. E., Algozzine, B., & Thurlow, M. L. (1992). *Critical Issues in Special Education*. Boston: Houghton Mifflin.

Ysseldyke, J. E., Thurlow, M. L., & Shriner, J. G. (1992). Outcomes are for special educators too. *Teaching Exceptional Children, 25*, 36–50.

Zedler, E. (1953). Public opinion and public education for the exceptional child court decisions. *Exceptional Children, 19*, 187–188.

References

Index

Index

193

Index

195

Index

About the Author

Herbert Goldstein earned his B.S. and M.A. degrees from San Francisco State College and in 1947 obtained his certification to teach elementary and special education with specialization in the education of students with mild mental retardation. He taught a special class in the San Anselmo, California, schools, and in 1950, he began graduate study as a student and research assistant at the Institute for Research on Exceptional Children in the College of Education at the University of Illinois at Urbana-Champaign. He was awarded an Ed.D. in 1957 and was appointed assistant and associate professor. In 1962, he was a Fulbright Scholar at the University of Oslo. In 1963, he was appointed chair of the Department of Special Education at Yeshiva University's Graduate School in the Social Humanities and Sciences, where he designed and directed the Center for Curriculum Development and Research in Mental Retardation. He moved with the center to New York University in 1975. Retiring from New York University in 1980, he became adjunct Professor of Education at Fairleigh Dickinson University.